SCHOLAS

Adams Twelve Five Star Schools
Rocky Mountain Elementary School
3350 W. 99th Ave.
Westminster, Colorado 80030

M000250551

Kindergarten Literacy

*

Matching Assessment and Instruction

By Anne McGill-Franzen

New York • Toronto • London • Auckland • Sydney
Mexico City • New Delhi • Hong Kong • Buenos Aires

Teaching *Resources*

Much of the impetus for writing *Kindergarten Literacy* came from my experience with several funded professional development and research projects:

Tennessee Higher Education Commission (THEC) Teacher Quality Grant (#EO11755030), an initiative funded by the state of Tennessee to support teachers' professional development and capacity building at the school level.

The William Penn Foundation and Children's Literacy Initiative (CLI), a funded evaluation of the CLI Philadelphia kindergarten literacy project.

Office of Educational Research & Improvement (OERI) Grant (#R305T010692), a research intervention designed to mitigate out-of-school reading loss among poor children.

Center for English Learning & Achievement (CELA), a national research center that supported collaborative curriculum projects among teachers and professors in order to develop research-based models of language arts teaching, learning, and assessment (#R305A6005).

The contents of the book do not necessarily represent an endorsement by any state or federal funding agencies, nor the positions of my colleagues and collaborators in the research and professional development projects.

Fry's 100 High-Frequency Words on page 116 excerpted from *Dr. Fry's Instant Words* by Edward Fry, Ph.D., Teacher Created Resources, Westminster, CA.

Excerpt of *Have You Seen My Duckling?* by Nancy Tafuri, Greenwillow, 1984. © 1984 by the author. Used by permission of the publisher.

The Barbecue by Jillian Cutting, Wright Group/McGraw Hill, used by permission of the publisher.

Shoes by Sarah Weeks, Celebration Press, 1997. © Used by permission of the publisher.

Scholastic Inc. grants teachers permission to photocopy the reproducible pages in this book only for personal classroom use. No other part of this publication may be reproduced in whole or in part, or stored in a retrieval system, or transmitted in any form or by any means, electronic, mechanical, photocopying, recording, or otherwise, without written permission of the publisher. For information regarding permission, write to Permissions Department, Scholastic Inc., 557 Broadway, New York, NY 10012.

Cover design and photograph by Maria Lilja
Interior design by LDL Designs
Professional interior photos © Ellen B. Senisi
Photos on the following pages by Anne McGill-Franzen: 174, 216, 234, 235, 261; by Theresa Wishart:142, 143, 144, 146, 151, 152, 169, 186, 187, 223; by Ruth Lindsey: 155; by Danielle Matheson: 43
Illustrations by Maxie Chambliss
Sort image concepts by Mac Wishart

ISBN 0-439-80034-X
Copyright © 2006 by Anne McGill-Franzen
All rights reserved. Published by Scholastic Inc.
Printed in the U.S.A.
2 3 4 5 6 7 8 9 10   23   12 11 10 09 08 07 06

Contents

Dedication

To the teachers, students, and children I have known—
thank you for all you have taught me.

Acknowledgements

I want to first thank Margery Rosnick, who believed in me and my idea for this kindergarten book, and Wendy Murray, whose keen eye for detail and ear for language helped make my work accessible to my audience.

Without the support and encouragement of my colleague Theresa Wishart, this book would not have been possible. Theresa is a tireless advocate for children—her life's work has been to provide opportunity to all children, especially the youngest learners, and to develop the expertise of teachers so that they might carry out this important work with confidence and commitment. I thank Linda Carr, former language arts supervisor in upstate New York, who not only pioneered early literacy assessments and interventions but also hired me to be a kindergarten teacher many years ago!

I owe a great debt to all the teachers who graciously shared their classrooms with me, and the children themselves, whose open, unabashed engagement with literacy inspired me to write this book.

As a college professor, I have had the fortune to work side-by-side in classrooms and research projects with amazing graduate students and colleagues. I thank all of them, but in particular, Jacqueline Love, the University of Florida; Rhonda Nowak, now at the University of Hawaii; Katie Solic, Danielle Mathson and Rebecca Payne, the University of Tennessee; and my former colleagues and professors in the Reading Department at the University of Albany, State University of New York.

Many researchers inspired me and provided direction for my thinking—Marcia Invernizzi, Marie Clay, Delores Durkin, Charles Temple, and many others whose ideas you will see many times over in this book.

Finally, I thank my family for their love—my colleague in literacy and life partner, Dick Allington, and my children, Maggie and Mike.   *—Anne McGill-Franzen*

Foreword

Anne McGill-Franzen sends three powerful messages in this book: Kindergarten is a critical year for literacy development, literacy instruction needs to align with children's strengths, and instruction must be differentiated in order to meet the various needs of kindergartners, especially those children who most need school-based literacy instruction. Drawing on her own research and the research of others, Dr. McGill-Franzen makes a compelling case that the progress children can make in reading and writing during the kindergarten year can change the rest of their entire academic lives. Kindergartners whose teachers help them begin to read and write are far more likely to go on to become proficient readers and writers than children who are not provided with these opportunities. By describing what motivates children to read and write and how their reading and writing abilities develop in actual classrooms, she convinces us that it is indeed developmentally appropriate to teach literacy concepts in kindergarten.

McGill-Franzen suggests that the centerpiece of kindergarten literacy programs and the entry point for crafting powerful instruction is assessment. Her discussion of related research on teacher professional development and literacy instruction radiates from this central concept of assessment-informed instruction. In her view, teaching that is dovetailed with reliable assessment data propels each child's learning forward better than a one-size-fits all approach to instruction.

In the first few chapters, McGill-Franzen lays out a plan of assessment using easily administered tools. These assessments are comprehensive, covering all critical aspects of early literacy development, and provide teachers with sufficient information to plan instruction to meet the needs of learners who come to kindergarten with a variety of background experiences in reading and writing.

Using the assessment plan provided in this book, teachers will find that their kindergartners will most likely fall into four categories: "letters and sounds kids," "sounds kids," "almost readers," and "readers." Teachers will find these categories provide a useful framework for making instructional decisions. Conceptually, understanding these groups of children both helps teachers gain insight into early literacy development and helps them use this insight for practical purposes of forming instructional groups, choosing appropriate materials, and developing differentiated lessons and activities.

McGill-Franzen shares the beginning of the year, midyear, and end-of-year assessments of two teachers in Tennessee, and walks us through how these practitioners looked at their class profiles and shaped their instruction around what they discerned. We see the writing and hear the voices of specific children; we are given big-picture details of guided reading lessons and individual portraits of children engaged in various literacy activities. McGill-Franzen's decision to give her readers this "ringside seat" gives this book energy, immediacy—and the level of detail we need to actually put its ideas into practice.

Fulfilling the promise of this book's subtitle, McGill-Franzen shifts in the second half of the book from assessment to instruction. Inviting us into classrooms in Tennessee and upstate New York, she provides information for using familiar kindergarten instructional routines including reading aloud, shared reading, guided reading, shared writing, interactive reading, writing workshop and conference, and word study using word walls and sorts. She provides guidelines for using each of these classroom routines and for using specific teaching strategies such as thinking aloud while teaching, prompting children to use what they know in strategic ways, stretching sounds, and linking reading and writing together. But what makes this book unique are suggestions for using these generic classroom routines and teaching strategies to meet the needs of four kinds of kindergarten learners. She successfully connects the dots so that we come away with a vivid picture of instruction matched to assessment.

This book is compelling because McGill's expertise and her passion for her work are evident on every page. I predict it will transform the profession's perspective on best-practice in kindergarten.

—*Lea McGee*

Part One

Teaching to Children's Strengths

*I once heard Marie Clay say that we must teach to
children's strengths, not to their weaknesses, if we want
to succeed. I believe that teaching to strengths is a
revolutionary idea. If you reflect for a moment on
everything a 5-year-old does not know about reading,
or a struggling reader of any age, you can see that
weaknesses do not help you know where to begin
teaching. To know where to start instruction,
you must know what the child can do. Effective
teachers build on what children know.*

Chapter One
Kindergarten Rules!

Toward an enhanced vision of kindergarten play—playing with language

Kindergarten teachers have always known how important they are in children's lives. They know they stand at the crossroads between home or community preschool and school, between family literacy and school literacy, between oral language and full-fledged literacy. They know that in creating a happy transition to school—immersing children in its routines, encouraging children's natural appetite to learn while nurturing their social-emotional development—they bring peace of mind to parents and limitless possibility for children. Nonetheless, I believe we have been slow to recognize the awesome contribution of a good kindergarten teacher to later academic success. I believe we may have underestimated the power of kindergarten to change the developmental trajectory of children who start school behind as well as sustain the motivation and engagement of children who start school with a wealth of experiences with language and literacy.

Federal policy, particularly "No Child Left Behind," arguably has changed the conversation in our schools from "Some children can't learn" to "How can we teach all children to read?" Many states, including my own state of Tennessee, require that schools publish not only the test scores and school grades that compare one school with another, but also the value or gain in achievement that accrues to children attending that school. Called either value-added or gain scores, these results are equally important for all children, including high-achieving children, who have a right to expect a year of progress for each year of school even though they may have started school with above-grade-level achievement.

As the importance of early language and literacy development for long-term success in school becomes more apparent with every new research study, we have turned our attention to kindergarten. Many states have expanded kindergarten from a half to a full day to enhance learning by all children. A longer kindergarten day makes possible more personal and effective instruction, leading to higher achievement as well as social and emotional benefits for all children (WestEd, 2005; Denton, West, & Walston, 2003).

Kindergarten in the Hot Seat: How Research Can Provide a Calm, Cool Direction

I believe that we need to teach kindergartners to read and write—that's what I mean by *Kindergarten Literacy*, the title of this book. And I believe that equipping kindergarten teachers with reliable literacy assessments is one of the single most powerful professional development tools we can hand them to attain this goal. Why? Because we have to know what children know in order to teach them what they need. Only then can teachers differentiate their instruction to meet each child's need. When kindergarten instruction matches assessment, rich literacy practices such as read-alouds, letter sorts, and interactive writing push each child's development forward, like gusts of wind hitting a sailboat at just the right angles. And finally, I believe that as kindergarten is transformed by the currents of society today—from the pluses of good preschools and the findings of neuroscience about early learning to the minuses of low family literacy—so, too, is the role of kindergarten teacher transformed, and that professional development is therefore critical. All too frequently, districts purchase new material and expect that teachers' instruction will automatically improve. As one of the teachers told me, "Often we are overwhelmed with an abundance of material we don't know how to use. Professional development matters, kindergarten matters. Kindergarten can rule!"

In the chapters that follow, I'll share the research that informs these beliefs, as well as ready-to-use assessments, step-by-step guidance on interpreting the results, and examples of how to use the results to plan your instruction. In Part Four, I'll detail the routines and practices that you draw from as you tailor your instruction. For now, here are a few of the foundational research findings that I'd like you to keep in mind as we explore the current climate of ideas about kindergarten.

Just Being There Makes a Difference for Some Children

We used to think that if children are behind at school entry, then they will learn at a slower rate throughout their schooling, never catching up to their more advantaged peers. Sociologist James S. Coleman used this theory to explain the impotence of schooling in the face of poverty. How else can we explain the ever-widening gap in achievement between many children of poverty and their peers, he reasoned. Nonetheless, Barbara Heyns, a researcher who studied achievement in the Atlanta public schools, published a study several decades ago (1978) challenging the Coleman hypothesis that children's gains during the school year are proportional to where children start. Instead, Heyns found that school makes a huge difference—it is the out-of-school time that accounts for the disparity in achievement for poor children. By studying longitudinal achievement patterns, including achievement upon school entry and over the summer months, sociologists Doris Entwisle, Karl Alexander, and Linda Olson further elaborated Heyns' work. They developed a "faucet theory" of schooling—the spigot of school resources is turned on when school is in session and off for children of low-income families during out-of-school time. For children of low-income families, just being in school makes a difference: "Home resources do not cause students to learn more during the school year. Rather, home resources provide students the opportunity [to learn] outside school [or] when schools are closed" (1997, p. 47).

Personalizing Instruction Is the Heart of It All

Children with few experiences with language and literacy outside of school—often called "school-dependent" children—need teachers to teach them. They need teachers who believe that they can accelerate the development of children who arrive "unready" for kindergarten, who can "bring them along," in the words of one teacher. Such teachers hold what researchers Mary Lee Smith and Lorie Shepard referred to as "interactionist beliefs," that is, they revise their instructional interactions, not their expectations for learning, when children do not make progress. Marie Clay, noted educator and Piagetian psychologist, and founder of the Reading Recovery movement in this country and the literacy program in New Zealand, said she herself was unprepared for the dramatic way that appropriate teaching in reading could accelerate young children's development.

As the "unready" children enter kindergarten, we cannot see their lack of literacy as something that will limit what they can accomplish as learners and what we accomplish as their teachers, but rather, as I wrote in *The Reading Teacher:*

> "...the individual and variable development of children is an opportunity to personalize our instruction. As teachers we must celebrate and affirm, but also extend and elaborate each child's developing knowledge of written language" (McGill-Franzen, 1992, p. 58).

Increasing the Intensity of Kindergarten Is Beneficial

Restructuring kindergarten to increase the time and intensity of instruction has profound, long-term beneficial effects on children's development. Entwisle, Alexander, and colleagues conducted a "beginning school study" in Baltimore (1987) to determine the influ-

ence of more time in kindergarten on children's social and cognitive skills and their attachment to school. They found that students who attended all-day kindergarten were absent
less, less often retained (two times as likely to avoid retention!), and achieved higher
teacher ratings and test scores than those who attended half-day programs (p. 156).

Policy maven Malia Villegas confirmed past studies and summarized what we current-
ly know about all-day kindergarten in the 2005 WestEd Policy Brief, *Full-Day
Kindergarten: Expanding Learning Opportunities* (available online: www.wested.org/policy).

A full kindergarten day provides teachers more flexibility to move children forward or
elaborate skills, depending on what individual children need, and makes possible more
autonomy and self-selection of activities by children. Children benefit academically, with
higher reading achievement, and socially and emotionally, with less frustration and deeper
attachment to school.

Bringing Home Literacy Practices to School Is Key

In a seminal intervention study, Delores Durkin (1974–75) restructured the kindergarten
classroom to more closely resemble the home literacy experiences of children who learned
to read early. She integrated read-alouds, talk about books, talk about writing, posting special words like names, and talk about spelling and letter formation in service of early writing. Whenever children learned a new letter, they were taught that knowing that letter
"would allow them to write words" (p. 13), and teachers demonstrated by writing words
with the same initial sounds. Letter names and sounds were taught in the context of familiar print and authentic purposes—to write and read children's names or bulletin boards in
the classroom; to respond to stories read aloud; to understand labels, street signs, birthdays,
addresses, and phone numbers. Because parents of early at-home readers reported reading
aloud frequently and taking time to talk about stories and respond to the children's questions, time was set aside each day for story reading and talk in the curriculum of the school.

Durkin's kindergarten schedule was divided into 15-minute, 20-minute, and 30-
minute blocks of time. One 20-minute time period was devoted to daily literacy instruction, with one day of the week devoted to reading, one day to writing, one to letter identification, and one to numbers; the fifth day was open, often spent on learning colors and

color words. A daily 20-minute free choice period included writing or drawing on slate boards as well as traditional play activities. Teachers allocated 30 minutes daily for art and 20 minutes daily for music. Because teachers wanted to infuse the school day with the language and literacy that early readers experienced at home, they typically taught art in service of language—art provided the context for writing. For example, children might print names on projects, write addresses on house pictures, draw and caption an experience, write name cards for clay figures they'd made, and label pictures. Just as home literacy experiences evolved from children's interest in and everyday uses of reading and writing, so, too, did the kindergarten curriculum.

Always sensitive to criticism that she was "hot-housing" youngsters, Durkin made clear in her research reports that there was no pressure on the children to achieve: "…[C]hildren's responses [were] always used as the criterion in making decisions about the content, pace, and duration of instruction" (p. 13). Durkin reported that it was better to go too slowly than too quickly—there was no goal of the highest possible achievement.

Even so, children who participated in Durkin's kindergarten classes significantly outscored comparison groups in first and second grade. Children in the treatment group were able to identify ten times as many words as children in the control. Amazingly, the effect size at fourth grade was between .50 and .41—a half of a standard deviation on test scores in reading. Translated into percentiles, the effect would move a kindergarten child from the 50th percentile to roughly the 70th percentile, or a below-average child into the average range, and in the Durkin study, that effect still held by fourth grade.

Kindergarten Reading Changes Lives

In other kindergarten studies, researchers supplemented teachers' regular classroom instruction with whole-class, small-group, and individual reading of "little books" and follow-up writing activities (Phillips, Norris, & Mason, 1996; Hanson & Farrell, 1995). The effect size of the Phillips et al. intervention at fourth grade was almost one-third of a standard deviation above average in reading for children who participated in the program. The effects of the second "little books" intervention reached way beyond fourth grade—the influence of the kindergarten year was still felt two decades later.

Perhaps the most compelling evidence that teaching children to read in kindergarten can change lives is that of a study of high school seniors carried out by researchers Ralph Hanson and Diane Farrell (1995). This study, one of the most comprehensive evaluations of kindergarten ever done, followed up on about 4,000 students from 24 districts in ten states who had been taught to read in kindergarten. By the time they were contacted and evaluated for the study, more than 12 years had passed between the kindergarten experience and their senior year, yet the researchers found "extraordinary" benefits for the children:

> "…[N]ot only did the students who received formal reading instruction in kindergarten exhibit a clear pattern of (a) showing superior current reading skills, (b) having higher grades and better attendance in school, and (c) needing and receiving significantly less remedial instruction in both elementary and secondary school, but they were also from families with a significantly lower social class status and parent education as compared to those in the other two comparison groups" (p. 923).

Thus, in spite of fewer family resources, students who received kindergarten reading still outperformed higher socioeconomic students (SES) who did not. However, kindergarten reading was a beneficial experience for all students, including the advantaged, in that it reduced poor readers in all groups. Across all groups, children who spent the most time in reading instruction experienced the greatest gains and long-term effects so that "the more reading instruction, the better" the results.

The reading instruction that these high school seniors experienced as kindergartners consisted of 52 story booklets sequenced developmentally into ten units that the children read aloud and took home; each story had discussion questions about the story characters and plots; students were assessed on skills at the end of each unit and provided with instructional support for skills not mastered (p. 912). Through group flashcards and games, children learned sight vocabulary and decoding (instruction focused on "sequencing and presentation of the critical sounds and words needed to gain initial competence in reading" (p. 912). Total instructional time was 20 to 30 minutes daily. The researchers argued that profound social benefits accrue as a result of this investment in kindergarten reading instruction: "How much does it save society when the proportion of illiterate high school seniors [defined as approximately fifth-grade reading level] is reduced by one-third?"

The impact of kindergarten is long-lasting and powerful. As the authors of the intervention chapter in the *Handbook of Reading Research* assert, kindergarten can be at least as potent as Reading Recovery, a program that has attracted more attention and funding: "The trace of the kindergarten intervention appears to be as resilient as the one for an intensive first grade intervention such as Reading Recovery" (Hiebert & Taylor, 2000; p. 477). The results of the Hanson & Farrell study of high school seniors suggest that large-scale focused professional development around well-developed instructional materials "can reap substantial benefits for students" (p. 478).

Let's All Get on the Same Page

Social development and literacy instruction needn't be an either/or proposition. If we are to improve literacy in our nation, we all have to embrace the belief that teaching reading to 5-year-olds can be a school experience that's every bit as playful, imaginative, inquiry-driven, and developmentally appropriate as anything John Dewey or Jean Piaget might have dreamed up. We have to stop casting the discussion as skill-and-drill versus joyful learning through play. Explicit literacy instruction is a relatively brief portion of a kindergartner's day.

All teachers want to do their personal best for every child. I wrote this book—and the assessments and teaching routines within—to help you accomplish that goal. I encourage you to use this book as a professional development tool—one that helps you identify children's strengths and needs, but also helps you gain deep knowledge of the process of becoming literate, as you observe and document children's growth over a kindergarten year. As I'll detail further in the next chapter, building more literacy into the kindergarten year requires careful, engaging professional growth for teachers. To maintain children's love of learning and the desire to communicate through talk and writing, we have to do much, much more than stock a teacher's shelves with basals and "little books" and standards.

Chapter Two

The Research That Informs This Book

Teacher Jasmine Cordero listens to a student read.

Approximately four million children attend kindergarten today—most in public schools and about half in all-day programs. Children bring with them the language and culture of the home, beliefs about themselves as readers and writers, and almost to a child, an intense curiosity about print and the desire to master its form. Depending on the resources of the home or preschool, children enter kindergarten with varying levels of experience with print and knowledge about print conventions and purposes for reading and writing. The National Center for Education Statistics (NCES), the U.S. agency responsible for collecting and analyzing data on priority areas in education, recently initiated the Early Childhood Longitudinal Study (ECLS-K)—the first national study of kindergartners, their schools, and their families. Although the NCES will follow this cohort of children through fifth grade, the portrait of America's kindergartners has generated much interest, particularly in the cognitive profiles of the entering children. Here, I share some findings from this and other studies that are useful to have tucked under your hat as you watch your pint-size print lovers amble through your classroom door and hang up their little backpacks. The findings underscore why it is so important to build literacy with more rigor in kindergarten.

Their Print Awareness

According to the study, two-thirds of entering kindergartners know their letters, almost a third can identify initial sounds, and about one-fifth can identify ending sounds! More than a third of kindergartners know that print moves left to right with a return sweep, and they are able to show where the story ends. However, there is great disparity between the highest- achieving children, whose mothers are likely college graduates, and the lowest-achieving, whose mothers may not have finished high school. As the level of the mother's schooling increases, so does the child's performance on measures of reading achievement, a correlation that speaks to the power of particular kinds of home experiences. On alphabet tasks, for example, 86 percent of children of mothers who are college graduates scored at the proficient level, whereas only 38 percent of children of mothers without even a high school diploma did so. Half of the children from well-educated families recognized initial sounds, but less than 10 percent of those from undereducated families were able to do so. More-advantaged children entered kindergarten knowing how to read at least six words; the least-advantaged children, in terms of their mothers' education, knew not a single word. Nor were the least-advantaged children familiar with print concepts—almost 40 percent of children of welfare mothers were unaware of all the print concepts evaluated in the study, whereas the average child was able to hold a book right side up and identify the front of the book and where to start reading.

Achievement Differences Among Entering Kindergartners

	Percent Letters	Proficient Beginning sounds	Known Sight-words
College-graduate mother	86%	50%	6
Mother without high school diploma	38%	9%	0

Source: NCES (April 2000). *America's Kindergartners*. Washington, D.C.: U.S. Department of Education (pp. 22–24).

Their Speaking and Listening Vocabulary

Not only do entering kindergartners differ in measures of the alphabet and print knowledge, but they also exhibit profound differences in the number of words in their speaking vocabularies. An oft-cited research study of children's language development, *Meaningful Differences in the Everyday Experiences of Young American Children*, asserted that a "30 million word gap by age 3" exists between children from professional families, similar to the college-educated mothers in the NCES study, and children from families on welfare, presumably those with the least-educated caregivers. Not only did poor children have smaller vocabularies, but they were adding words at a much slower rate than the other children, making the vocabulary gap wider with each passing year. The authors of the study, Betty Hart and Todd Risley (1995), identified the 30-million word gap by extrapolating children's four years of language experience based on their hourly observations of the number of words heard by children in different home environments. A frequently cited statistic from that study holds that the preschool children of professional parents had larger speaking vocabularies than the parents in welfare families. Sadly for children in poor families, preschool vocabulary predicted later language achievement, even reading comprehension, in third grade. In other words, children's use of language at age 3 predicted about half the variance in measures of language development—listening, speaking, word meaning, and syntax—and one-third the score on a standardized test of reading comprehension.

Why would this be so? According to Andrew Biemiller (2003), oral language comprehension sets a ceiling on reading comprehension for children. Listening comprehension begins to develop at about 12 months and grows steadily throughout elementary school and beyond. Reading comprehension develops in kindergarten but lags far below listening comprehension. In fact, it is not until seventh or eighth grade that average children are able to read and understand what they would understand without difficulty if they heard it instead (p. 3). This is a special problem for children who enter kindergarten with speaking and listening vocabularies that are far smaller than those of their peers. Although they may start school only a year behind, with each passing year children in the bottom quartile may fall farther behind so that by the time they are sixth graders, their listening comprehension is similar to average fourth graders. At the same time, children in the top quartile of their sixth-grade class may understand information presented orally at a level far above their age. Unless teachers give special attention to individual differences among children in the prior knowledge and experiences they bring to school, some children may be bored while others will struggle. Kindergarten teachers, with their background in child development and their sensitivity to social and emotional factors, can provide the special attention that our diverse 5-year-olds need. One very important contribution of research describing the vast disparities in the language experiences of our preschoolers, and the later influence of these disparities on reading achievement, is that we now know how much good teaching needs to take place once children reach school and our kindergarten classes.

Listening Comprehension Among High- and Low-Achieving Children at Kindergarten and Third Grade

AT KINDERGARTEN
The 25th percentile of entering kindergartners are already a full year *behind* 50th percentile kindergartners.
The 75th percentile of entering kindergartners are already a full year *ahead* of 50th percentile kindergartners.

AT GRADE 3
The 25th percentile of third graders are on par with average second graders or younger.
The 75th percentile of third graders are on par with average fourth graders.

Source: Biemiller, A. (Spring 2003). Oral comprehension sets the ceiling on reading comprehension. *American Educator*. Available online: www.aft.org

---

What's Behind Good Teaching?
Good Professional Development

In 1999, my university colleague Richard Allington, and Marcia Moon and Linda Katz of the Children's Literacy Initiative, and I demonstrated in a true experimental study (the U.S. Department of Education's "gold standard" for research) that providing kindergarten teachers with professional development and new materials can have a much greater effect on students' gains than simply providing teachers with new materials. Professional development—developing teachers' expertise in early literacy—mattered more than materials (McGill-Franzen et al., 1999).

To demonstrate my point, I will describe the achievement of kindergartners in two Philadelphia schools—just a block or so from each other—in the same high-poverty community. Kindergarten teachers in one school received a new classroom library of 250 good children's books and another 150 books in a parent lending library, plus about 30 hours of professional development (ten of them before school started and the rest in side-by-side coaching in the classroom). Kindergarten teachers in the other school received the same books but no professional development. (Of course, there were teachers in another school who received neither professional development nor books, at least not until the end of the school year—these teachers were the controls, the ones without any special treatment.)

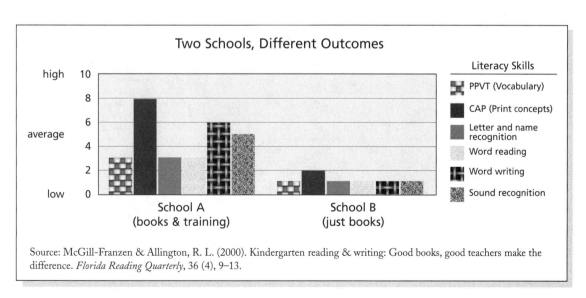

Source: McGill-Franzen & Allington, R. L. (2000). Kindergarten reading & writing: Good books, good teachers make the difference. *Florida Reading Quarterly*, 36 (4), 9–13.

As the bar graph shows, teachers who received professional development and the new libraries outperformed the teachers who received only the libraries, even though these schools served children from exactly the same backgrounds.

Overall, children from classrooms where teachers received books but not professional development performed no better than the children in classrooms with no new books at all. But kindergartners in classrooms with new books and teachers who were trained in their use performed like first graders on all the literacy assessments that we administered.

Notice that the biggest gains pertained to children's print concepts and spelling. The next greatest gains—almost one standard deviation—pertained to children's ability to read and write words. One standard deviation in test scores is an enormous *real* difference in children's ability to read and write. Think about the "normal curve"—most children perform at an average level, that is, the 50th percentile; some perform at the lower end of the curve, at the 25th percentile; and others, the high achievers, perform at the top end of the curve, or at the 75th percentile. An intervention that is able to improve children's achievement by one standard deviation is powerful indeed: It would move a child scoring in the bottom quartile into the average range of achievement (50th percentile) and an average child into the top quartile (75th percentile).

We were not surprised that the intervention had such a strong influence on several of the literacy measures—we expected kindergartners to learn what they were taught. On the other hand, we were astounded that the intervention was related to increased scores on the Peabody Picture Vocabulary Test (PPVT). Because the PPVT is a vocabulary test, and vocabulary is highly correlated with intelligence, it is often a proxy, or substitute, for more thorough and time-consuming individual intelligence tests. In fact, the PPVT provides an IQ score as well as a vocabulary score. Tests of intelligence are typically considered very stable and resistant to change, so we were surprised and very pleased that the kindergartners in the classrooms with teachers who received books and professional development performed substantively better than those in the other classrooms. The improved score on the PPVT is significant because educators often look upon it, and other proxies for intelligence, as a measure of what children can learn. That a relatively modest intervention in terms of cost and time could have such an influence on the vocabulary score speaks volumes about the power of good teaching and good books in kindergarten.

We further examined differences in the classrooms—the display of books and print, the integration of reading and writing, and the ways teachers read books aloud to children and engaged them in conversations about the readings. Teachers clearly displayed their books differently. Teachers who had professional development created attractive displays that were accessible to the children; teachers without this support were likely to still have their new books stacked, even unopened, in their classrooms. Teachers with professional development also displayed children's drawing, writing, and word work; teachers without the support did not. Teachers with professional development support reported that their children participated in daily read-aloud and writing activities that were explicitly linked; they reported using multiple resources to plan; they more often planned themes or topic study instead of strictly relying on the district reading curriculum of a letter of the week.

Our observations of teachers prompted an in-depth examination of the way they interacted with children about the books that they read aloud. Teachers who participated in the professional development read the books in a way that promoted vocabulary and comprehension, as you'll see in the sample lessons in Part Four of this book.

A Decade's Research:
What I've Learned About Children's Literacy Understandings

Over the past decade I have been a participant observer in many early childhood and primary grade classrooms, most prominently in the Albany, New York, area, where I collaborated with urban primary grade teacher Jill McClement for several years. I met Jill in her third year of teaching at an urban elementary school that for decades had reported some of the lowest test scores in the state of New York. I was beginning my third year of a longitudinal study of the development of literacy understandings among children from 4 to 7 years old. Several of the children in Jill's kindergarten class were children I had observed since they were 3 and 4 years old. Jill was alarmed that her kindergarten children were not progressing—they could not learn from the reading curriculum that the district had purchased: The materials were too difficult, contained too many words, required too many skills, and went into too little depth. It was heartbreaking for me to watch the children fail to learn to read.

Earlier, I had discovered the work of two literacy researchers: Israeli educator Dina Feitelson, who wrote about the influence of read-alouds on young children's language development, and Darrell Morris, who theorized about the importance of matching voice to print in the beginning stages of learning to read. Together, Jill and I created a literacy curriculum based in large part on read-alouds of books with familiar characters, notably Clifford books and Curious George books, and the reading back of children's writing. We did not know it at the time, but the cut-up sentences we used to develop children's "concept of word in text," and the cut-up words from the sentences that we had the children manipulate and sort, presaged many of the strategies that the National Research Council identified as important in preventing reading failures. Against great odds—impoverished neighborhood, rigid curriculum, high mobility, and poor attendance, Jill created a

Books with familiar characters and patterned, simple text begin children's journey to reading.

Books with pictures, labels, and captions support kindergartners.

community of young readers and writers in her inner-city kindergarten.

Not long afterward, I took a position as a kindergarten reading teacher working in the classrooms of two new kindergarten teachers in suburban upstate New York. With Jill's assistance, I taught my new colleagues what we had learned. My new colleagues, particularly Angela Anderson, taught me the importance of embedding kindergarten literacy strategies in well-rehearsed classroom routines. The experiences in upstate New York and Philadelphia and my research on young children's literacy development prepared me for my work with kindergarten teachers in a large east Tennessee district that served urban, suburban, and rural populations.

The Tennessee Kindergarten Literacy Project

Building on what I learned in my earlier work teaching kindergartners, I helped develop a project to make literacy development more prominent in east Tennessee kindergarten classrooms. I present this work here because I believe it can serve as a model for literacy instruction for kindergartners in other schools and districts. The Tennessee Kindergarten Literacy Project involved the entire kindergarten teacher and student population within the school district, including 200 kindergarten teachers, 37 curriculum generalists, and approximately 4,000 children in 50-plus elementary schools. During year one of the project, a district committee consisting of teachers, the district reading specialist, Theresa Wishart, and an elementary supervisor reviewed or "mapped" the kindergarten curriculum against the new state standards, gathered research on kindergarten, and observed current practice in each kindergarten class. The committee found little consistency in kindergarten literacy instruction among schools in the district or even among classrooms in the same school. Although teachers made children aware of the alphabet and corresponding sounds through weekly themes and "letter-of-the-week" activities, students were not expected to know these concepts by the time they left kindergarten, nor were they ever asked to write letters or words in the classroom. Teachers used predominantly whole-group methods to teach the letter of the week with little attention to individual development.

The overwhelming emphasis of the kindergarten curriculum was on what was considered "social" development—getting along with others, developing responsibility for belongings, doing group work, completing assignments. There was little awareness that social dimensions are broader than simply acclimating children to classroom routines or that social dimensions interrelate with cognitive and emotional dimensions of children's development. Thinking, problem solving, experimenting, manipulating, and observing have relevance for all dimensions of children's development, and none more so than literacy development. When children play, they engage in all of the above—they explore, attempt, question, predict, analyze, and reflect. As they learn to read and write, they play with language—they orient lines and circles in space to make letters, they segment sounds in the speech stream they hear, they map sounds onto letters, manipulate letters to make words, and arrange words to compose messages for friends and family.

Children "grow into the intellectual life around them" (p. 88) as the famous developmental psychologist Lev Vygotsky suggested, and adults should teach them at the "growing edge of the [their] competence" (Bruner, 1986, p. 77). But to teach them at the edge, teachers have to be informed and sensitive observers of children. Only then can they provide exactly the right kind of assistance to children in the beginning stages of literacy development and move that development forward. At the time of the Tennessee project, few teachers in the district reported that they observed children systematically, used observations to inform instruction, or documented the progress of individual kindergartners in literacy development.

A few pages back, we noted that putting new books in classrooms without professional development for teachers is of little value. Similarly, literacy instruction that is not based on careful observation of individual development will not help all children gain the ground they need to reach their potential. In the next section, I'll describe teachers and students who prospered.

The Case for Systematic Observation

Based on recommendations of the committee, the district initiated a plan to develop a set of curriculum-based assessments to be used along with ongoing professional development in research-based practices in early literacy instruction for kindergarten children. Elaborating on assessments created by many educators before me, I developed a series of authentic, emergent literacy observations that inform instruction at the earliest levels. The tasks are aligned with the joint IRA/NCTE statement of developmentally appropriate practice (1998), and they have been validated against PALS-K. I was influenced by the seminal work represented by the following educators: Marie Clay's Concepts About Print and Observation Survey (1993); *The Beginnings of Writing* by Charles Temple et al. (1993); the Phonological Awareness Literacy Screening developed by Marcia Invernizzi and her colleagues at the University of Virginia's McGuffey Reading Clinic (PALS, Invernizzi, Meirer, Swank, & Juel, 2000); family literacy observations created by Greg Brooks and his colleagues at the UK's National Foundation for Educational Research (Gorman & Brooks, 1996); and many locally developed district assessments, particularly the South Colonie, New York, assessments created by the district's talented language arts supervisor, Linda Carr.

My assessments, which are presented in the sections that follow, constitute a systematic way to document individual development in *alphabetic knowledge, phonological awareness, blending and segmentation, print concepts, word reading and word writing*, and *text reading and text writing*.

Enhancing Teachers' Early Literacy Expertise

In addition to the observation tools, I developed a framework for professional development that has been successfully implemented and reported in the research literature (McGill-Franzen et al., 1999/2000; McGill-Franzen & Goatley, 2001). The organizational components of professional development include flexible grouping, that is, appropriate use of whole-class, large- and small-group, individual work/conferencing, and independent or workshop-group modes of teaching, depending on children's needs and instructional purposes. Instructional routines, that is, those everyday formats for engaging in literacy practices, include read-alouds and discussion, shared and guided reading, shared and interactive writing, and word work. The emphasis throughout my framework (see pages 28–29), and indeed, throughout this book, is on the use of scaffolds, in particular, explicit language that supports children's developing literacy. The professional development that I conducted for the Tennessee Kindergarten Literacy Project and its success in enhancing teachers' early literacy expertise and children's early literacy knowledge is the impetus for and the substance of this book.

Framework
For Kindergarten Literacy

Systematic Assessment of Literacy Development

Work samples

* ✴ Writing and spelling drafts
* ✴ Oral reading records

Observed behaviors

* ✴ Sorts
* ✴ Word reading and writing fluency
* ✴ Print and book handling concepts
* ✴ Voice-print match

Reading Support Provided by Teacher

Classroom routines

* ✴ Read-alouds
* ✴ Shared reading
* ✴ Guided reading
* ✴ Reading and discussion groups
* ✴ Independent reading

Teaching strategies

* ✴ Reading aloud
* ✴ Thinking aloud
* ✴ Prompting
* ✴ Linking reading to writing

Writing Support Provided by Teacher

Classroom routines

* ✴ Read-alouds
* ✴ Dictated writing

* Shared writing
* Interactive writing
* Writing workshop and conferences
* Independent writing

Teaching strategies

* Thinking aloud
* Prompting
* Linking writing to reading

Word Study Embedded in Reading and Writing

Classroom routines

* Name work
* Wall words work
* Sorting
* Hunting

Teaching strategies

* Sound stretching
* Thinking aloud
* Prompting

Inquiry-based Content Study

* Family and community knowledge
* Thematic units and integrated curricula

Points to Note:

* The reading and writing support ranges from very directed and explicit support (reading aloud to students or taking dictated writing from students), to minimal teacher support (independent reading and workshop writing, and inquiry-based content study). In the chapters that follow, I'll describe this continuum in greater detail.
* Knowing how much guidance to provide to a student, and when, is an art that you develop with experience and reflection.
* Traditionally, theme-based inquiry is the bedrock of the early-childhood curriculum. That doesn't change, even in this "new" notion of more strategic literacy instruction in kindergarten. In fact, teaching reading and writing in the context of this inquiry is ideal.

Teachers Try New Pedagogy

An open-ended survey of teachers' practices suggested that prior to using the assessments, most teachers had not taught reading or writing in kindergarten, only letters and sounds. As the bar diagram suggests, experienced teachers who then used the assessments taught many more areas of literacy than they had previously. Not surprisingly, letters, letter sounds, beginning sounds, and rhyme were not new—the great majority of teachers were already teaching this information to kindergartners. What was new was attention to the middles of words—the patterns within words—and word families, and the strategies children needed to be able to actually read and write, decode and spell.

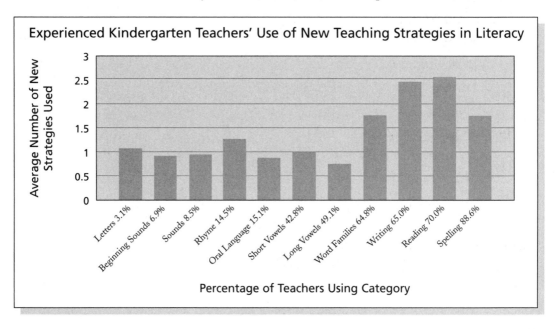

Experienced Kindergarten Teachers' Use of New Teaching Strategies in Literacy

Extending the Day for Children Who Struggle

Despite the positive accomplishments of the Tennessee Project, many children in these schools continued to leave kindergarten without the requisite literacy skills needed to achieve success in first grade. To address this literacy gap, the district initiated the Extended Day Kindergarten Literacy Program, first at a single elementary school and gradually increasing participation to about 35 teachers. Again, the Tennessee experience can provide a model for extending teaching and learning time for struggling kindergartners in other schools and districts. Depending on the way kindergarten is scheduled, the extended day can take many forms—overlapping lunch hours for half-day programs, a structure that several upstate New York schools initiated, or before- or after-school time for full-day kindergartners. In the east Tennessee model, a small number of children stayed for approximately an hour after the school day ended. Teachers were able to provide intensive and personalized instruction to these children, because they regularly observed and documented students' progress using the literacy assessments.

Program assessment data showed that students made substantive literacy progress after participating in the Extended Day Kindergarten Literacy Program (Bunker & Luna, 2003). In addition, survey results showed all kindergarten teachers believed the program was worthwhile and had a positive impact on the children served.

An Invitation to You

The Tennessee teachers I've talked about here were "lucky" in that they were given support as they changed their practice. A number of them even participated in university seminars where they shared their experiences—and their challenges. This collaborative talk with fellow teachers built both their confidence and their knowledge. Said Melissa Tatum:

> "In the beginning I was concerned that I would not be able to help my at-risk students. I was afraid that I would not provide the 'right' kind of instruction. I had heard about positive results, but I wasn't sure that I could be successful with my students. Meeting regularly with my colleagues gave me a chance to hear that other teachers were facing many of the same fears and struggles. Other teachers were struggling to get some students to retain the simplest high-frequency words, too. Other teachers sometimes started out with leveled readers that were also too hard. I was able to see how other teachers responded to these challenges. We compared notes. We learned from one another."

It is so liberating—and instructive—to hear the lowdown on others' experiences. This is something we know in our lives outside of school, but we underestimate its value in our professional lives. So where does this leave you, the teacher who is sitting with this book in your lap, very much on your own? With this invitation: Invite in your colleagues. Make this book the impetus for an ongoing professional-development support group with other teachers in your school and/or district. (Turn to page 267 for more on collaborative professional study.)

The shoptalk has a joyous effect, too—it's a place to share triumphs. As teacher Deanna Allen exclaimed, "The difference I saw in my kindergarten students at the end of the year amazes me! But even more amazing is the joy I felt as I listened to my colleagues—each one of us reported such tremendous growth in our students!"

Part Two

Timely Assessments of What Children Know

Unlike the once-a-year high-stakes standardized testing that we all love to hate, the assessments that I share in this section are easy to implement, flexible, and timely. They provide a system of observing, documenting, and interpreting what children know. If you believe, as I do, that teachers can and must move kindergarten children's development forward, regardless of what they bring to school, then the place to begin is not with the curriculum but with the child.

The Assessments

Chapter Three

Ten Minutes That May Change a Life

Individual attention, big gains.

Many early childhood advocates often equate good assessment with simply "kid watching," and kid watching we do, but to describe assessment as only "watching" somehow doesn't reflect the interactivity of the process of learning about children's development. We must purposefully engage children in reading and writing tasks that are the components of literacy in order to describe where children are—and where they need to go. Becoming literate has been likened to a journey along a road, and although the metaphor does not capture the complexity of literate development, particularly the ways that family and community shape our values and behavior, the idea of a journey does express movement, destination, and signposts. In fact, leading researchers describe children with reading disabilities as children who somehow got "offtrack" on the road to learning to read (Spear-Swerling, 2004).

As kindergarten teachers, we stand at almost the beginning of the journey. It is an awesome responsibility. Not only must we acknowledge what children bring to school from family and community, but we must also be smart enough to know how to use that knowledge to transform teaching and learning in our classrooms. In order to keep all children on-track, we need to be knowledgeable about literacy, what it looks like along a developmental continuum, how reading, writing, speaking, and listening are related and reciprocal, one language process supporting another, and how written language is different.

But despite the fact that the term "systematic assessment" sets off in our brains red flashing alarms—*Overwhelming! Can't do it! Don't have time in the day!*—finding out what your kindergartners know when they enter your classroom in September isn't hard. In short, each assessment takes about ten minutes per child—ten minutes that can enhance your instruction tenfold and set a child on his way to becoming a proficient reader and writer, rather than someone who gets permanently stamped with the label of "struggling learner." You're out to get answers to two questions: *What does this child know about literacy?* and *What can this child do?* Armed with this information, you'll know where to start instruction.

Purposes of the Assessments

Take a look at the Assessment Schedule on the next page. You will administer most of the tasks at the beginning and end of the school year an,d when appropriate, check children's progress at any point in time. The timing and purposes of the assessments vary:

* The beginning-of-the-year assessment provides a starting point for instruction.
* The midyear assessment—and assessment at any point during the school year—informs your instruction and gives you insights to share with parents.
* The end-of-year assessment helps you document progress during the school year and provide information for parents and first-grade teachers.

Suggested Schedule for Kindergarten Literacy Assessment

The 8 Skills		Beginning of Year To inform instruction	Midyear and as Appropriate To communicate to parents and inform instruction	End of Year To document progress and to communicate to parents and first-grade teachers
Letter and Sound Association Use card stock or letter tiles	Names and Sounds	Assess	Assess unknown letters and sounds	Assess unknown letters and sounds
	D'Nealian			*Your Purpose*
Phonological Awareness Use picture sorts	Rhyme	Assess	Assess unknown concepts	Assess unknown concepts
	Beginning Sounds	Assess	Assess unknown concepts	Assess unknown concepts
Print Concepts Use a Level A book		Assess all concepts, depending on book	Assess unknown concepts	Assess unknown concepts
Phonemic Segmentation and Representation Use paper and pencil or letter tiles	Spelling List 1	Assess	Assess	Assess
	Spelling List 2	*You select these lists (see sample, page 77)*		Assess if all words on List 1 are spelled correctly
Word Reading Use card stock or word cards	List 1	Assess	Assess unknown words	Assess unknown words
	List 2		Assess only those students who know most of List 1 words	
Word Writing "Write all the words you know"		Administer prompt and record number of words in writing vocabulary		
Text Reading Ask the child to read a text— • a "pretend reading" of a familiar book or story, such as *Have You Seen My Duckling?* or • the child's own writing, or • an appropriate guided reading leveled book, depending on what level of text is appropriate		Record observations as appropriate *See pages 103–113*		
Text Writing "Draw a picture and write all about yourself"		Administer prompt and analyze writing sample		

In general, assess only things child missed on previous assess.

Tips for Getting Started

✳ **Set aside 30 minutes each morning** during the first few weeks of school to assess children's literacy knowledge. If there is a parent helper or paraprofessional available, take advantage of the extra pair of hands. Parents and paraprofessionals can read the rest of the class a story, model an art project, or provide a snack while you work with individual children or small groups on the literacy assessments in another part of the room.

✳ **Set up the materials at a small table** where you can monitor the class without turning around. You can work at the table for individual assessments, or you can gather a small group there for assessments that can be administered to a group.

✳ **Conduct the assessments in the order in which I present them,** but feel free to adjust to your own needs. As you become used to doing them, you may find you like to do the tasks in a different order.

✳ **Give the one-on-one assessments a full ten minutes**—or more, depending upon how much or little knowledge children have at that point in time. Even though the one-to-one administrations take a lot of time, it is time well spent. How often can you say that you spend ten minutes focusing on a single child? As a parent, how many times have you walked away from a parent-teacher conference thinking, "She doesn't know my child"? Or, conversely, "She really captured my child." Personal interactions, such as the individual assessments, offer opportunities for us to observe individual children and take stock of their unique personalities as well as their performance on the literacy tasks.

✳ **Keep track of student progress.** Document individual student progress on the Student Profile Sheet (see page 41). Following is a sample of a completed one. Enter the scores for the entire class on the Class Record Sheet (see page 42):
- Write students' names.
- Next to each student's name, enter his or her score on the tasks and observations.
- Record the date on each Class Record Sheet.

- Plan to fill out a Class Record Sheet three times a year—beginning of the year, midyear, and end of year (although you will not administer every assessment this much).
- Assess progress any time you need information on learning and development.
- Use the Class Record Sheet to help you organize small, flexible groups for targeted instruction.

Student Profile Sheet

Student _____   Teacher _____

		Observation Dates		
		Beginning of Year	Midyear	End of Year
Letter and Sound Association	Names	+ 7/54		
	Sounds	+ 0/26		
	D'Nealian	+ 0/52		
Phonological Awareness	Rhyme	+ 4/10	+ 7/10	
	Beginning Sounds	+ 0/12	+ 1/12	
Print Concepts	Book	yes		
	Directionality	yes		
	One-to-one Match			
	Word			
	Letter	yes		
	First & Last			
	Punctuation			
	Total Concepts	+ 4/12	+ 13/14	+ 13/14
Phonemic Segmentation and Representation	Spelling List 1	+ 0/20	+ 4/20	+ 15/20
	Spelling List 2			+ 12/18
Word Reading	List 1	+ 0/16	+ 9/16	+ 16/16
	List 2			+ 11/16
	List 3			+ 10/16
Word Writing "Write all the words you know"			2 words	14 words
Reading				
Reads from Memory		yes		
Reads Own Writing				
Reads Leveled Text	Book Title			
	Guided Reading Level		A	A
	Accuracy		87 %	100 %
	Rate/Word Correct per Min.		20 WCPM	40 WCPM
Writing "Draw a picture and write about yourself"				
Drawing & Letter-like Forms				
Copied & Random Letters				
Name			yes	
Words				
Sentence				yes
Text				

Kindergarten Literacy Assessment Class Record Sheet

Teacher ___ **Ruth** ___ School _____ Date ___ **Fall** ___

Student Name	Letters: Name	Letters: Sound	Letters: D'Nealian	Phon. Aw.: Rhyme	Phon. Aw.: Beginning Sounds	Print Concepts	Spelling List 1	Spelling List 2	Word Reading List 1	Word Reading List 2	Word Reading List 3	Word Writing	Reading: Memory	Reading: Own Writing	Guided A	Guided B	Guided C	Guided D	Writing: Drawing & Letter-like Forms	Copied & Random	Name	Word	Sentence	Text
Allen	51	13		10	12	5	10		4			6	M								N			
Maddy	50	26		7	12	9	0		10			1					X				N			
Rose	49	23		8	12	7	5		2			3			X							W		
Walt	49	14		6	8	8	11		2			3			X						N			
Lea	49	25		9	12	9	5		8			4	M								N			
Zack	48	19		7	4	8	4		4			5	M								N			
Olivia	47	21		9	12	4	1		2			3	M								N			
Don	45	24		8	10	8	13		2			2			X							W		
Mike	44	5		4	8	8	7		2			3	M								N			
Emma	41	14		7	8	10	0		0			3			X							W		
Greg	38	17		4	8	8	7		2			3	M								N			
April	37	1		10	12	10	6		2			2	M								N			
Sy	34	4		10	12	8	3		0			1	M								N			
Charles	28	24		4	4	3	2		0			0	M								N			
Caden	25	5		7	10	9	0		1			1	M								N			
Jake	16	1		10	12	10	6		2			2	M								N			
Blair	13	5		10	12	10	5		4			6	M								N			
Jack	7	0		4	0	4	0		0			0	M						Ͻ					
Ashley	3	0		0	0	6	0		0			1							Ͻ					
Luke	2	0		9	0	6	0		0			1									N			
Sam	1	0		0	0	6	0		0			1									N			

A beginning-of-the year profile

Student Profile Sheet

Student _____   Teacher _____

		Observation Dates		
		Beginning of Year	Midyear	End of Year
Letter and Sound Association	Names			
	Sounds			
	D'Nealian			
Phonological Awareness	Rhyme			
	Beginning Sounds			
Print Concepts	Book			
	Directionality			
	Voice-to-print Match			
	Word Concept			
	Letter Concept			
	First & Last Word			
	Punctuation Total Concepts* (period, question mark, exclamation point)			
Phonemic Segmentation and Representation	Spelling List 1			
	Spelling List 2			
Word Reading	List 1			
	List 2			
	List 3			
Word Writing "Write all the words you know"				
Reading				
Reads from Memory				
Reads Own Writing				
Reads Leveled Text	Book Title			
	Guided Reading Level			
	Accuracy			
	Rate/Word Correct per Minute			
Writing "Draw a picture and write about yourself"				
Drawing & Letterlike Forms				
Copied & Random Letters				
Name				
Words				
Sentence				
Text				

* Your total will be between 12 and 14, depending upon the punctuation in the book you use.

Kindergarten Literacy Assessment Class Record Sheet

Teacher _____   School _____   Date _____

Category	Sub-category		Student Name → (blank columns)
Writing Text Levels	Text		
	Sentence		
	Word		
	Name		
	Copied & Random		
	Drawing & Letter-like Forms		
Reading Text Level	Guided Reading	D	
		C	
		B	
		A	
	Own Writing		
	Memory		
Word Writing			
Word Reading	List 3		
	List 2		
	List 1		
Spelling	List 2		
	List 1		
Print Concepts			
Phonological Awareness	Beginning Sounds		
	Rhyme		
Letters	D'Nealian		
	Sound		
	Name		
Student Name			

Kindergarten Literacy © 2006 Anne McGill-Franzen

Tips for Using Portfolios

In addition to the Kindergarten Literacy Assessments, maintain portfolios of children's work. Portfolios are organized and systematic collections of students' work that show individuals' efforts, improvements, or achievements over time. Portfolios may include tasks or observations from the Literacy Assessments, the core reading program, or any other work that you or the students may wish to include. Portfolios allow you to:

A portfolio with dated writing samples, reading logs, and word-bank words from cut-up sentences.

* Select items for inclusion in the portfolio in collaboration with students.
* Send the portfolio home at the end of the school year or pass it on to the student's first-grade teacher.
* Emphasize what students can do.
* Use the portfolio to show steps along the way to mastery (process) as well as final achievements.
* Talk through the selection of items with the student to teach self-evaluation strategies.

Two of the most persuasive reasons for using portfolios are that they involve students in their own learning and that they allow your students and you to compile samples of students' work that represent development over time. As students examine early examples of their work and compare these with more recent examples, they develop the capacity to monitor their progress, set goals, and engage in self-assessment. Portfolios are very effective ways to communicate progress with students themselves, their parents, and first-grade teachers.

Teachers often use portfolios as documentation to support their judgment that children have met grade-level standards. In some states, children who fail high-stakes standardized tests may be promoted to the next grade via "good cause exemptions," which often include portfolio evidence (including samples of students' work and assessment results) of having met grade-level standards.

I make several suggestions below for items to include in the portfolio. One way to promote students' self-evaluation is to ask them to explain why they selected each item for the portfolio and what they want to learn next. The following items may be included in their portfolios:

* Student self-assessment forms
* Pages from core program workbooks
* Personal word banks
* Personal dictionaries or "Words I'm Learning How to Write" charts
  (see example below)
* Reading logs
* Word-study notebooks
* Writing samples
* Pages from journals or writing logs

Words I'm Learning				How to Write			
Aa *a* *and*	Bb	Cc *can*	Dd	Ee	Ff	Gg *go*	Hh *Have*
Ii *I* *in*	Jj *Jackson*	Kk	Ll *Like*	Mm *My*	Nn	Oo	Pp *pig* *Play*
Qq	Rr *ride*	Ss *See*	Tt *The* *This*	Uu	Vv	Ww	Xx
Yy	Zz	__ed	__ing				

Assessing
Letter-Sound Identification

Did you know that the number of letters a child knows at the beginning of kindergarten will predict how easily he will learn to read? In research terms, letter-name knowledge is the most potent correlate of later reading achievement, meaning that the more letters kindergartners know now, at the start of school, the more likely they will be readers down the road. The strong relationship between letter knowledge and later reading achievement holds true even now, in an era when children have been attending preschool in record numbers. In the Tennessee Kindergarten Literacy Project, knowing at least ten upper- and lower-case letters in the fall predict-

ed that the child would be reading at least guided reading level A books by spring. By the same token, knowing only a few letters in the fall of kindergarten meant that the child was at risk of not learning to read, and in the Tennessee Kindergarten Literacy Project, the child was selected for intensive support.

Many educators caution, however, that knowing many or most letters of the alphabet may be a proxy for other kinds of preschool or home experiences, such as lis-

Bianca! A child's name is usually the first word she learns to spell.

tening to and talking about books, exploratory message writing, and opportunities to draw, write, and manipulate letters. For sure, children are socialized into the practice of literacy by adults and significant others within their home and school lives, and they often imitate the adult writing they see and pretend to read books with intonation and story language long before they can do either in a conventional sense. Children who have had access to books and book language and supportive adults to lead them into an understanding of the purposes and functions of literacy in our everyday lives certainly have a context within which learning the alphabet makes sense.

Nonetheless, knowing only the names of the letters provides children—who are quintessential pattern detectors—with a good deal of information to begin to crack the code. Letter sounds are embedded within most letter names; for example, the sound /b/ is the first phoneme that is articulated when saying the name of the letter *B*. Prior to an alphabetic or letter-name stage, marked by awareness of the association between the letter name, or symbol, and the sound, children use strictly visual information to try to remember words. In this stage, familiar to all parents, children may "read" the golden arches sign as "McDonalds" but cannot recognize the word outside the context of the arches. Without the insight that the sound /m/ is represented by the letter *M*, children read the "McDonald's" sign as a picture or logograph. When children grasp the alphabetic principle—that sounds or phonemes are represented by letters—they begin to notice the letter patterns that make up words. Similarly, when children first try to write, they use what they know—the names of the letters—to create or "invent" spellings.

LETTER-SOUND ASSOCIATION TASK

PURPOSE: To determine whether a child understands that letters represent sounds

TIME: About 10 minutes

SETTING: One-to-one

MATERIALS: Prepare the following:

- a laminated sheet with the letters of the alphabet, both upper- and lowercase, clearly printed in columns (as shown below and on Appendix page 281).

- an index card, which the child may use to frame the rows of letters as he reads them.

- a sheet for recording the child's answers, with the letters of the alphabet, upper- and lowercase, with space for checking off both the identification of the letters and the sound (see page 50).

DIRECTIONS:

Beginning of the Year

In the fall, test for both upper- and lowercase letter identification but only ask children for letter sounds, or words that begin with the sound, when assessing uppercase letters. These are more familiar to children just beginning kindergarten.

Kindergarten Literacy Assessment

1. Letter-Sound Identification

A	F	K	P	W	Z	B
H	O	J	U	C	Y	L
Q	M	D	N	S	X	I
E	G	R	V	T		
a	f	k	p	w	z	b
h	o	j	u	**a**	c	y
l	q	m	d	n	s	x
i	e	g	r	v	t	**g**

This chart for students includes two fonts for *a* and *g* that commonly appear in children's books. (You can add a column for D'Nealian font, too.) Students read across the rows on the chart, much like they would taking an eye exam.

Uppercase Letters and Letter Sounds

1. Say: "Start with the top row, and move your finger across the row of letters" (or "move the index card across the row of letters"). Show the child where to start and how to move his finger across the row of letters from left to right.

2. Say: "Tell me the name of the letter. What sound does it make?" If the child hesitates, you can prompt him by asking: "What word begins with that sound?" Accept either long vowel or short vowel sounds.

3. After the child reads across each row of letters, say: "Move your finger down to the next row of letters." Show the child the next row, or slide the index card down as the child reads each row.

Lowercase Letters (and font specific *a* and *g*)

In the fall, ask children to identify only the names of the lowercase letters and the extra *a* and *g* letters in specific fonts, but do NOT ask them for letter sounds again.

4. Say: "Tell me the name of the letter."

Recording and Scoring Uppercase Letter Names and Letter Sounds and Lowercase Letter Names

5. Record the child's responses in the appropriate column. If the child named the letter, put a check next to the letter under the Letter Name column.

6. Add up the total number of checks for both upper- and lowercase letters to obtain the total number of letter names that the child identified. Total Names: ___/54.

7. If the child provided the appropriate sound, put a check in the Sound column for that letter. If the child provided a word that begins with that letter sound, write the word in that column.

8. Add up the total number of sounds or words that the child provided for each letter and record the total. Total Sounds or Words: ____/26.
9. Write any incorrect responses that the child makes in the Letter Name or Sound or Word columns next to the letter.

Directions:

Midyear and End-of-Year

At midyear, assess only those upper- and lowercase letters and letter sounds that children did not know in the fall. In the spring, assess only those upper- and lowercase letters and sounds that the students did not know midyear. Record responses the same way you did in the fall.

What If? Answers to Common Questions

- *What if the child doesn't seem to know very many letters?*
  Say: "Look across the letters in the front row. Tell me any you know." Note the letters on the record sheet.

  For any known letters, ask: "What sound does it make?" If the child does not know, prompt for a word that begins with the letter. Ask: "What word begins with that letter?" Record the child's responses in the Sound and Word column.

  Continue this series of prompts until the child has scanned all the rows on the chart.

- *What if the child says he doesn't know any letters?*
  Find the first letter in his name and say, "Tell me the name of the letter." You want each child to be able to identify at least one letter.

Letter-Sound Record Sheet

Student _____ Teacher _____ Date _____

Uppercase Letters

Assess Date	Letter Name	Sound or Word
A		
F		
K		
P		
W		
Z		
B		
H		
O		
J		
U		
C		
Y		
L		
Q		
M		
D		
N		
S		
X		
I		
E		
G		
R		
V		
T		
Total		

Lowercase Letters

Assess Date	Letter Name	Sound or Word
a		
f		
k		
p		
w		
z		
b		
h		
o		
j		
u		
c		
y		
l		
q		
m		
d		
n		
s		
x		
i		
e		
g		
r		
v		
t		
Total		

D'Nealian Uppercase

Assess Date	Letter Name	Write
A		
F		
K		
P		
W		
Z		
B		
H		
O		
J		
U		
C		
Y		
L		
Q		
M		
D		
N		
S		
X		
I		
E		
G		
R		
V		
T		
Total		

D'Nealian Lowercase

Assess Date	Letter Name	Write
a		
f		
k		
p		
w		
z		
b		
h		
o		
j		
u		
c		
y		
l		
q		
m		
d		
n		
s		
x		
i		
e		
g		
r		
v		
t		
Total		

Jackson: What He Teaches Us

In Chapter Four we'll delve into how to use the assessments to plan lessons and activities in whole class, small group, and individual settings. Until then, I'll provide brief snapshots of particular students to give you a general sense of how assessments inform teaching decisions. Ruth Lindsey, a kindergarten teacher in east Tennessee, noted that one of her students, Jackson, identified no sounds and four uppercase letters of the alphabet at the beginning of the school year. Not surprisingly, the letters he identified were J-A-C-K—the first four letters of his name and his nickname at home. Ruth built initial instruction on what Jackson knew—the four letters in his name, and his interest in his name, and the names of the other kindergartners. She invited Jack to practice with the following activities. Generally, Ruth had Jackson devote about ten minutes a day to letter work practice.

* Jackson cut up the letters in his name and the names of his friends, making and breaking each name so that he could recognize them on sight.

* Jackson "used what he knew"—the way his name started and those of his friends—to identify and remember initial letters in other words.

Letter-Sound Record Sheet

Student _____ Teacher _____ Date _____

Uppercase Letters		Lowercase Letters		D'Nealian Uppercase		D'Nealian Lowercase	
Letter Name (AUG)	Sound or Word (AUG)	Letter Name (AUG / DEC)	Sound or Word (DEC)	Letter Name (MAY) / Write (MAY)		Letter Name (MAY) / Write (MAY)	
A ✓	✓	a ✓ (AUG)	✓	A ✓ ✓		a ✓ ✓	
F ✓	✓	f ✓ (AUG)	✓	F ✓ ✓		f ✓ ✓	
K ✓	—	k ✓ (AUG)	—	K ✓ ✓		k ✓ ✓	
P ✓	✓	p ✓ (AUG)	✓	P ✓ ✓		p ✓ ✓	
W ✓	✓	w ✓ (AUG)	✓	W ✓ ✓		w ✓ ✓	
Z ✓	✓	z ✓ (AUG)	✓	Z ✓ ✓		z ✓ ✓	
B ✓	✓	b ✓ (DEC)	✓	B ✓ ✓		b ✓ ✓	
H ✓	hen	h ✓ (DEC)	✓	H ✓ ✓		h ✓ ✓	
O ✓	okra	o ✓ (AUG)	✓	O ✓ ✓		o ✓ ✓	
J ✓	jumprope	j ✓ (DEC)	✓	J ✓ ✓		j ✓ ✓	
U ✓	umbrella	u ✓ (DEC)	✓	U ✓ ✓		u ✓ ✓	
C ✓	cup	c ✓ (AUG)	✓	C ✓ ✓		c ✓ ✓	
Y ✓	yellow	y ✓ (AUG)	✓	Y ✓ ✓		y ✓ ✓	
L ✓	Lizzie	l ✓ (DEC)	✓	L ✓ ✓		l ✓ ✓	
Q ✓	—	q ✓ (AUG)	✓	Q ✓ ✓		q ✓ ✓	
M ✓	—	m ✓ (AUG)	Jemma	M ✓ ✓		m ✓ ✓	
D ✓	—	d ✓ (AUG)	dont	D ✓ ✓		d ✓ ✓	
N ✓	✓	n ✓ (DEC)	—	N ✓ ✓		n ✓ ✓	
S ✓	snake	s ✓ (AUG)	✓	S ✓ ✓		s ✓ ✓	
X ✓	—	x ✓ (AUG)	✓	X ✓ ✓		x ✓ ✓	
I ✓	✓	i ✓ (AUG)	—	I ✓ ✓		i ✓ ✓	
E ✓	Emily	e ✓ (AUG)	✓	E ✓ ✓		e ✓ ✓	
G ✓	green	g ✓ (AUG)	✓	G ✓ ✓		g ✓ ✓	
R ✓	✓	r ✓ (AUG)	✓	R ✓ ✓		r ✓ ✓	
V ✓	violin	v ✓ (AUG)	✓	V ✓ ✓		v ✓ ✓	
T ✓	team	t ✓ (AUG)	✓	T ✓ ✓		t ✓ ✓	
Total 26	21	Total 20	22	Total 52 52		Total 52 52	

* He sorted letters from names into many different categories.
* He hunted for letters in words that were the same as letters in names and not the same.
* He found letters in words that started the same as names, ended the same.
* He matched upper- and lowercase letters.
* He matched letters in names to letters in alphabet books.
* He created his own alphabet book.
* He wrote letters to fluency on whiteboards [that is, they write them until they can spell them conventionally without looking at a model].
* He wrote every day, using what he knew to compose messages, and read back what he wrote.

Jackson's progress at midyear

Jackson, at midyear, had almost mastered the letters and sounds of the alphabet! Still, he confused some letters and sounds when most of Ruth's other students fluently identified letter names and sounds. Using midyear performance on the letter and sound identification assessments, Ruth listed Jackson's confusions.

What do his errors tell us?

Let's look closely at the pattern of errors. Jackson's confusions make perfect sense! Not only do *Uu*, *Ww*, and *Yy* look similar, but *U* and *W* sound similar, and the name of the letter *Y* is formed in a similar place in the mouth.

Similarly, we form the lowercase letters *q*, *p*, and *d* the same way—using "balls and sticks." Only the way we orient these letters in space distinguishes one from another. To further confuse Jackson, the phonemes /p/ and /d/ also sound similar. In some fonts, including many magnetic letters used in core reading program materials, whether the letter is supposed to be a *p*, *b*, *q*, or *d* is almost impossible to ascertain—it depends completely on how the child orients the magnetic letter in constructing words.

Another source of confusion is the lowercase *l* and the uppercase *I*. Again, in some fonts the letters look identical. To further muddy the waters for Jackson, both the lowercase letter *i* and the lowercase letter *j* have dots and are distinguishable only by the "tail" on the *j*.

Letter:	Jackson Confused With:	Sound:	Jackson Confused With:
W	U	/w/	/y/
w	u	/w/	/y/
U		/u/	/y/
u	a	/u/	/y/
V	u	/v/	/u/
p	d	/p/	/d/
Q	P	/ku/	/p/
q	p	/ku/	/p/
i	j	/i/	/j/
l	I	/l/	/j/

Font sorts help clear up confusion

Using font sorts, Ruth helped make explicit the features that distinguish these highly confusable letters. In order to "anchor" Jackson's visual memory, Ruth first taught one letter of the confusing pairs to mastery. Again, building on what Jackson knew, Ruth used a "key word" that he already automatically recognized and spelled—*pig*—to help anchor Jackson's memory and to serve as a reference for him. Whenever Jackson was confused about the directionality of the letter *p* versus *q*, he referred to his alphabet book and the drawing of the pig. By contrasting *p* with *q*—the two visually similar letters, Ruth explicitly pointed out the directionality of the "ball" and "stick" in the two letters, and the orientation in space—that is, what makes a *p* a *p* and not a *q*? Jackson hunted for *p*'s and *q*'s, wrote words with these initial letters in his word study notebook. Ruth used the same strategies to teach Jackson to differentiate lowercase *i* from *j* and *w* from *u* and *v*. By the end of the year, Jackson—now a reader and writer—no longer confused *p* with *q* but still had some difficulty differentiating lowercase *l* from uppercase *I* when these letters were presented to him in isolation.

Phonological Awareness

By now, most of us have heard the call to develop children's "phonological awareness"; we know that phonological awareness is critical to kids' reading. But what exactly does the term mean? Before moving on to a description of the assessments, here is salient background about this much-touted term.

Phonemes are the smallest units of sound in our language. For example, the word *cat* is made up of three sounds or phonemes—/c/ /a/ /t/. There is not a one-to-one correspondence between phonemes or sounds and letters. The word *cake* also has three sounds or phonemes—even though it has four letters. Phonological awareness, then, refers to our conscious attention to the sounds or phonemes of spoken language. As skilled speakers and readers, it is often difficult for us to step back and analyze the phonemes or sounds in words we already know how to spell.

For a child learning to talk, however, speech is a continuous stream of sounds that he miraculously learns to parse into units that have meaning. In learning to read, the child not only has to segment the speech stream into the smallest units—phonemes—but also must match phonemes to the letters

Discerning the sounds of words

that represent them. For the kindergarten child, a major task of learning to read is understanding that the phonemes or sounds of our language map onto the printed letters in fairly predictable ways.

One of the first patterns that children discover about language is rhyme. Being able to detect rhyming patterns supports children's emerging insights into the predictable ways that speech maps onto print. Another aspect of phonological awareness that develops early, along with knowledge of the alphabet, is the ability to distinguish among initial sounds in words. In the beginning stages of learning to read, children attend first and foremost to the initial letter in words. Therefore, it is important to assess children's ability to attend to and differentiate beginning sounds in words, and to develop this awareness along with rhyme in children without such knowledge. I constructed the sorting tasks that follow based on the sound contrasts used to tap phonological understandings in the PALS-K, a screening instrument for identifying kindergartners at risk across Virginia and other assessment and teaching materials typically included in core reading programs for kindergartners.

Sorts: What Are They?

Sorts are hands-on tools for categorizing pictures and words according to particular criteria. In some cases, as in the phonological awareness assessments described here, students select pictures that rhyme or have the same beginning sound. I like the sort format, rather than a paper-and-pencil task, for evaluating children's awareness of rhyme and beginning sounds, because sorting is not only an assessment tool but also a problem-solving strategy that helps children detect patterns. In the process of observing what children know, teachers are also teaching them to categorize sounds and search for common elements.

RHYME SORT

PURPOSE: To discern whether the child can hear rhyme in common words

TIME: About 10 to 20 minutes

SETTINGS: One-to-one

MATERIALS: 24 blackline picture cards for the rhyme sort—four practice picture cards, 20 picture cards for students' independent sort—and a sheet for recording students' responses (see Appendix, pages 277, 278). (The blackline pictures suitable for laminating are on Appendix pages 279, 280.)

DIRECTIONS:

Again, I standardized the administration and scoring of the phonological sorts so that you can document students' learning over time.

1. First, model how to sort picture cards into rhyming pairs:
    *   Place the four practice picture cards faceup, saying the name of each picture (*hen*, *bag*, *ten*, *tag*).
    *   Say: "I am listening for the rhyme." Put the two sets of pictures together that rhyme. Say: "*Hen* and *ten* rhyme, so I am putting them together. *Bag* and *tag* rhyme, so I am putting them together."

Practice cards

2. Next give the student ten picture cards, saying the name of each picture (*rug, tube, fan, mail, dig, can, bug, cube, pail, pig*).

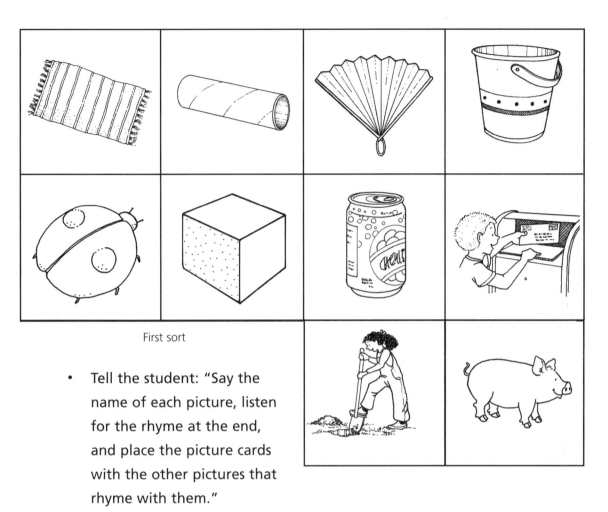

First sort

- Tell the student: "Say the name of each picture, listen for the rhyme at the end, and place the picture cards with the other pictures that rhyme with them."

3. After the student has finished the sort, ask the student to check his work.
    - Tell the student: "Say the name of the picture in each rhyming pair, and make sure that there is a match."
    - If the student does not accurately match all rhyming pairs, do not continue with the assessment. Record the score. You do not want to frustrate the student or get a score that represents pure guessing. You have already determined that he needs to develop his ear for rhyme.
    - If the student accurately matches the rhyming pairs, give him the remaining ten picture cards, identify each picture (*feet, cake, moose, seat, rake, goose, tie, sock, pie, lock*) for the rhyme at the end, and

Second sort

place each picture with the picture that has the same rhyme.

• Record the student's score.

Key pictures for beginning sound sort (see next page)

BEGINNING SOUND SORT

PURPOSE: To determine whether the child can distinguish among initial sounds in common words

TIME: About 10 to 20 minutes

SETTINGS: One-to-one

MATERIALS: 4 picture cards to be used as headers (key pictures) in the sort, 4 practice picture cards and 12 picture cards to be used in the independent sort, and a student record sheet. (See blackline masters in Appendix, pp. 277–280).

DIRECTIONS:

1. First model how to do a picture sort for beginning sounds:
   - Place the key pictures (*needle, penguin, fairy,* and *game*) faceup in a header (or top of the column) position.
   - Say: "I am listening for the beginning sound."
   - Point to each picture as you say the name of the picture, stressing each beginning sound. Ask the student to repeat the name of each picture, again stressing the beginning sound. Take out the four practice pictures (*nine, peas, garden,* and *fan*).
   - Place each practice picture card faceup underneath each key picture as you say the name of the practice picture card, and the name of each key picture, stressing the beginning sound.
   - Model your thinking by saying: "I am listening for the same sound at the beginning. *Ggg-ame* and *ggg-arden* both sound the same at the beginning, so I am putting *garden* under *game*."
   - Continue in the same way with the other practice picture cards.

2. Next, set up the independent sort. First, take away the practice picture cards and leave the key picture cards (*needle, penguin, fairy,* and *game*) on the table.
   - Give the student six picture cards, saying the name of each picture (*goose, feather, pencil, note, neck,* and *pizza*).

- Tell the student: "Say the name of each picture, listen for the beginning sound, and place the picture card under the key picture that sounds the same at the beginning."
- After the student finishes, ask the student to check his or her work.
- Tell the student: "Say the name of each picture placed under the key pictures. Check to make sure the beginning sound matches the beginning sound of the key pictures."
- If the student does not accurately match the beginning sounds for four out of six, do not continue with the assessment but do record the score.
- If the student accurately places four out of six pictures, give him or her the remaining six picture cards, and say the name of each picture (*frog, pan, fish, guitar, nest, gate*).
- Tell the student to sort the remaining picture cards in the same way.
- Remind the student to listen for the beginning sound, and place each

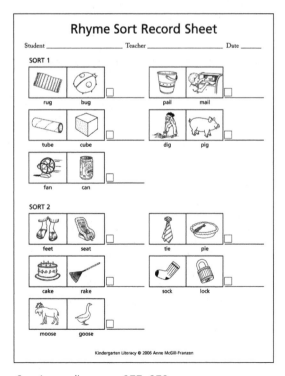

See Appendix, pages 277, 278.

Beginning Sound Sort Practice Cards

picture under the key picture that sounds the same at the beginning.

- Record the student's score.

3. To score this task, mark the Student Record Sheet with a check if the picture is appropriately placed.

4. Add the number of checks and record the number. Beginning Sounds Total: _____/12.

Phonological Awareness: Tips for Analyzing It

At the beginning of kindergarten, most children can match some rhyming pictures and sort some pictures that begin with the same sound on the literacy assessment. Whole-class routines like shared reading, poetry reading, choral reading, and memorized songs provide many opportunities for children to develop an "ear" for rhyme and beginning sounds and an appreciation for wordplay. Kindergartners not only have to attend closely to the sounds of language so that they can segment speech, but they also have to have an understanding of the vocabulary we use to refer to language. Asking a child to listen for "rhyme" or a "beginning sound" is a meaningless exercise unless she understands the concept we are referring to.

Teacher Mandy Taylor had a child in her kindergarten who did not understand the concept of rhyme. At the beginning of the year, Megan was unable to match pictures that rhyme or identify pictures that start with the same sound. By midyear, Megan could segment and stretch the sounds in words; she could distinguish sounds at the beginning of words but had made no progress with rhyme. By teaching Megan word families, starting with short /a/ families, Mandy gave Megan a visual strategy for understanding rhyme— the idea that words that sound alike at the end or "rime" usually are spelled with the same pattern. By early spring Megan had made progress in every area of reading and writing— she could fluently read high-frequency words, she was spelling, she was writing, and she was a reader. Megan had made some progress in being able to identify rhyme, as well. Despite Mandy's best efforts to focus on rhyme as an area of study, Megan matched only a few rhyming pictures on the literacy assessments. Mandy, however, decided to move on. Because rhyme is the means to an end—reading—and not an end in itself, and because Megan was already a reader and writer, Mandy determined that hearing rhyme was not important for this particular child's development.

Assessing Print Concepts

When learning to read, there is a kind of all-or-nothing principle at work: Children must be able to use all sources of information in a text in order to self-correct their errors and become "self-teaching" or, as Marie Clay put it, "a self-improving system." If children have had sustained experiences with reading and writing outside of school, they are likely to demonstrate at least book handling and print orientation skills upon entry to kindergarten. These are a few of the concepts of print that you'll evaluate with the assessments in this section.

These print awareness concepts may strike us as obvious when we think about our bookish kindergartners, but for children who cannot yet read or have little experience with print, we can't take for granted the "metalanguage," or language about language, that we use to describe the literacy process. Terms such as *letters*, *sounds*, *words*, *sentences*, *paragraphs*, and *pages* are abstract concepts that only convey meaning once a youngster is learning to read.

Learning to read and learning to talk are analogous in many respects. The most striking similarity, I think, has to do with segmenting: Learning to talk requires that the child segment the speech stream into meaningful units; similarly, learning to read requires that the child segment a line of print into meaningful units—words.

Teacher Debra Burke assesses concepts of print.

Syntax and sentence meaning—what sounds right and makes sense—support children's nascent ability to recognize and remember words. *Context* is the term that we typically apply to the information supplied by sentences in a book and by the story as a whole, and in books for beginning readers, the illustrations provide contextual support, as well. Determining what your students get—and don't yet understand—about books will give you the insights you need to move their literacy forward.

About the Concepts of Print Assessment

The education field is indebted to Marie Clay for her insight into the fact that print awareness is critical in learning to read, and for her creative measure of children's awareness of print. I adapted Marie Clay's original Concepts About Print (CAP) because I wanted to use real books rather than the more contrived ones used in CAP. I have seen many such adaptations and tried to incorporate the most salient of the print concepts in the most efficient way, as these observations must be made on an individual basis.

Sitting with a child one-on-one is a giant bonus to a child—a special opportunity for him or her to attend closely to the process of reading with an interested and skilled adult by his side. In a single meeting, a child can learn critical concepts about book orientation, distinctions between illustration and text, directionality of text, the meanings of *letter*, *word*, *first*, and *last*, and the function of common punctuation marks.

Voice-to-print match. One of the most important of the print concepts that Clay originally assessed is the voice-print match, that is, the ability to point to each word in the text as the words are spoken. A one-to-one correspondence between the spoken words and the printed words suggests that the child has grasped the concept that words are units separated by white spaces and that words are not syllables or "beats" in the cadence of a line of text read aloud. According to researcher Darrell Morris, and his mentor Ed Henderson, both of whom have written extensively on this topic, understanding a concept of word in text figures prominently in the child's ultimate ability to decode. Using information from letter names, the child first notices beginning consonants in words, an understanding that contributes to his ability to read the spaces between words.

Once a concept of *word* is established and the child notices both beginning and ending letters, the word itself is "frozen" in the line of print, and thus available for the child to inspect (the word's vowels and vowel patterns). Being able to "hold" the word in text leads the child to letter or letter-cluster matches with sound, which is the ability to decode and spell. The ability to decode frees the child from having to visually memorize every new word according to shape or other kinds of configurations, and instead enables controlled decoding of new words. Repeated exposures to simple text lead to more rapid word recognition, a growing repertoire of words known at sight, and fluent oral reading.

The following assessments uncover children's print awareness and ability to voice-print match a line of familiar text. A sample sheet for recording students' responses is provided on page 69.

PRINT CONCEPTS ASSESSMENTS

PURPOSE: To evaluate the child's knowledge of how print works

TIME: About 10 minutes

SETTING: One-to-one

MATERIALS:

Autumn: A predictable book of about 8 pages and 25 words, such as *The Birthday Cake* by Joy Cowley. (Generally, these are guided reading level A books.) Text should include at least periods and question marks. Pictures should clearly support text.

Midyear or Spring: A different book of about 8 pages and 10 words per page. For example, *My Butterfly Garden* by Stefanie Langer. Text should have periods, question marks, and exclamation points.

SETTINGS: One-to-one

DIRECTIONS:

1. To get a sense of a child's book orientation skills, hand the book to the child with the spine or back of the book facing the child. Do not open the book for the child. Say:
   - "Show me the front of the book."
   - "Point to the title." Note the student's actions on the record sheet (p. 69).

2. Next, open the book to a page with both text and pictures or a place in the book with a page of print opposite a page of illustrations. Say:
   - "Show me where you start reading." Note whether the child points to pictures or print. You want to discern whether the child realizes that print, not pictures, carry the story.
   - "Which page do we read first?" Note whether the child points to the upper left-hand corner or the beginning of the text on the page.

3. In English, unlike some other written languages, readers' eyes follow a line of text from left to right and, at the end of the line, return to the beginning of the next line of text. To assess directionality and return sweep, say:
   - "Show me with your finger which way you would go when you read." Note whether the child understands the left to right sequence of reading a line of text.

   1   —————————————————▶   2

   - "Show me where you would go when you get to the end of the line." Note whether the child understands that he returns to the beginning of the next line.

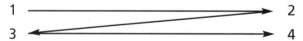

4. Read a page or two of text, pointing to each word. Reread the print, asking the child to point to each word as you read. Say:
   - "Point to each word while I read."
     Note whether the child points to each word. Observe whether there is an exact match between the words spoken and the printed words to

which the child pointed. Record your observations.

5. If you wish to further evaluate children's understanding of the concept of word in context, you can ask the child to find particular words in the text that was read, asking him to point, read, and search for the word(s).

6. Continue reading the book.

7. After the reading, give the child two index cards to frame words and letters in the text. Show the child how to move the index cards. Say:

   - "Show me one word."
   - "Show me the first word on the page."
   - "Show me the last word on the page."
   - "Show me one letter."

8. There are other words that constitute the language of instruction in beginning reading, for example, *top*, *bottom*, *beginning*, *middle*, and *end*. You may wish to evaluate the child's understanding of these words as well as the words identified here. If so, follow the format as above.

9. Turn to a page with a period. Say:

   - "What is this?"

10. Turn to a page with a question mark. Say:

    - "What is this?"

11. Turn to a page with an exclamation point. Say:

    - "What is this?"

12. There may be other punctuation marks in the text, for example, quotation marks. You may want to assess the child's knowledge of other punctuation by following the same format as above. Remember, though, that kindergarten children may have trouble articulating the function of punctuation even if they can recognize and name the marks.

TIPS FOR SCORING:

As you review each child's performance on the assessments, consider what the students need more exposure to and practice with. How can you build these concepts into your literacy routines? Let's look at what Mary, a magnet school teacher, in an urban area in east Tennessee did with her assessment results. Mary had kindergartners from widely divergent literacy backgrounds. There were some children in her class who would be considered very well "read-to" and advantaged by any standard and others with little preschool experience with books. Nonetheless, on the literacy assessments, almost one-third of her class was unable to track print with

Kindergarten Literacy Assessment — Print Concepts				
Student: Tikea	Teacher:			
Directions	Scoring & Concept Analysis	Date	Date	Date
Hand the book to the child with the book spine toward the child.	Put a check over the concept and the date mastered.	Aug	Dec	May
Before opening the book, say:	**Book Concepts**			
"Show me the front of the book."	Front cover	✓		
"Point to the title."	Title	✓		
"Show me where you start reading."	Print carries the message (not illustrations)	✓		
	Directionality			
"Which page do we read first?"	Beginning of text	✓		
"Show me with your finger which way you would go when you read."	Left to right sequence	✓		
"Show me with your finger which way you would go when you read."	Return sweep	—	✓	
During reading, say: "Point to each word while I read." Observe whether the child points to each word as the teacher reads. Is there an exact match between number of words spoken (read) by the teacher and the printed words to which the child points?	One-to-one match between speech and print Observations: Until May, she needed my guidance to match. Now can locate words. *Memorized words*	—	—	✓
After reading, ask the child to use index cards to:	**Word Concepts**			
"Show me one word only."	One word	✓		
"Show me the first word on this page."	First word	—		✓
"Show me the last word on this page."	Last word	—		✓
"Show me one letter."	Letter concept	✓		
"What is this?" [.]	Punctuation concepts (period)	—	—	
"What is this?" [?]	(question mark)	—	—	✓
"What is this?" [!]	(exclamation mark)		—	

Fall book title: The Birthday Cake
Winter book title: My Butterfly Garden
Spring book title: My Butterfly Garden

Total points 7/12 8/14 12/14

their fingers as she read a familiar, predictable book.

Mary used singing as a strategy to support the voice-print match, singing books instead of reading them (for example, *Lazy Mary Will You Get Up*, *On Top of Spaghetti*, *Mary Wore Her Red Dress*), and pointing to each word. Kindergartners reread and sang the books during center time, using pointers. Their concept of voice-print match improved.

Mary made the other print concepts accessible to all her students during classroom literacy routines by emphasizing good reader behaviors and the concept of word in text. Here are some of the routines for you to consider:

- Model left-to-right voice-print match and directionality during

Kindergarten Literacy Assessment
Print Concepts

Student _____ Teacher _____

DIRECTIONS	SCORING & CONCEPT ANALYSIS	Date	Date	Date
Hand the book to the child with the book spine toward the child.	Put a check over the concept and the date mastered.			
BEFORE OPENING THE BOOK, SAY: "Show me the front of the book."	**BOOK CONCEPTS**			
	Front cover			
"Point to the title."	Title			
"Show me where you start reading."	Print carries the message (not illustrations)			
	DIRECTIONALITY			
"Which page do we read first?"	Beginning of text			
"Show me with your finger which way you would go when you read."	Left to right sequence			
"Show me with your finger which way you would go when you read."	Return sweep			
DURING READING, SAY: "Point to each word while I read." Observe whether the child points to each word as the teacher reads. Is there an exact match between number of words spoken (read) by the teacher and the printed words to which the child points?	**ONE-TO-ONE MATCH BETWEEN VOICE AND PRINT** Observations:			
AFTER READING, ASK THE CHILD TO USE INDEX CARDS TO:	**WORD CONCEPTS**			
"Show me one word only."	One word			
"Show me the first word on this page."	First word			
"Show me the last word on this page."	Last word			
"Show me one letter."	**LETTER CONCEPT**			
"What is this?" [.]	**PUNCTUATION CONCEPTS** Period			
"What is this?" [?]	Question mark			
"What is this?" [!]	Exclamation point			

Fall book title _____

Winter book title _____

Spring book title _____

Total print concept points	_____	_____	_____

Total will be between 12 and 14, depending on punctuation in book you use.

Kindergarten Literacy © 2006 Anne McGill-Franzen

shared reading.

- Model spacing, linearity, capitalization, and punctuation during interactive writing.

- Make writing and reading tasks authentic and engaging.

- Encourage partner reading and rereading of familiar, easy books, tracking print with their fingers.

- Always ask children to read back their own writing, and have them point to each word.

If you're not familiar with routines like shared reading and interactive writing, I describe them in more detail in section four. See the box at right for other resources on these practices.

Next, we'll look at how children stitch together their emerging understandings of spelling to get down in writing all they want to say.

Books With a Wealth of Literacy Lessons

Getting the Most Out of Morning Message by Mary Browning Schulman and Carleen Payne

Guided Reading: Good First Teaching for All Children by Gay Su Pinnell and Irene C. Fountas

Guided Reading: Making It Work by Mary Browning Schulman and Carleen daCruz Payne

The New Kindergarten: Teaching Reading, Writing, & More by Constance J. Leunberger

Reading and Writing in Kindergarten: A Practical Guide by Rosalie Franzese

Reading and Writing With Word Walls by Janiel M. Wagstaff

Shared Reading for Today's Classroom by Carleen deCruz Payne

Shared Writing Lessons by Carleen deCruz Payne and Mary Browning Schulman

Teaching Kindergarten: CDs/ Songbook by Bonnie Brown Walmsley et al

Assessing

Spelling: Segmenting Sounds and Representing Sounds With Letters

Wouldn't it be something if we could get a Grand Canyon–vast view of a kindergartner's mind, to see exactly what they know about written language? When children spell—or try to spell—we get quite a fantastic vista. We say that kindergarten children "invent" spelling, but actually there is nothing invented about the letters they choose—they are using what they already know about letters and sounds to spell words.

The assessments in this section provide you with ways to see beyond the seeming randomness of children's spellings to their coherence—to all they have to tell you about their developing knowledge of how words work. But first, a bit of background on the synapses that are firing when little Susie spells *chair hr* or *jr*.

The sorting tasks in the previous section helped you to see whether your students were able to identify rhyme and distin-

Segmenting sounds to spell

Chapter Three: Ten Minutes That May Change a Life

guish sound—phonemes—at the beginnings of words. The ability to do those things are considered early markers of phonological awareness. The spelling of words is a more advanced category of language in that spelling requires children to *segment* the phonemes in a spoken word and represent those phonemes with letters. As the child begins to spell a word, he must slowly stretch out the sounds, trying to forge a connection between what he hears and the letters he knows.

If the child perceives a match—the name of the letter, when spoken, feels the same as the sound as it is stretched—the child represents the sound with the letter.

3 Sources of Kids' Spelling Sense

There are three sources of a child's early knowledge about spelling:

1. The names of the letters
2. The way a sound feels in the mouth when it is spoken or articulated
3. The way the letter names feel when they are spoken or stretched

Spelling: Part of a Desire to Write

Moms, dads, and caregivers write a fairly continual stream of purposeful messages—lists, calendar jots, invitations, e-mails—and practically from birth, children are watching their every move, like ace detectives on a hot trail. They pick up on writing's purpose, and are eager to crack the code of written communication. By kindergarten, children are more than ready to begin the process of spelling conventionally. To them, it's all part of the delight of purposeful reading and writing.

Spelling, it turns out, is linked to later reading achievement, as well. Recently, researchers have demonstrated that kindergarten spelling is both a predictor of first-grade reading achievement and possible precursor to word recognition (Morris, Bloodgood, Lomax, & Perney, 2003). This may be so because the desire to write, and consequently, to spell, may *precede* an interest in reading. Or more specifically, wanting to write out a message may provide the impetus for children to attend to print—which ultimately leads to learning to read. Durkin, whose work I cited in Chapter One, called children who learned to read early "paper-and-pencil kids" because of their intense desire to write. Paper-and-pencil kids probably come from high-literacy backgrounds, too, which may account for their later proficient reading.

The Stages of Spelling Development

Beginning on page 83, we'll look at some actual student examples of spelling at various stages and the kinds of activities that can move students' understandings forward. For now, here is an overview for you to keep in mind as you assess what your students know.

Emergent Stage

If children confuse drawing and writing, use letterlike forms, letters, or random letters to represent words but without attention to letter and sound correspondence, they are at the Emergent Spelling Stage (Bear et al., 2004, p. 11).

Letter-Name Stage

The next stage, Letter-Name, is associated with spelling that clearly represents letter-sound correspondences, beginning with control over most initial consonants, some digraphs and blends, and confusion over short vowels. Often, children in the Letter-Name stage of development substitute the alphabet letter name that feels closest to the point of articulation for short vowel sounds, as in these examples from Bear et al. (p. 14).

BAD	for	bed
SEP	for	ship

Within-Word Stage

The Within-Word Stage is characterized by spelling that correctly represents initial and final consonants, blends and digraphs, and short vowels, but not long vowel patterns. Children in this stage "use but confuse" long vowel markers, such those at right (Bear et al., p. 16).

FLOT	for	float
PLAIS	for	place
SPOLE	for	spoil
DRIEV	for	drive

Tips for Using the Phonemic Segmentation Assessment

I constructed this assessment using the spelling assessments developed at the University of Virginia McGuffey Reading Clinic and PALS-K as my guide.

* At the beginning of kindergarten, we do not expect children to spell conventionally. So on the scoring sheet for the first two spelling lists, you'll notice that I've included "allowable phonemes" in addition to the conventional spelling.

* Phonemes, or sounds, are represented in brackets, e.g., the phonemes in the word *rag* would be represented this way: /r/ /a/ /g/. There are three sounds, and those are represented by three letters. The phonemes, or sounds, in the word *coat* would be represented this way: /c/ /o/ /t/. There are three sounds, but in conventional spelling, these are represented by four letters. The letters *oa* represent a single sound.

* Your goal is to evaluate whether your kindergartners can hear sounds in words and represent these sounds with letters. To keep the task of printing the letters and words from becoming onerous, provide each kindergartner with an alphabet strip to help scaffold the formation of the letters. For children whose fine motor coordination isn't as developed, you may want to administer the assessment to them one-on-one, using magnetic letters (see page 80).

* Allowable Spellings List 1 (page 77) assesses the child's knowledge of letters that represent consonants in initial and final position and short vowels in a medial position in three-letter words. We refer to this spelling pattern as Consonant-Vowel-Consonant (CVC).

* Allowable Spellings List 2 (page 77) assesses the child's knowledge of consonant blends and digraphs and long vowel patterns. There are various configurations of these patterns: Consonant-Vowel-Vowel-Consonant (CVVC) and Consonant-Vowel-Consonant-Silent *e* (CVCe) are the most common. *Administer it only to those children who spelled all the words in List 1 conventionally.*

SPELLING LIST 1

PURPOSE: To determine whether the child can hear sounds in words with short vowels and represent each of the sounds with letters.

TIME: About 10 minutes

SETTING: Whole-class or small-group administration

MATERIALS: Students will need an alphabet strip and a blank sheet of paper. (Or you can use the reproducible in the Appendix, p. 281.)

DIRECTIONS:

1. Model for the students how to listen for sounds in words and how to represent each sound with a letter:

   • Say: "Please write your name at the top of the paper. Today you are going to spell some words. I will show you how. Please listen and watch me. I want to spell the word *bat*. First,

---

Kindergarten Literacy Assessment
Spelling

Student _____ Teacher _____ Date _____

a b c d e f g h i j k l m n o p q r s t u v w x y z

A B C D E F G H I J K L M N O P Q R S T U V W X Y Z

1. _____

2. _____

3. _____

4. _____

5. _____

Total Phonemes _____

I will say the word slowly and listen to each sound. *Bb-aa-tt*. I hear a /b/ sound at the beginning of *Bb-aa-tt* so I am going to write a *b* [write on a white board or chart paper]. *Bb-aa*. In the middle of the word I hear an /a/ sound so I am going to write an *a* next to the *b* [write *a*]. *Bb-aa-tt*. At the end of the word I hear a /t/ sound so I am going to write a *t* at the end of the word [write a *t* after the *a*]. Now I want you to spell some words. I want you to listen carefully, say each word to yourself and then write down a letter for each sound you hear. You can use the alphabet at the top of the page to help you remember how to write a letter."

- Say: "The first word is *rag*." Do not assist children except by encouraging them. You may prompt by saying: "What other sounds do you hear?" Continue the assessment as suggested below.
- Say:

  "The next word is *mob*. . . ."

  "The next word is *fun*. . . ."

  "The next word is *sit*. . . ."

  "The next word is *jet*. . . ."

- Thank students, and say something that encourages them about their spelling. Collect their papers. You can either score papers as you get them or wait until you've given the assessment to everyone.

TIPS FOR SCORING:

1. Examine the child's spelling of each word.

   - Compare the child's spelling with the Allowable Spellings List 1 (next page).
   - Note that most of the sounds may be represented by more than one letter. For example, in the first word, *rag*, /r/ may be represented by *w* or *y* as well as by *r*. In the middle of the word *rag*, the /a/ may be represented by *e* as well as by *a*. And at the end of the word *rag*, the /g/ may be represented by *k* as well as by *g*.

2. Record your observations on the student's record sheet. For each spelling word, put a check over the letter that represents the sound (phoneme), even if it is not the "correct" letter in terms of the conventional spelling of that word and even if the letter is written backward or out of order. (Each word has 3 phonemes, for a total of 15.)

Kindergarten Literacy

Allowable Spellings List 1	
Word	Phonemes Represented By Letters
1. rag	/r/ /a/ /g/ r a g w e k y
2. mob	/m/ /o/ /b/ m o b u p i
3. fun	/f/ /u/ /n/ f u n v o
4. sit	/s/ /i/ /t/ s i t c e d
5. jet	/j/ /e/ /t/ j e t g a d ch h
Total _____ /20	

Allowable Spellings List 2	
Word	Phonemes Represented By Letters
1. coat	/c/ /o/ /t/ c o a t k o d ow
2. plate	/p/ /l/ /a/ /t/ p l a t e b e d ae
3. sheep	/sh/ /e/ /p/ sh ee p s e b ea
4. bump	/b/ /u/ /m/ /p/ b u m p p o b
Total _____ /18	

- Assign an extra point for each conventional spelling.
- Count the total number of checks for all the words, and record this number next to Total (___ /20).

3. For each of the five spelling words, write comments about the student's ability to hear and represent sounds—jot down notes anywhere on the record sheet. Use the following questions to prompt your thinking:

   - Does the child write only letterlike forms or random letters?
   - Does the child represent some consonant sounds by an appropriate letter?
   - Does the child attend to sounds at the beginning of the word? The middle of the word? The end of the word?
   - Does the child represent the word by writing a single letter?
   - Does the child include any vowels?

SPELLING LIST 2

PURPOSE: To determine whether the child can hear sounds in words with long vowel patterns and represent each sound with a letter. (Give this assessment only if the child spells all the words in List 1 conventionally. You don't want to frustrate children by presenting too many words for them to spell.)

TIME: About 10 minutes

MATERIALS: Students will need an alphabet strip and a blank sheet of paper

SETTINGS: Whole-class or small-group

DIRECTIONS:

1. Model how to spell words as you did before giving students List 1.
   - Say: "Now I want you to spell some words. I want you to listen carefully, say each word to yourself, and then write down a letter for each sound you hear. You can use the alphabet at the top of the page to help you remember how to write a letter."
   - "The first word is *coat*." Do not assist children except by encouraging them. You may say: "What other sounds do you hear?"

2. Continue the assessment as follows.
   - Say:

     "The next word is *plate*. . . ."

     "The next word is *sheep*. . . ."

     "The next word is *bump*. . . ."
3. Thank students and collect their papers.

TIPS FOR SCORING:

1. Score students' spelling on List 2 as follows:
   - Words 1 and 3 are worth a total of 4 points—one point for each sound (phoneme) that is represented by an allowable letter and one extra point if the word is spelled conventionally.
   - Words 2 and 4 are worth 5 points. There are four sounds (phonemes) in each of these words. One point is awarded for each phoneme that is represented by an allowable letter and one extra point for conventional spelling.
2. Examine the child's spelling of each word.
   - Compare one child's spellings with the Allowable Spellings List 2 (page 77).
   - Note that some sounds may be represented by more than one letter and that some letter combinations are represented by only one sound. For example, in the first word, *coat*, /o/ may be represented by *oa* or *o* as well as by *ow*.
3. For each spelling word, put a check over the letter that represents the sound (phoneme), even if it is not the "correct" letter in terms of the conventional spelling of that word, and even if the letter is written backward or out of order. Write on the student's record sheet.
   - If the word is spelled correctly put an extra check in the space beside the word.
   - Count the total number of checks for all the words and record this number next to Total (___ /18).

4. Record your observations (with a comment) about the student's ability to hear and represent sounds anywhere on the student record sheet.
   - Note whether the student was able to represent consonant sounds, consonant blends, and digraphs with appropriate letters.
   - Note whether the student attended to sounds at the beginning of the word, the middle, or the end.
   - If the student tried to spell using long vowel patterns, note that, as well.
   - For students who have difficulty with the fine motor coordination required to write, you may wish to administer this assessment individually, using manipulatives so that the child can demonstrate his ability to represent sounds with letters.

ASSESSING INDIVIDUALLY WITH MANIPULATIVES

PURPOSE: To observe the child sound-stretch words with short vowels and select a letter to represent each sound

MATERIALS: Large and small magnetic phonics or word-building boards; magnetic letters or tiles, both upper- and lowercase, arranged alphabetically for the student

SETTING: One-to-one (this setting is preferable if a child has difficulty with the fine motor coordination needed to write letters)

DIRECTIONS:

1. As in the whole-class paper-and-pencil task, model how to listen for sounds in words and represent each sound with a letter.
   - Say: "Today you are going to spell some words. I will show you how. Please listen and watch me. I want to spell the word *bat*. First, I will say the word slowly and listen to each sound. *Bb-aa-tt*. I hear a /b/ sound at the beginning of *Bb-aa-tt*, so I am going to put a *b* at the

beginning [find a lowercase *b* and place it on the first line on the large magnetic board]. *Bb-aa*. In the middle of the word I hear an /a/ sound, so I am going to put an *a* next to the *b* [find an *a* and place it next to the *b*]. *Bb-aa-tt*. At the end of the word I hear a /t/ sound so I am going to put a *t* at the end of the word [find and place a *t* after the *a*]. Now I want you to spell some words. I want you to listen carefully, say each word to yourself, and then find a letter for each sound you hear. You can say the alphabet to help you find the letters."

2. Score the assessment and analyze the results as in the paper-and-pencil administration, making sure to record the child's responses as he spells words with the manipulative letters.

The Spelling Analysis Guide

Okay, you have your students' performance on List 1 and List 2 words. Now what? The Kindergarten Spelling Analysis Guide (see next page) will help you see the sound-letter correspondences your kids are using—or confusing—and which patterns would be a sensible starting point for instruction.

Notice that the guide shows consonants and consonant blends and digraphs in initial and final position, short vowels, and the long vowel patterns that were included in the assessment. You can see at a glance the developmental sequence in spelling as the children move from using only the names of the alphabet letters and the way they feel when they say them to including visual information, or how words look, in their spelling attempts. Although children typically move through developmental spelling stages in this sequence, it is important to keep in mind that they may start at different points. For instance, kindergartners may present themselves as emergent spellers, letter-name spellers or, in the case of more experienced writers and readers, within-word spellers. By looking closely at the student's spelling, you can see what letters or patterns she or he is "using but confusing" in his or her attempts to represent different sounds. Where the student is using but confusing spelling patterns is an excellent place to begin word study.

Kindergarten Spelling Analysis Guide

Students begin by understanding these three elements of spelling

This knowledge develops later

Spelling Words	Consonants		Blends & Digraphs		Short Vowels CVC	Long Vowels CVCe	Long Vowels CVVC	Other Vowel Patterns	Adding -ed -ing	Prefixes & Suffixes
List 1	Initial	Final	Initial	Final	Middle	Middle	Middle			
1. rag	r	g			a					
2. mob	m	b			o					
3. fun	f	n			u					
4. sit	s	t			i					
5. jet	j				e					
List 2										
1. coat	c						oa			
2. plate			pl			a-e				
3. sheep		p	sh	mp	u		ee			
4. bump	b									

Students then develop more complex understandings about the insides of words

Tikea, Jacob, and Olivia: What They Teach Us

Tikea is in the Letter-Name Stage. She was able to represent initial consonants and some final consonants fairly consistently but did not represent any vowels in the three-letter phonograms that comprised List 1. Her teacher, Elizabeth Bunker, a Reading First literacy coach, stepped up rhyme activities, especially songs and chants, so that Tikea would notice onset and rime in rhythmic prose. At the same time, Elizabeth introduced word families, pointing out that if words sound the same at the end, they are likely to have the same letters, or rime, at the end. First, Elizabeth introduced the –at family, then compared –at words with other short a- word families.

At midyear, Jacob spelled two words on List 1 conventionally and spelled the other three words with plausible representations of the phonemes, including each short vowel. In this case, his teacher, Mandy Taylor, compared and contrasted words across word families. Jacob was in the late Letter-Name Stage. At the end of the year (second column), Jacob had mastered short vowels, as illustrated by his performance on the same words.

Olivia, who correctly spelled all the words on List 1 and several of the words on List 2 (second column), knows short vowels in three-letter words and consistently represents initial consonants and blends, including consonant

Kindergarten Literacy Assessment
Spelling

Student _____
Teacher I'Keah

a b c d e f g h i j k l m n o p q r s t u v w x y z

A B C D E F G H I J K L M N O P Q R S T U V W X Y Z

+1 1. H
+1 2. m
+2 3. f N
+2 4. ʒ f
+2 5. J J
    +8

Kindergarten Literacy Assessment
Spelling

Student Jacob D   Date _____
Teacher _____

a b c d e f g h i j k l m n o p q r s t u v w x y z

A B C D E F G H I J K L M N O P Q R S T U V W X Y Z

4 1. Rag | Rag 4
3 2. MoSP | Mob 4
4 3. BuL FuN | fun 4
                        4
3 4. Set | Sit
                        4
4 5. Jet | Jett

18/20   20/20

Kindergarten Literacy Assessment
Spelling

Student Olivia   Date _____
Teacher _____

a b c d e f g h i j k l m n o p q r s t u v w x y z

A B C D E F G H I J K L M N O P Q R S T U V W X Y Z

1. rag   Cot   (3)
2. mob Plat   (4)
3. fun Sheep   (5)
4. Sit BuP   (3)
5. Jet
   20/20   15/18

blends in final position, but needs instruction in digraphs and vowel patterns. Olivia is in the Within-Word Stage. She is able to segment words and identify the long vowel sound inside the word, but she is confusing the long vowel patterns that represent that sound. Her teacher, Ruth Lindsey, showed her that different spelling patterns can represent the same long vowel sound and helped her sort and record the common ways to represent the long /a/ in her word study notebook.

Kindergarten Spelling: What to Expect

Typically, in kindergarten, most students will look like Jacob in their spelling. Early in the year, kindergartners usually can represent at least a few phonemes with the appropriate letters, usually consonants in an initial position in the word. Next, students represent consonants in the final position. Like Jacob, many kindergartners "use but confuse" short vowels late into the school year, needing picture-sound sorts to distinguish among short vowel sounds in the middles of words and plenty of practice to consolidate that learning. By the end of kindergarten, most children will be able to segment the sounds in consonant-vowel-consonant (CVC) words and represent these sounds with appropriate letters, although they may not always spell these words conventionally. We can support kindergartners' spelling development by engaging them in reading and writing, by making explicit the patterns that distinguish words, and by providing opportunities for them to manipulate, categorize, and study words. In section four, I'll detail activities that support children's development.

Assessing
Text Writing

"**C**omposing is a gathering of ideas to share," states Charles Temple et al. in their brilliant book on early writing, *The Beginnings of Writing* (1993). It's a simple but rich statement to ponder as our kindergartners embark on writing. It reminds us that writing is a social act, and like so many endeavors kids engage in, it's worth the effort because it connects them with others. Temple et al.'s words remind us that children aren't excited to write unless the act involves meaningful ideas, unless it lets them have their say. "Composing is a gathering"—yes, and that's what makes it a challenge, as it requires a child to sift among many ideas, and select, and then find a "right" order to communicate the things that matter to him.

And to up the ante further, *written* composition is "making marks that call to mind the ideas you had…" (p. 13). It adds a whole other layer for a child to attend to. For writing to be read by others, it must be conventional. For children to write conventionally, they need to be aware of others' points of view—what others need to know in order to understand. And they need to be aware of the conventions of spelling as well as the different forms—or genres—

Brianna tells us something about herself.

of writing to fit their ideas into. As Temple puts it, children have to master three aspects of convention:

* What does writing look like, or "How to make marks that look like letters?" After all, letters are arbitrary, conventional symbols related to spoken words and the sounds, or phonemes, within words.

* How do letters work to make words? Certain sequences of letters make words, and the conventions that govern these sequences are spelling patterns.

* How does writing organize ideas? ". . . [T]here are certain patterns around which ideas can be organized, that give writing a certain form, which is put to a certain purpose"—to convey feelings, inform, persuade, or entertain (p. 14).

The Predictable Way Children Learn to Write

As is true of reading, learning to write is analogous in some respects to learning to talk. Children learn to talk by paying close attention to the communication around them and attempting to make their needs and wants heard within this communicative framework. They create a set of internalized "rules" to account for the language they notice, and through trial and error, construct their own utterances based on these rules. Adults, mostly parents, support children's acquisition of appropriate language by modeling and simplifying the structures they use to make them more accessible to children.

Children learn to write in school through a similar interplay with adults. Teachers scaffold children's developing proficiency in writing by modeling various writing structures, providing engaging examples of various forms, encouraging children to try out what they are learning on others, and systematically teaching conventions that children lack. Just as children learn the "rules" of speech in roughly the same sequence, as Roger Brown described in his studies of oral language, children demonstrate control over written language conventions in predictable ways. In the previous chapter on spelling, we explored children's movement through orthographic stages, and how to measure growth. In the task that follows, I present a rubric for evaluating children's position along a developmental sequence for written language mastery.

The observations by Marie Clay in her insightful foray into writing, *What Did I Write?*

(1975), Gertrude Hildreth's analysis of writing published at least a decade earlier (1964), and Charles Temple's incisive description of early writing (1993) each have informed the construction of my rubric. It is critical for teachers to document children's developing control over the conventions of writing as they move through successive approximations to proficiency. The most efficient way to do so is by collecting multiple samples of an authentic writing task at specified points in time, but first we must know:

The desire to write may precede the desire to read.

* what features of writing to look for
* what adaptations signal progress
* where the child needs to go next

Early writing and early reading are reciprocal processes, with writing supporting reading and learning to read supporting writing. In acknowledgment of that relationship, the writing that children produce in response to this task provides the text that children will "read back" in order to help teachers evaluate children's reading development (see Reading Level Assessments, p. 103).

TEXT WRITING TASK

This task taps into the familiar, encourages children to use what they know about writing, and all children, regardless of their developmental level or experience, can participate equally in the assignment.

PURPOSE: To learn what children know, using writing to communicate

TIME: About 15 minutes

MATERIALS: Paper, pencil, markers

SETTINGS: One-on-one, small-group, or whole-class

DIRECTIONS:

Begin the writing task after giving students paper and pencils or markers.

1. Say: "Draw a picture and write all about yourself."

2. Tell the children that you cannot help them, but they should use all the resources they have to help them write.

3. Say: "You can use the word wall, the alphabet chart, the vowel chart, the 'Words I Use When I Write,' list, or your personal dictionary. Think of the things that you would like to say about yourself: your name, how old you are, what you like to do, your favorite food or book or things to do in school. You can tell about your pets or brothers and sisters or mom and dad. You can write where you live and who your friends are. Make sure to put your name on your paper."

4. Date the papers, rewrite what the student has written—have the student tell you what he wrote—for future reference. Record other observations.

TIPS FOR SCORING:

1. Using the rubric on the following pages, examine the students' writing. On the Student Profile Sheet (page 41), mark the highest level of writing according to the rubric—drawing (D), copied or random letters (C), name only (N), words (W), sentences (S), and text (T).

Writing Rubric

Drawing and Letterlike Forms

Writing that mixes drawing and distinct letters or letterlike forms is the first kind of emergent writing—it suggests that the child knows that "squiggles," "waves," and circles, humps, crosses, and other letterlike forms of print convey the message, not the drawing or picture.

"I am at home."

Copied and Random Letters

Once the child recognizes the alphabet as a series of letters, he tries to copy them. By repeating letter string patterns or creating random strings of letters, numbers, and some letterlike forms, the child gains mastery over the formation of letters. The child likely can differentiate numbers from letters and knows that letters of the alphabet are used to create messages.

"I love snow."

Adams Twelve Five Star Schools
Rocky Mountain Elementary School
3350 W. 99th Ave.
Westminster, Colorado 80020

Name Only

What the child learns in mastering his name—that sounds map onto letters, that letter names carry sound, and control over fine motor skills—he applies to all other attempts to write and read. Give credit for the name category even if the child reverses letters and uses upper- and lowercase letters in inappropriate positions (see "Courtney"). If the child does not write his name in a linear, left-to-right direction or mixes "mock-letters" with actual letters, do not give credit for this category of development (see Levantay).

"Courtney"

"Levantay"

Words

At this level, the child may include memorized words and words spelled with single letters, missing vowels, incorrect vowel patterns, or other invented spellings. The message may be primarily one- or two-word labels, captions, or lists.

"My dad. My dog."

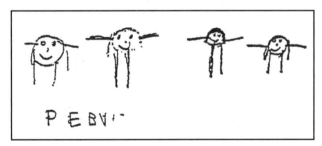

"People"

Sentences

This category includes at least one line of words (conventionally spelled or invented spellings), written from left to right, with some spacing between words, and may include punctuation (not necessarily appropriate punctuation). Notice in the Barbie™ example, the child writes a number of unrelated sentences; thus, she hasn't achieved text level yet but is still writing at the sentence level.

"I go to ride my bike."

"I like to play with my friends."

This student writes well, but is not yet able to compose a series of sentences that sustain an idea.

Text

This category includes more than one sentence (as defined above) with ideas that are related. The child's sentences can be the beginning of a narrative, as in the first example, with an event or episode described in a simple setting. Or the child's sentences can be the beginning of informational or expository writing, as in the second example, with a simple listing of attributes of a person or a whale. Notice in the whale example, the sentences relate to each other.

"It is sunny today. I went out to play."

"The whale can't come out of the water.
I can get out of the water."

Tikea: What She Teaches Us

Tikea made remarkable progress in her writing. In the fall, she was able to write her name and random letters and letterlike forms. Clearly, Tikea had few "anchor" or high-frequency words that could support her reading and writing. Besides the attention to letters, letter patterns, and the sounds that represent these patterns, Tikea's teacher wrote predictable chart stories with sentences that Tikea cut apart, sorted, and reconstructed. Tikea practiced writing these high-frequency words to fluency and added them to her personal word wall for easy reference in her writing. By spring, Tikea was writing text—an amazing achievement.

* Analysis of her text writing suggests that she has a memorized store of high-frequency words that she is able to spell fluently.
* She can sustain a topic over four sentences with appropriate punctuation and capitalization.
* Tikea made a single reversal—the lowercase letter *g*.

Tikea's Fall Writing

Tikea's End-of-Year Writing

Assessing

Word Writing

"Kids say the darndest things!" How many times have we chuckled over the uncensored comments that kids make? Well, when children have another venue—writing—for off-the-cuff observations, look out! I'm thinking, in fact, of my 5-year-old, who posted signs all over her bedroom door the day her little brother learned to walk—"No babies allowed!" Or my nephew, who described his mom in his school Mother's Day card by writing, "Her eyes are the color of dirt." Kindergartners express unmitigated glee at being able to write a message in the first place, and if the recipient laughs, hugs him, or gets mad, so much the better.

I am always surprised at the very first words children write—look at Olivia's words on page 99—*Olivia*, *red*, and *God*! You will be surprised, and usually delighted, by the first words your children haltingly write in the fall of kindergarten and amazed at their word writing fluency just a few months later.

You can administer this assessment in a small-group or whole-class setting. It requires only a student record sheet and provides a great deal of information to you about children's literacy development. I adapted the task from Clay's "Write All the Words You Know" assessment in the Observation Survey (1993). Taking into account that writing for ten minutes can be a formidable task for a kindergartner, I suggest you provide kids with an individual alphabet strip in case they can't remember how to print certain letters.

Discovering the power of words

WORD WRITING TASK

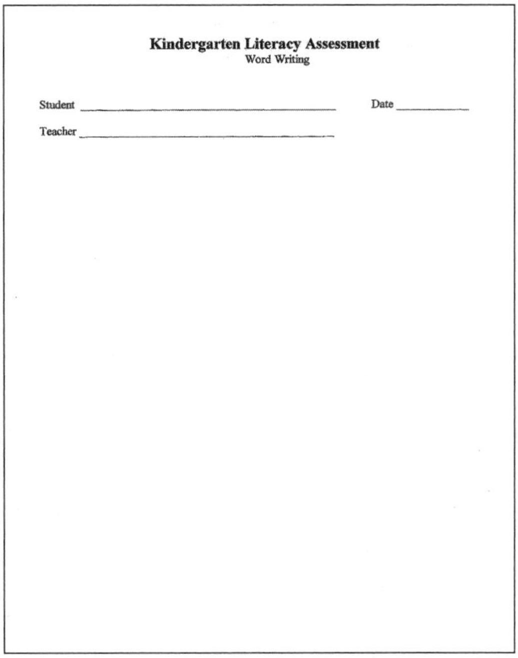

Kindergarten Literacy Assessment
Word Writing

Student ______________________ Date __________

Teacher ______________________

PURPOSE: To observe the child's word writing fluency

TIME: About 10 minutes

SETTINGS: Small-group or whole-class

MATERIALS: Make up a sheet like the one shown at right, or provide an individual alphabet strip for the child's reference

DIRECTIONS:

1. Model how to write all the words you know by talking about your thinking as you write:
   - Say: "Put your name on the top of the paper. Today you are going to write all the words you know. Watch me. I am going to show you what words I would write."
   - On the white board or chart paper, write your own name.
   - Say: "The first word I would write is my own name."
   - "Now I write the names of people in my family or the name of one of my friends." Write another name.

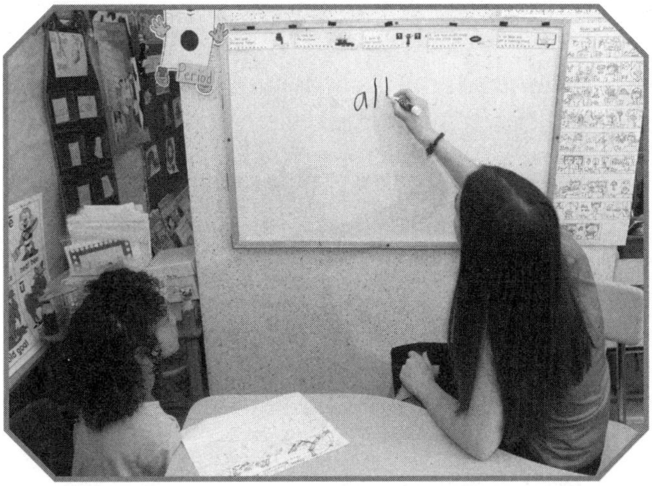

Model word writing before giving the assessment.

- Say: "If I know how to write my mother's name or my father's name, or the words *mom* or *dad*, I would write that." Write *mom*.
- Say: "I would write the name of my pet or any other words I know, like *dog* or *cat*." Write another name. Write *cat*.
- Say: "I can use words I know to make new words. If I take the *C* off *cat,* I can make the word *at*." Write *at*.
- Say: "I also know how to write the word *no*. Write *no*."
- Say: "You will have ten minutes to write all the words you know."

2. Erase the board or remove the chart paper.

3. Do not assist the children. Prompt, if necessary, by again suggesting the child's name, names of family members, pets, friends, family words such as *Mom* or *Dad*, words for pets such as *cat* or *dog*, color words, and words likely to be known, such as *yes* and *no*.

4. Prompt the student to use words he or she knows to make new words.

5. Allow only 10 minutes.

6. Gather student papers.

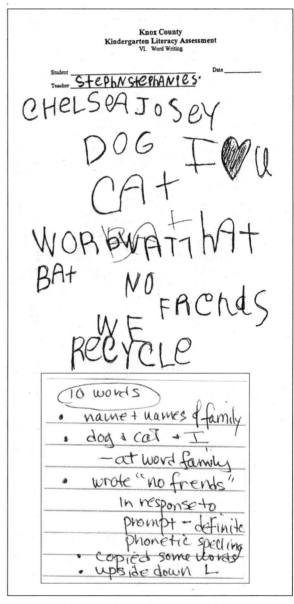

You can write your observations on a sticky note.

TIPS FOR SCORING:

- Count the number of words the child spelled conventionally, and write that number on the child's student profile sheet (and class record sheet, if you wish). Generally, kindergartners write just a few words in the fall of their kindergarten year, but by spring their word writing vocabulary has grown by leaps and bounds.

- If you notice that the child copied some words (for example, from wall charts or the class rules, like Stephanie's "We Recycle" on page 96), ask the child to read the words back. If the child can read the words, give credit for the writing. If not, write "copied" next to the words.

- Do you notice any patterns or confusions? Record on the record sheet what you discern. You might note, for example, whether the child wrote memorized sight words—this provides information about the extent of the child's bank of known high-frequency words. At the beginning of the year, the child may have few words that he or she learned from reading, but as the year progresses, and the child has more exposure to high-frequency words, he or she should be able to fluently and accurately write such words in a timed task.

- Note whether children appear to use letter-name knowledge to spell the words, as in invented spelling. For example, a child may invent the spelling of *of* as *AAV* because the short *o* vowel is very close to the letter name *A* in sound and the way it feels when spoken. Try it! The letter *V* is very close to the consonant *f* in *of*, especially if the child is stretching the word to hear the sounds.

- Note if a child can use known words to write new words. For example, does the child manipulate onset, or consonant, and rime, or the vowel and any subsequent letters, to write new words? Take a look at Stephanie's word writing task. In addition to her own name and the names of family members, she wrote *cat, bat*, and *hat*, changing the initial consonant to write other *–at* word family words. Stephanie knows how to make and break a familiar word to write other words.

- Note whether a child uses—or uses but confuses—short vowel or long vowel patterns and, if so, which ones. For example, many kindergartners who have a lot of experience with reading may write the word *they* as *THAY* because they remember the *-ay* pattern in words such as *play* or *day*. In other words, they know the sound that they want to represent (the long *a*), but they are "using but confusing" the letter pattern that spells that sound in *they*. Kindergartners need to be taught flexible strategies for writing words. Long *a* can be spelled with *-ay* as in *play*, *-ai* as in *rain*, with a final *e* as in *cake*, and *-ei* as in *eight*, as well as *-ey* in *they*.
- Note confusions in letter formation, including reversals.

Olivia: What She Teaches Us

To give you a picture of what understandings a kindergartner's word writing might showcase for you, let's look at the work of one child, Olivia. At the beginning of kindergarten, Olivia wrote three words; at midyear, her teacher Ruth counted 21 conventionally spelled words. Now, on the one hand we can applaud that Olivia is much more prolific in her word writing after several months of school—the number increased seven-fold. But with Olivia, and your own students, pause to consider the kinds of words she has written. In the fall and spring, Olivia wrote memorized words:

- ✳ color words (*white, pink, yellow, red, purple, blue, green, brown, orange, black*)
- ✳ high-frequency words encountered in her reading materials at school (*the, to, go*)
- ✳ words used in daily writing in school (*I like*)
- ✳ words from her family and community (*God, Mom, Dad, Emily*)

A growing bank of memorized words culled from life experiences is great, but what's lacking in Olivia's assessment words is evidence of *word making*. That is, Olivia does not use what she knows about the structure of words (for example, word families) to make new words. This will probably be the case for a number of your students. So, what's your

Olivia's Fall Word Writing

Kindergarten Literacy Assessment
Word Writing

Student _____   Date _____
Teacher _____

OLIVIA

RED

GOD

Olivia's Midyear Word Writing

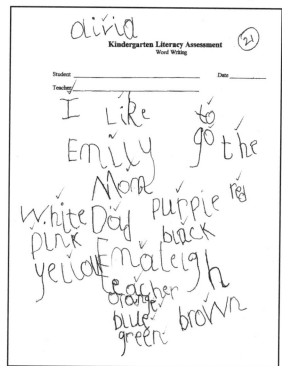

olivia   ㉑
Kindergarten Literacy Assessment
Word Writing

Student _____   Date _____
Teacher /_____

I Like   to
Emily   go the
         Mom
White Dad Purple red
Pink   black
yellow Emaleigh
      teacher
      orange
      blue brown
      green

next teaching move for kids at this stage?

A useful strategy is "making and breaking" words, substituting initial letters, medial letters, and final letters to build new words. Because Olivia can write so many words already, as many other kindergartners can also do by midyear, a good place to start is the child's own writing vocabulary. What words—already known—can help Olivia and others learn to write more words? Words such as *like*, *Dad*, and *red* are good words for making and breaking because they have a common spelling pattern. By substituting other consonants for the first letter in *like*, for example, Olivia can make *bike*, *Mike*, and *dike*; using the word *Dad*, she can make *bad*, *mad*, *sad*, *fad*, and several other new words. By adding the letter *i* to the letters *r-e-d* in the word *red*, Olivia can make several new words, including *rid* and *ride*. Magnetic letters, laminated or magnetic letter tiles, letter rods, and plastic overhead letter tiles are all excellent tools for little hands to manipulate letters and build new words.

Assessing
Text Reading

Think of some amazing circus act—someone crossing a high wire on a unicycle while juggling flaming torches, a hundred feet above loud music and lions. Whew, lots of skills in simultaneous action! Now think of learning to read. Which is the more impressive feat? With all due respect to the high wire artists of the world, reading is.

Reading requires an awareness of language by ear and language by eye—you have to hear the sounds while processing the visual cues, or spelling patterns, that match the sounds. Reading requires as well many other understandings about language–an intuitive knowledge of what "sounds right" in a sentence and what words "make sense" and match visual and meaning cues. We must attend to other signals in print, too—sentence and phrases boundaries and punctuation—so that we read with fluency and appropriate intonation.

Reading is strategic, meaning we have to activate an array of cognitive strategies to pull it off. We have to relate new information to known information, and in doing so, construct, monitor, and repair our understandings as we read. It's quite a high-wire act that goes on in our brains.

Reading is quite a feat for a 5-year-old.

Wading Pools and Rapids

Now let's switch metaphors. When I think of children's development as readers, I often have an image of kids playing in a stream, one with stretches of fast-moving water alternating with quiet pools. Some children may need time to consolidate early reading strategies at a particular level before moving on, to wade and

Young readers develop at their own pace.

splash around in a big, round puddle of concepts before they're ready to jump to the next pool. Such children may read many, many books at guided reading level A, where they are supported by highly predictable language patterns, illustrations, and words repeated over and over, before they tackle level B. Others children seem to ride swiftly down the stream, moving from nonreader to reader in no time at all. Such children gain insight into decoding fast, and it may carry them from level A to level C within a week. The point is, children's development is so fluid in the early stages and full of surprises as to who is going to "catch the current" and who is going to need more time. And so I think it's vital to observe reading behavior closely and frequently in order to provide the best possible instruction.

In the assessments that follow, you'll use leveled books to help you observe where each student is in the process of learning to read a text conventionally. On the next page, I've sequenced the tasks to set up a continuum of reading levels, similar to those of learning to write.

Continuum of Reading Levels

Reads From Memory: This is the earliest stage of reading. As you observe children at this level, notice what language features they have internalized about reading. Do they use "book language"? Do they create a story from memory?

Reads Back Writing: This is often the first actual—conventional—reading a child does. It is the easiest text for a child to read because is comes from him—both the ideas and the printed message that communicates those ideas. The child draws a picture to represent what he is thinking, then uses what he knows about letters, sounds, words, and print concepts to create a written text that explains his drawing. By looking at a child's writing, as we did in previous sections, we can see what he knows about writing words. Take, for example, the charming little text about the whale on p. 92: "The whale's can't cm out aav wwdr. I can get out aav wwdr." What is striking here is that the child wrote the same invented spelling for both "aav" and "wwdr," demonstrating that he knows a word is spelled with the same letters regardless of where it appears. If a child is able to read back his own writing, saying, for example, the same word whenever he sees a particular combination of letters, or reading the text back in exactly the same way, regardless of how often you ask him to do it, he is demonstrating the same principle: words are invariant. Being able to read back writing is actual reading—the child points to each word, making a voice-print match; he uses initial letters to help support his memory for words; he uses the drawing he created to support his memory for the ideas he wishes to communicate.

Reads Text: Once the child has a small store of "sight" words—words like *the*, *I*, or *in* that appear over and over in reading materials—and can use these words, initial letters, and the spaces between words to match voice to print, he is ready to try easy, leveled books. Of course, the child must simultaneously orchestrate any number of strategies to successfully read even the simplest little book, but writing and reading back his own writing will prepare him well for this task. As I show you on p. 106, books vary in the level of support they offer the emergent reader, most noticeably in the illustrations, the familiarity of the topics and words, and the predictability of the language used. The easiest books are also the shortest books, with the fewest number of words and the shortest sentences.

READING LEVEL ASSESSMENTS

PURPOSE: To determine the level of text the child is able to read

TIME: 10 to 20 minutes, depending upon on child's ability

SETTINGS: One-to-one

MATERIALS:

If you suspect the child's level is:

- **Reads From Memory**: Use a level-A wordless picture book such as Nancy Tafuri's *Have You Seen My Duckling?* (Greenwillow, 1984) or a book with which the child is very familiar

- **Reads Back Own Writing**: You will need the child's text writing assessment (see page 88)

- **Reads Text**: Use books spanning guided reading levels A through D

DIRECTIONS FOR USING A WORDLESS PICTURE BOOK:

1. Take an initial picture walk through the book. (I'll use Tafuri's as an example.)
   - Read aloud the title, pointing to each word.
   - Say: "I wonder what's going to happen in this story?"

2. Invite the child to picture walk through the book.
   - Ask the child to suggest what might be going on in the story.
   - Ask the child to identify the various animals that the mother duck meets.

3. Next, model a "reading" of this or another wordless picture book, reading any text that is there and creating a story that reflects what's shown on the wordless pages. (For *Have You Seen My Duckling?* you might say: "Early one morning, a baby duck saw a pretty butterfly and swam away from the other ducks.")

4. Now ask the child to "read" the story.

5. Note the child's use of book language such as "one day" and "once upon a time." Note the child's use of memorized phrases, such as "Early one

Early one morning...

morning..." or "Have you seen my
duckling?" Note the child's ability
to create a story that reflects the
illustrations on each two-page
spread.

DIRECTIONS FOR USING A FAMILIAR BOOK:

1. If using a book that has been read during shared reading, ask the child if he or she remembers the story.

2. If so, ask the child to take a picture walk through the book to help remember what happens.

3. Then ask the child to "read" the story.

4. Note whether the child uses book language and can recreate a story that matches the illustrations even though the child is not reading conventionally.

Three opening pages from the wordless picture book *Have You Seen My Duckling?* by Nancy Tafuri (Greenwillow, 1984)

TIPS ON SCORING:

- If the child points to the words and reads them, he or she is not "reading from memory" but actually reading the text. Give the child a book from a higher guided reading level and assess his or her reading of that (see guidelines below).
- If this is the highest level of text reading that the student can do, then indicate that the student is "reading from memory" on the Student Profile Sheet and/or Class Record Sheet (page 40).

DIRECTIONS:

1. After the child completes the Text Writing Task of "Draw a picture and write all about yourself," ask, "Can you read what you wrote?"
2. Note the child's reading behaviors, e.g., looking at the illustration, re-reading his words, pointing, matching his voice to the print, and self-correcting his mistakes.

TIPS ON SCORING:

- If the child is able to point and read back his or her own writing, then he or she is at the easiest level of conventional text reading. At this point, the student knows that words are invariant, that is, the word *the* will always be spelled with the same pattern of letters, regardless of where it appears.
- Give the child a book at the next reading level, guided reading level-A, and assess.
- If level A is too hard, indicate that the student "reads back own writing" on the Class Record Sheet.

Leveled Books: A Through D

These A–D levels, typically considered "readiness" or "preprimer" levels in core reading programs, represent the range of difficulty that the average kindergartner would read. (The average kindergartner in the Tennessee research project was able to read text similar to level B by the end of the year.)

Level A books typically have very few words on the page and the words may be inferred by the illustrations.

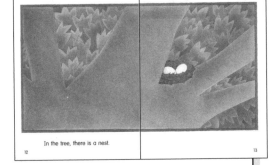

The chicken.   The steak.

2   3

A purple kite flies across the sky.

12   13

Level B books have more words, usually a phrase or sentence heavily repeated, with strong support from the illustrations.

Level C books have longer sentences that may sound more like "book language" than language in easier books. Opening and closing sentences may also differ from the sentence patterns in the rest of the book. Topics in level C books are familiar and the illustrations help the reader identify unknown words.

In the tree, there is a nest.

12   13

"Ready or not, here I come!" he called.

4

He looked in the closet.

5

Level D books may introduce more literary elements, like dialogue and quotation marks. Unlike easier books that repeat a single sentence, level D books may have a two-sentence pattern that is repeated over two pages. The reader may have to infer a story line from the illustrations, which offer limited support for word recognition.

DIRECTIONS FOR USING AN A-LEVELED BOOK:

Before you assess: When you assess students who you have surmised are at this stage, you'll have to keep a few things in mind as you listen to them. So, using an easy level-A book, *The Barbecue*, and a slightly more difficult level A, *Shoes*, as models, first I'll highlight for you some of the things a kindergartner needs to know in order to successfully read these books. I'll then provide you with a model for how you would assess a child reading this book—or any book at this level. The model assessment (see page 100) provides a standard way for you to collect information on your students' oral reading behavior. The components include:

 * a script and directions for what to do and say in the introduction before the child reads
 * the story text for making notations during the child's oral reading
 * what to say during reading
 * what to say after reading
 * a scoring matrix and suggested criteria for determining instructional level

What a Child Needs to Know: In order to read guided reading leveled texts, the student must have a small core of sight vocabulary, including high-frequency words and decodable words, that is, words that follow a "regular" spelling pattern (e.g., CVC, CVCe, CVVC). The easiest books, referred to here as level A, are basically captioned illustrations with one or two words on each page. The student must be able to recognize at sight only one or two words, but these books also require strategic reading on the part of emergent readers.

General guidelines:

 * Make a photocopy of the book for yourself, so you can make notations that capture your students' oral reading behavior record errors, and note use of early reading strategies.
 * When you select books to use for assessment, I recommend that you not use them for instruction. In this way, the observation of oral reading is standardized; the books become benchmarks of the reading levels.
 * After the child reads aloud the text, ask the child to retell the "story," as if to a friend who had not heard the story before. Given that there is little memorable narrative to

interpret, or even to retell, in these books with few words, I believe it is enough for the child to simply give the gist of the book without naming every detail.

* To see whether the child can go beyond the text to make associations with other books or with his or her own experiences, you may ask: What does the story remind you of? At this level, I am assuming that if the child is able to read the words, the child can understand the book. There is one caveat, however. At this level, children may have to make inferences based primarily on the illustrations in order to construct a coherent "story" from so few words and so spare a text.

* Recording student's performance: If level A text is the highest level of text that the student can read at an instructional level, indicate that level on the Class Record Sheet. If the student is able to read higher levels of text independently (B, C, D, etc.), record the highest level of independent reading on the Class Record Sheet.

A Model Assessment: The Barbecue by Jillian Cutting

Reading strategies required: *The Barbecue* requires that a child be able to recognize *the*. Other words—*salad, corn, potatoes, plates*—can be identified by the following strategies:

* Activating prior knowledge about barbecues and the kinds of food found at them
* Using picture clues
* Using knowledge of consonant sounds at the beginnings of words
* Cross-checking all information to make sure that the word matched all available information. The last words in the book—*Yum! Yum!*—can be decoded using knowledge of phonograms or short vowel CVC patterns.

The Barbecue
Story by Jillian Cutting

The chicken.

The steak.

The salad.

The corn.

The Barbecue is an easy book—the easiest level of conventional text. It is a series of illustrations with captions, and the words are fully supported by the pictures.

The potatoes.

The plates.

Yum! Yum!

Model Assessment

Sample Record Form for Guided Reading Level A (Easier)

Student's Name: _____**Tikea**_____ Date: __**August**__

Title: *The Barbecue*   Word Count: 14

Introduction: Read the title aloud. Point to each word. Say, "This book is about a barbecue. Look at the pictures to see what you would find at a barbecue." If the child does not know what an illustration represents, e.g., the steak, tell the child what it is. Say, "Now you read the book by yourself to see what you would find at a barbecue." Reread the title.

During reading: Note oral reading errors and strategies used. If the student stops reading altogether because of an unknown word, prompt him to continue by saying, "Try it." If the student stops reading because he knows he misread a word, prompt him to continue by saying, "Try that again." An alternative prompt that may be used to urge the student to continue to read is: "What do you know about that word that can help you?"

After reading: Say, "Tell me about this book as if I were your friend and I had not heard it before. What happens? What does it make you think of?"
Possible summary: "It's about the things you could have at a barbecue." Note either Y/N next to "Can summarize."
Possible interpretation: "I went to a barbecue." Note either Y/N next to "Can interpret."

Text   **Notes**

The chicken. ✓   She read the pictures. She has few strategies
(The) steak. ✓   beyond using picture information and pointing to
(The) salad. ✓   the print. She has no sight word vocabulary—
(The) corn. ✓   didn't know "the" and did not decode "yum."
(The) potatoes. ✓   She remembered my introduction and said
(The) plates. ✓   "Yummy!"
(Yum)! Yum!

Errors	0	1	2	3	4	5	6	7	(8)
Accuracy	100%	93%	87%	79%	71%	64%	57%	50%	43%

(Between one and two errors allowed for instructional level)

Can summarize: (Y)/N   Can interpret: Y/N

Rate **Didn't** (Number of correct words / number of minutes to read)
really read the words

too hard to read but
she got the gist—
"It's a barbecue!"

Model Assessment: Shoes *by Sarah Weeks*

Reading strategies required: *Shoes*, a somewhat harder level-A book, requires strategic reading and prior knowledge as well. Students who rely solely on decoding each word will not be able to successfully read *Shoes*, nor will students who depend solely on memorized sight words. Rather, a combination of strategies is necessary:

✳ The title is given; the student has to remember the word *shoes*.

✳ As color words, *red*, *blue*, and *green* may be known at sight, but if not, the illustrations provide support.

✳ *Four* may be known as a sight word, but if not, the illustrations also support this number word.

✳ *Little* is a high-frequency word and may be a known sight word.

✳ *Muddy*, *old*, and *new* are also supported by the illustrations but to a lesser extent.

✳ Initial letters, in conjunction with picture support, may help the emergent reader identify all the above words.

✳ In addition, familiar and/or decodable word parts, such as *mud* in *muddy*, may help the reader decode this word.

As is true with most books, no one reading strategy, to the exclusion of others, is sufficient for an emergent reader to read *Shoes* at an instructional level.

Making Notes During Oral Reading

Along with colleagues, develop a notational system for recording the kinds of errors that students make when they read orally. A simple system of taking notes follows.

<u>Correct words</u>	Put check (or no mark)
<u>Errors</u>	
Substitutions	<u>Substitution</u> Text word
Attempts to read	(Note phonetically)
Added words	<u>Added word</u> Insert word ----- (or ∧)
Omitted words	------ (or circle) Text word
Words told by teacher	T (Next to text word)
<u>Problem-solving strategies</u>	(Not errors)
Self-corrections	SC (Next to the substituted word)
Repetitions	R (At the beginning of the line)

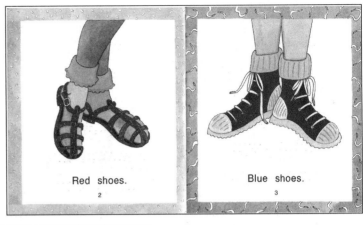

Red shoes.

2

Blue shoes.

3

Old shoes.

4

New shoes.

5

Shoes is also an easy book—level A—but in order to read it success-fully, the child must use initial letters as well as picture information

Four little green shoes!

8

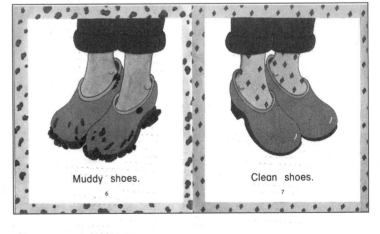

Muddy shoes.

6

Clean shoes.

7

Model Assessment

Sample Record Form for Guided Reading Level A (Harder)

Student's Name: **Olivia**   Date: _____

Title: *Shoes*   Word Count: 16

Introduction: Read the title aloud. Point to each word. Say, "This book is about shoes. Look at all the pictures and tell me what kind of shoes you see." After the picture walk, say, "Now you read the book *by yourself* to find out about the different ways that shoes can look." Reread the title.

During reading: Note oral reading errors and strategies used. If the student stops reading altogether because of an unknown word, prompt him to continue by saying, "Try it." If the student stops reading because he knows he misread a word, prompt him to continue by saying, "Try that again." An alternative prompt that may be used to urge the student to continue to read is: "What do you know about that word that can help you?"

After reading: Say, "Tell me about this book as if I were your friend and I had not heard it before. What happens? What does it make you think of?"

Possible summary: "There were different kinds of shoes—different colors, old, new, so on." Note either Y/N next to "Can summarize."

Possible interpretation: "It was a silly book because dogs don't wear shoes." Note either Y/N next to "Can interpret."

Text	Notes
✓ ✓ Red shoes.	Remembered my language from picture walk (old, new, muddy, clean)
✓ ✓ Blue shoes.	
dirty ✓ SC Old shoes.	Used initial letter to self-correct dirty.
✓ ✓ New shoes.	Instructional level– can try level B
✓ Mu(ddy) shoes.	
✓ ✓ Clean shoes.	
✓ ✓ ✓ ✓ Four little green shoes!	

Errors	0	①	2	3	4	5	6	7	8
Accuracy	100%	94%	88%	81%	75%	69%	63%	56%	50%

(Between one and two errors allowed for instructional level)

Can summarize: ⓎN "lots of shoes"   Can interpret: ⓎN "I like shoes"

Rate __**31**__ (Number of correct words / number of minutes to read)

> Olivia read *Shoes* in 31 seconds. When a child's rate is less than one minute, first divide 60 seconds by the number of seconds the child took, then multiply that number by the number of words in the text.

Making Notes on Student's Fluency

Fluency is the ability to read text quickly, accurately, and with prosody. Fluent reading sounds natural, like speaking, only more formal. Fluent readers pause appropriately at phrase and clause boundaries, changing emphasis and tone where warranted. Fluency is important because it is related to comprehension.

Readers who are not fluent may read accurately, but because they labor over word recognition or decoding, they may be extremely slow. By the time the passage has been read, slow readers may have forgotten the meaning of the text as a whole. In the most recent National Assessment of Educational Progress (NAEP) study, researchers found that fourth graders who scored low on fluency also scored low on comprehension. For kindergartners, however, disfluency may be a good sign—a sign that they are beginning to attend to initial letters and the letter sequences inside words, a sign that they are beginning to decode, not memorize words.

The table below represents a rough estimate of fluency norms for early readers. Fluency norms should be interpreted with caution for kindergartners, however. Given Marie Clay's observation that word-by-word reading among emergent readers may be a good thing, an indication that children were beginning to notice the spaces between words, it may be more important for teachers to look for strategy use rather than speed or prosody.

<u># of Words Read Correctly</u> x 60 = Words Read Per Minute

Listening to kindergartners read helps us see what problem-solving strategies they are using to navigate a leveled book, what strategies they need to be taught, and what book level is appropriate for us to use in our teaching. A typical kindergartner will be

Age	Reading Rate (WCPM)
6	50–70
7	60–80
8	70–90
9	80–100

able to read guided reading level A and B books at an instructional level by the end of the school year and many will read books that are much more challenging. Through careful observation and note-taking we can monitor each child's progress, making sure each and every kindergartner has a "just-right" book to read and enjoy.

Assessing
Word Reading

"I do not like green eggs and ham, I do not like them, Sam I am!" —Dr. Seuss

"Miss Mary Mack, Mack, Mack, all dressed in black, black, black…" —Mary Ann Hoberman

Even the most wonderful, verging-on-nonsense children's narratives have a coherence of ideas, of course. And these gems of meaning can't be comprehended unless a child can read each word—and read them fast, fast, fast.

Why? The more words a child immediately recognizes, the easier it is for him to swiftly find his way across a line of print in order to construct meaning. Immediate word recognition is called *automaticity*. Automatic word recognition is fast and effortless: it is a necessary condition for fluency, though fluency is more than automaticity. Words that are recognized automatically, without analysis, are called *sight words*. Words that appear frequently in our reading

On the road to fluency

materials are called *high-frequency words*. Typically, high-frequency words are learned as sight words simply because students see them more often.

To assess sight word knowledge and automaticity, select a target word list. The most commonly used word lists are those constructed independently by Ed Fry and E.C. Dolch several decades ago. Both the Fry Word List and the Dolch 220 Word List are divided into gradients of frequency with the most frequent words listed first. For example, Fry identified the "first 100 most frequent words" in a list, the second 100 words, and the third 100 most frequent words. Dolch divided his words into grade level lists to roughly correspond to reading materials at that grade level, for example, preprimer through third grade. Core reading programs, or basals, typically identify the most commonly used words in reading materials at each grade level and construct another kind of list—a list of words that are specific to a particular published curriculum.

Take a glance at the next page, where I share Fry's list of the 100 most frequent words.

These words appear over and over in reading materials for beginners. The words in kindergarten core reading programs that differ may be thought of as "content" words, or words that carry the weight of the information in reading materials. Content words are unique to the texts, they may be outside the typical curriculum, and they rarely repeat across stories or publishers. In reading materials for beginners, content words would likely be predictable from the illustrations and initial letter information and not known at sight, nor decodable at the kindergarten grade level.

A child's name is a powerhouse of a teaching tool.

Fry's First 100 High-Frequency Words

the	or	will	number
of	one	up	no
and	had	other	way
a	by	about	could
to	word	out	people
in	but	many	my
is	not	then	than
you	what	them	first
that	all	these	water
it	were	so	been
he	we	some	call
was	when	her	who
for	your	would	oil
on	can	make	now
are	said	like	find
as	there	him	long
with	use	into	down
his	an	time	day
they	each	has	did
I	which	look	get
at	she	two	come
be	do	more	made
this	how	write	may
have	their	go	part
from	if	see	over

Excerpted from *Dr. Fry's Instant Words* by Edward Fry, Ph.D., Teacher Created Resources, Westminster, CA.

Now look below, at the list of 22 words (Clay, 1993), plus the child's name, that are highly useful to the emergent reader and should be taught to fluency—that is, children should be able to recognize these words automatically, at sight, and should be able to use them in their writing. I recommend that these words be sung, stomped, spelled, and showcased. It is important to track children's progress in acquiring a basic reading vocabulary of these high-frequency words.

I've divided the words below into two lists, with List 1 easier and List 2 harder. You can use your own list of targeted words, the Fry words (p. 117), or combine my Lists 1 and 2.

Useful Initial Reading and Writing Vocabulary

List 1			List 2	
Child's name	to	can	on	
I	come	me	up	
a	like	we	this	
is	see	and	look	
in	the	at	go	
am	my	here		

WORD READING ASSESSMENT

PURPOSE: To determine which high-frequency words students can read

TIME: About 10 minutes individually; about 20 minutes to a group

MATERIALS: Identify an appropriate word list, such as the one above or one that includes words introduced in your core program materials.

SETTINGS: Group or individual format.

DIRECTIONS:

1. If assessing one-on-one, put each sight word on flash cards
   - Ask students to identify each word
     Say: "Read aloud each word," or
   Give the student a list of the targeted sight words, and then:
   - Ask the student to read the words on the list, beginning with the top row.

Kindergarten Literacy Assessment
Word Reading Student Record Sheet

Student _____ Teacher _____

Directions: Check correct response and record incorrect responses. Once the student identifies the word correctly, it is not necessary to retest.

WORD	DATE	DATE	DATE
I			
a			
is			
in			
am			
to			
come			
like			
see			
the			
my			
can			
me			
we			
and			
at			
here			
on			
up			
this			
look			
go			
TOTALS	_____ / 22	_____ / 22	_____ / 22

Kindergarten Literacy © 2006 Anne McGill-Franzen

- Allow three to four seconds per word, then move to the next word
- If the child misses a number of words in a row, e.g., five words, ask the child to scan down the list for words he knows

2. In either case, record students' responses on a sheet (see p. 119).
   - If the child makes an error, write the word that the child said. This information will help you analyze errors and develop instruction.

3. For a group test, prepare a sheet with each sight word represented in a row (see p. 121 for an example):
   - Use the first row as practice. You can have students move an index card or blank paper down the page to help them keep their place. For example, for list 1:

     Say: "Put your finger on the first row." (Model this.) "Look across the row at each word."

     Say: "Find the word *I*." (Model this.) Check responses. "Now move your finger down to the next row. Find the word *a*. Circle the word."

     Continue with each target word from List 1 in order (*is, in, am, to, come, like, see, the, my*) and, if needed, List 2 (*can, me, we, and, at, here, on, up, this, look, go*).

TIPS FOR SCORING

1. It is important to record not only whether children can recognize basic reading vocabulary automatically, and which ones, but also to record the hesitations and the substitutions or attempts made in trying to identify high-frequency words. If, for example, the child says or circles words as kindergartner Charlie did, he is just guessing based on words he may know how to write:

Word	Charlie said:
am	cat
like	dog
the	I

Sample Group Assessment of Sight Words

Student _____ Date _____

List 1

I	see	the	my
am	to	a	at
to	is	here	we
in	the	to	on
like	up	see	am
see	my	me	to
the	come	like	here
my	up	at	like
me	am	my	see
the	go	me	here
and	my	am	come

List 2

at	can	on	a
here	me	look	my
on	up	we	in
up	and	here	can
this	the	at	and
I	here	in	see
on	to	a	come
see	up	in	I
this	look	the	in
the	go	on	look
can	to	I	go

Kindergarten Literacy © 2006 Anne McGill Franzen

2. If, by contrast, the child substitutes words as Andrew did, he is using visual memory, mostly first letters to identify the words (see p. 122):

Word:	Andrew said:
am	and
like	look
the	the

   Also articulate for the child the good reader strategies that he is using; for example, I'd praise Andrew's use of initial letters before prompting him to look inside the word, or see if the ending sound matches the last letter in the word.

3. Because sight words should be recognized "at sight," children should have only a couple of seconds to identify the word. If the children take more than a few seconds to identify the word, they may be trying to decode the word, not recognizing the word at sight, and it is important to note this. These words, although identified, would not be considered known "sight words."

4. Some high-frequency words are also words with regular spelling patterns that can be decoded, and some are not. For those that may be decoded, it might be efficient to teach them as decodable units (but to also provide enough experience with the words so that they are recognized at sight). Also use these words to help children read and spell new words with the same patterns.

5. In other words, many sight words can be decoded; that is, the letter-sound correspondences are regular, such as in CVC words that contain a short vowel in the middle, or CVCe words that have a long vowel in the middle and silent *e*. Of the basic reading and writing vocabulary that I presented earlier, the following words represent examples of regular spelling patterns and lend themselves to initial learning by decoding:

it	in	at	am	and	me	we	like

Part Three

What Patterns Do You See?

Planning Literacy Activities Based on the Assessments

Just like adults, children want to do things that they're good at, and like us, they avoid what is frustrating. Allen came to school eager to do "grown-up reading," but armed with only bits and pieces of information about how those squiggly marks on the page get read, he fell behind and became silent. Until his teacher took a close look at the pattern of his development and saw little knowledge of print concepts despite almost perfect letter-name knowledge, she was at a loss to help him. Armed with Allen's assessment data, she took the time to individualize instruction for him. Allen became successful and engaged, and moved on to first grade.

Chapter Four
What Counts as Progress?

The Fuzzy Caterpillar

The fuzzy caterpillar

Curled up on a leaf

Spun her little chrysalis

And then f...

"Know the child
to teach the child."

A s we've seen, young children differ dramatically in the literacy skills and disposi-
tions they bring to school—and the gap between the literacy-rich kids and the
literacy-deprived kids tends to widen as they experience reading and writing in
school. As teachers, we've got to do everything we can to lessen this great divide.

One of many valuable things about administering literacy assessments like the ones in this
book is that it galvanizes us all to hold ourselves accountable for learning gains among *all* stu-

dents. Indeed, Peter Johnston, reading researcher and evaluation specialist, holds that the ultimate purpose of assessment is to provide instruction that is optimal for all children. To achieve this ideal, Johnston points out, teachers must become "evaluation experts" (p. 46, 1987). Looking at early writing, Johnston notes that experts see signs of writing development where non-experts see only scribble-scrabble. Listening to a kindergartner read, an expert hears self-correction and monitoring behavior, but the non-expert hears only dysfluency and errors.

In this chapter, we'll look at some class profiles and learn to view them through an expert's eyes. We'll notice patterns that help us to adapt the "dance steps" of our instruction for every child's understandings. Each child moves forward, each child is swept off his feet at a tempo that is right for her. At the classroom level, the literacy profiles help us better choreograph our whole-class and small-group instruction so that no one feels sidelined, unchallenged.

New research demonstrates that it is not only struggling children who need differentiated instruction (Olson, 2005). According to William Sanders, architect of value-added assessment adopted by many states, even high achievers will lose ground in classrooms where instruction is geared to the lowest achievers. By contrast, teachers who can "teach kids at three levels on the ramp" increase the learning rate of high achievers as well as those starting far behind. But before we dive into how two teachers examined their class profiles, a brief digression on the "big picture" potential that these assessments have for changing kindergarten instruction in your area on a wider scale.

Experts See Patterns Over Time

Over time, teachers and principals everywhere develop expectations about the kinds of experiences children in their communities normally bring to school. Another word for these expectations might be "norms"—that is, what children typically are able to do upon entering kindergarten. Even though these norms are often implicit and not written down, teachers, and principals, too, hold these norms or expectations in mind as they do "kindergarten roundup" or kindergarten screening of incoming 4- and 5-year-olds. Checking to see how many letters of the alphabet children can identify and whether children can write their names are usually among the tasks given to children at these first parent-teacher meetings or during the first few days of kindergarten classes. Experienced teachers often have their own benchmarks for behavior and skills that they use as "norms" to evaluate children's development and to guide them in planning and grouping for instruction in the first few weeks of school. Often kindergarten teachers within a school or across schools in a district try to codify the benchmarks they use to evaluate development in literacy, math, and social development, and they express these benchmarks in checklists, report cards, or other ways that communicate with parents and first-grade teachers what children have learned.

Constructing Local Norms

Let's look for a minute at how one district used the literacy assessments as the basis for developing a sounder sense of what they expected of kindergartners. Their story is an interesting glimpse into how you might work with colleagues to have assessment match instruction in a wider context.

In a large southeastern district, the director of research, Mike Winstead, and Theresa Wishart, district specialist in reading, examined the scores of more than 4,000 kindergarten students in 47 schools to develop local norms—that is, they asked: What do incoming kindergartners look like in alphabet knowledge and all the other domains of literacy at the beginning of the year, midyear, and at the end of the year? The large county district covers a diverse student population. It includes the center city as well as the suburban and rural areas. Schools in center city differ substantively from suburban schools, and these in turn differ from the rural, mostly Appalachian, schools that serve sparsely populated areas. Schools differ in the income and educational levels of families they serve, the percent minority and ESL, size, and the numbers of students with special needs.

By weighing these contextual factors, Mike determined a number of different categories of schools. Teachers in each school can look at children's performance at the beginning of the year, midyear, and end of year in schools that are like their own in important characteristics. Teachers can also compare the profile of their own class with that of the school, other like-schools, or the district as a whole. Within each class, teachers can compare individual student profiles with that of the class as a whole as well. Besides enabling teachers to compare entering performance across classes and schools, local norms enable teachers to compare gains in performance as well. The table that follows shows beginning of the year (fall) and midyear assessment scores for children who scored in the top quartile of all students in the district, the mean or average score, and the score obtained by children in the bottom quartile.

District Students	Letter Names		Letter Sounds		Rhyme		Beginning Sounds		Print Concepts	
	Fall	Mid-year	Fall	Mid-year	Fall	Mid-year	Fall	Mid-year	Fall	Mid-year
Top Quartile	43	52	10	23	9	10	10	12	8	13
Mean	26	40	6	16	6	8	5	10	6	11
Bottom Quartile	7	32	0	10	2	7	1	9	3	10

Teachers, Teachers, Teachers!

In Tennessee, the children who are getting hammered the hardest are the early high-achieving African-American children. They do well in the early grades but decline in later grades. This comes from their higher likelihood of being in a succession of classrooms where the instruction is geared to lower achievers. Any children who have a likelihood of being in such an environment will experience what I call a shed pattern: declining like the roof of a country shed. . .

Of course, those who start low need a faster growth rate. They need to grow at 110 percent or 120 percent. That is, they need to achieve 1.1 or 1.2 years of growth each year. We find that the top 20 percent of teachers are helping kids do that. They know how to teach children who are at three different levels on the ramp within the same classroom. We find inner city and rural schools that are doing a magnificent job. They're on the ramp at 120 percent.

Source: Sanders, W. DLC; *Blueprint* Magazine; September 1, 1999; http://www.ndol.org

However, these average scores for the district as a whole mask considerable differences in children from different schools. For example, children in low-risk schools, that is, schools with very little poverty, typically know ten more letters of the alphabet than do children from high-poverty schools. Similar disparities in beginning literacy development exist in all the literacy categories.

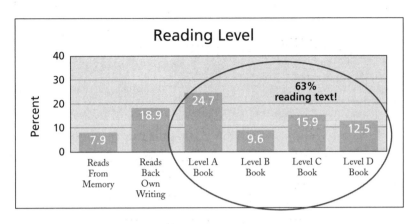

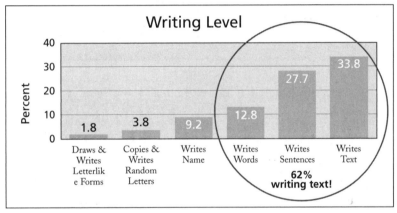

By the end of the year, however, the majority of kindergartners were reading and writing text—62 percent were writing text; 63 percent were reading text—at least at guided reading level A.

Determining Average Progress

In addition to local norms, Mike developed predictive indices so that teachers could see what "average yearly progress" looked like for kindergarten children with widely divergent entering knowledge of the alphabet letters.

Number of Alphabet Letters Known at Beginning of Year	Kindergarten Reading Level Achieved by End of Year
0–10	Reads Back Own Writing
11–24	Reads Guided Reading Level A
25–41	Reads Guided Reading Level B
42–47	Reads Guided Reading Level C
48–54	Reads Guided Reading Level D (or higher)

Using these predictive indices enables teachers to identify which children may not learn to read the easiest level of text, level A, by the end of kindergarten, and to develop instruction especially for them. Level A books are basically a series of illustrations on a topic with one or two words or captions about the pictures underneath. (See page 106 for a description of books at this level.) In the year that these local norms were developed, only 8 percent of the kindergartners were still "pretend reading" or reading a familiar book from memory by making up the story to go with the illustrations. About 20 percent were able to read only their own writing, but the majority were reading in a conventional sense, using sight words, beginning letters and other decoding strategies as well as the illustrations, to identify the words in a book that was not familiar to them. Children who could read unfamiliar text were considered "proficient" according to the district norms. The district's benchmark designating proficiency correlated with another widely used kindergarten test, PALS-K. In order to meet the guidelines for funding under the Reading Excellence Act (REA), participating schools needed to establish validity by correlating the scores obtained on their assessments with scores obtained on previously approved assessments. Elizabeth Bunker, Reading First coach at a high-risk elementary school and co-director of the REA grant, provided data showing that students who demonstrated proficiency on the Kindergarten Literacy Assessment also achieved proficiency as defined by PALS.

Different Kinds of Assessments

Most commercial materials include assessments. Unfortunately, these assessments may be tied to just one area of development, for example, phonemic awareness, and may not give teachers critical information about children's learning in other domains of literacy. As teachers, we need to examine assessments with a discerning eye.

On the one hand, assessments may be strictly assessments of content, for example, how many words can children read from a particular commercial program, but not assessments of process—that is: What strategies do children use to decode a word that is unfamiliar? The former assessment—that of content—tells the teacher the number of words the child has memorized; the latter tells the teacher whether the child can independently use what he or she knows about words to figure out unknown words.

On the other hand, some assessments may be only measures of process. Two examples of kindergarten assessments that come immediately to mind are "rapid letter naming" or "rapid decoding of nonsense words." Such assessments show fluency, or rapidity in processing, but little relationship to the content of instruction. Another assessment that falls into this category is a timed retelling assessment that simply counts the number of words spoken—clearly not a useful test for the teacher who wants to use information from assessment to improve children's comprehension. There are clear differences in assessments that allow teachers to examine strategy use and those that are strictly assessments of content. Teachers need assessments that do both: assessments that demonstrate mastery of content and provide a window on children's thinking.

Assessments help us tailor our instruction to the needs of every child.

Two Teachers, the Moves They Made

Now let's look at how two kindergarten teachers used the results of the assessments to group students for initial instruction in the fall. Their results are quite typical of what you'll find—that is, that even within a single school community, there is rarely a "typical" kindergarten profile.

Mandy Taylor and Ruth Lindsey, who teach at the same school, obtained strikingly different class profiles after administering the assessments. Look at the chart below—half of Ruth's class of 20 students entered kindergarten knowing more than 40 upper- and lowercase letters of the alphabet and many letter sounds. Five of these students met the district's standard for proficiency, that is, they were able to read level-A text, on the first day of school!

Half the class knows 40+ letters!

Strong sound knowledge too!

4 kids were already proficient readers

Kindergarten Literacy Assessment
Class Record Sheet

Teacher___Ruth_____   Date__Fall_____

School_____

Student Name	Letters Name	Letters Sound	D'Nealian	Phonological Awareness Rhyme	Phonological Awareness Beginning Sounds	Print Concepts	Spelling List 1	Spelling List 2	Word Reading List 1	Word Reading List 2	Word Reading List 3	Word Writing	Memory	Own Writing	Guided Reading A	Guided Reading B	Guided Reading C	Guided Reading D	Drawing & Random Letter-like Forms	Copied & Random	Name	Words	Sentence	Text
Allen	51	13		10	12	5	10		4			6	M								N			
Maddy	50	26		7	12	9	0		10			1				X					N			
Rose	49	23		8	12	7	5		2			3			X							W		
Walt	49	14		6	8	8	11		2			3			X						N			
Lea	49	25		9	12	9	5		8			4	M								N			
Zack	48	19		7	4	8	4		4			5	M								N			
Olivia	47	21		9	12	4	1		2			3	M								N			
Don	45	24		8	10	8	13		2			2			X							W		
Mike	44	5		4	8	8	7		2			3	M								N			
Emma	41	14		7	8	10	0		0			3			X							W		
Greg	38	17		4	8	8	7		2			3	M								N			
April	37	1		10	12	10	6		2			2	M								N			
Sy	34	4		10	12	8	3		0			1	M								N			
Charles	28	24		4	4	3	2		0			0	M								N			
Caden	25	5		7	10	9	0		1			1	M								N			
Jake	16	1		10	12	10	6		2			2	M								N			
Blair	13	5		10	12	10	5		4			6	M								N			
Jack	7	0		4	0	4	0		0			0	M								D			
Ashley	3	0		0	0	6	0		0			1									D			
Luke	2	0		9	0	6	0		0			1										N		
Sam	1	0		0	0	6	0		0			1										N		

Now look at Mandy's class profile (below)—her kindergartners fell mostly in the mid-range of letter-name knowledge. Ten of her nineteen students identified between 15 and 30 letters, whereas in Ruth's class, there were only three children in that category. Nonetheless, there were children in both classes who struggled to identify even a few letters of the alphabet at the beginning of the year. Four of Ruth's children and two of Mandy's named fewer than 10 letters, falling into the district's "at-risk" category.

What Can We Learn?

While I don't intend to put two kindergarten classes in Tennessee up on a pedestal as a perfect window of what you'll find, there are some clear patterns that we can note and that you can safely apply to your own thinking.

Kindergarten Literacy Assessment
Class Record Sheet

Teacher___Mandy_____   Date__Fall_____

School_____

Student Name	Letters: Name	Sound	D'Neillian	Phon. Aware.: Rhyme	Beginning Sounds	Print Concepts	Spelling List 1	List 2	Word Reading List 1	List 2	List 3	Word Writing	Memory	Own Writing	Guided Reading A	B	C	D	Writing: Drawing & Letter-like Forms	Copied & Random	Name	Words	Sentence	Text
Tom	54	18		10	12	9	16		16	16	16	4						F			N			
Jeremy	47	18		1	12	10	4		3			0	M							C				
Harriet	47	19		10	12	8	5		3			0	M								N			
Ellen	45	14		9	12	9	0		0			0	M								N			
Mary	43	16		10	12	8	6		1			0	M								N			
Wes	41	14		0	12	10	3		1			1	M								N			
Sherry	39	0		0	0	4	0		0			0	M							C				
Kelly	30	0		0	0	0	0		0			0	M							C				
Kara	26	3		0	0	5	0		0			0	M								N			
Diane	25	5		0	0	6	0		0			0	M							C				
Nancy	22	0		5	0	0	5		0			0	M								N			
Terry	27	4		0	6	4	0		0			0	M								N			
Rachel	25	4		3	0	6	0		0			0	M								N			
Arthur	21	4		0	0	4	0		0			0	M							C				
Sarah	19	2		7	0	3	0		0			0	M								N			
Caroline	18	0		3	0	4	0		0			0	M							C				
Josh	16	0		5	0	6	0		0			0	M								N			
Dalton	5	2		0	6	0	0		0			0	M								N			
Harry	3	0		0	2	4	0		0			0									N			

Majority in mid-range

✓ Clearly, in either class, pursuing a "letter-of-the-week" curriculum would bore children who already know most of the letters and the several children who can read.

✓ Even those children who know only a few letters wouldn't be well-served by a letter-of-the-week approach; it would be midyear before all the letters of the alphabet were taught.

✓ Children who lack letter-name knowledge need intensive instruction, focused on letter font sorts and personal alphabet books. Offering only whole-class shared reading and writing activities would confuse them.

✓ Likewise, kindergartners in Ruth's and Mandy's classes who already read need small-group guided reading instruction with leveled books to support their development.

As these two profiles show, classes of kindergarten often show a vast range of letter-sound knowledge as well as letter-name knowledge; and children who are strong in one area are usually strong in the other.

✳ On the profiles, children who identified 40 or more letters also identified most letter sounds.

✳ Children who identified more than 40 letters also were able to identify rhyming pictures and to match pictures with the same beginning sounds.

✳ Most of the children who knew many letters were able to represent at least some phonemes with appropriate letters in the spelling task and they could typically read and write at least a word or two. Clearly, these children had well-developed phonological awareness skills that put them on the road to reading, and six of the children did, in fact, read.

✳ Conversely, with some exceptions, children who identified fewer than 40 letters demonstrated inconsistent knowledge of letter sounds.

✳ In *both* classes there were children who could not provide a single letter sound, and half the children provided five or fewer sounds. Beyond whole-class routines, they need targeted small-group instruction that highlights distinctions in beginning sounds and helps them associate sounds with letters.

Early Literacy Development

Early literacy follows a continuum of loosely defined stages: pretend readers and writers, beginning readers and writers, and conventional readers and writers. When the two teachers and I studied the kindergartners' literacy understandings, we found ourselves sorting our students into the three stages, but with nicknames that better described the spirit of the stage. And like many nicknames, these labels stuck and so I offer them to you as ones you may wish to adopt: Readers, Almost Readers, and Sounds Kids. Ruth and Mandy refined the last group—they called the children who were still learning alphabet names plus the sounds "Letters & Sounds Kids"; they called the children who had more solid alphabet knowledge but were missing the concept of letter sounds, "Sounds Kids."

How Should Mandy and Ruth Proceed?

Mandy, Ruth, and virtually any kindergarten teacher will look at a class profile and see that each student needs something distinct. Such a profile gives a bird's-eye view on the need to make instruction a dynamic blend of individual, small-group, and whole-class work, the last of which provides kindergartners with a predictability that is precious to them at this age. The trick is to infuse the whole-class literacy routines with the knowledge gleaned from the profile. For example, during interactive writing, a child who is struggling with the formation of the lowercase *b* would be invited to take the pen and, with support, display what he has learned. The teacher would invite a child who needs practice putting spaces in his writing to place two fingers on the class white board to show the space between words. Within that same lesson, the child who can write every letter accurately and fluently would be challenged by reading back the message, pointing to each word as he reads. Wow, armed with the profile, a teacher can teach a lesson with laserlike precision.

But whole-class instruction, no matter how nuanced, cannot provide the intensity and targeted teaching that individual and small-group venues afford. And so let's see how Ruth and Mandy use the profile as a basis for organizing one-one-one tutoring, independent practice, and small-group instruction.

The Stages of Early Literacy Development

STAGE 1: LETTERS & SOUNDS KIDS and SOUNDS KIDS
Pretend readers and writers

* Make up a story based on memory, and using the pictures as a guide, pretend to read with intonation and book language

* Hold a book right side up

* Realize that print, not pictures, carries the message and point to the print when asked, "Where do I begin reading?"

* Know some letters

* Recognize own name in print

* Write letters or letterlike forms ("scribbles") to represent a message, but "read" the message differently each time, as they do not yet know that print is constant

* May ask an adult to read their scriptlike messages by saying, "What did I write?"

STAGE 2: ALMOST READERS
Beginning readers and writers

* Understand that a written message is constant, and demonstrate this understanding by "reading back" own writing

* Track print from left to right when asked, "Show me with your finger which way you would go when you read"

* Know most letters and sounds

* Can distinguish rhyme and initial sounds

* Recognize a few words in reading

* Use a few memorized words in writing: their own names; anchor words such as *the, mom, dad*; and names of pets or siblings. These words help anchor the student' first attempts at matching spoken words to printed words.

* Often spell with single letters as they try to represent their ideas in writing. The sounds conveyed by the names of letters and the way the letter names feel to the students when articulated become the building blocks for beginning spelling.

STAGE 3: READERS
Conventional readers and writers

* Read familiar books and fingerpoint to each word, making an exact match between words spoken and the printed words

* Know all letters and sounds

* Have memorized at least 25 highly frequent or phonetically regular words that they can read and write

* Rely on initial letters and letter sounds to recognize unfamiliar words in reading

* Use sight words from reading in writing

* Use letter names and some vowels to spell words

* Are able to use what they know about familiar words to decode and spell words that they have not seen before (often called a "self-extending system")

* Use some punctuation in writing; plan and edit simple texts.

Beginning of the Year: Grouping for Initial Instruction

Let's look at Ruth's and Mandy's class profiles and see how they might group children for small-group instruction.

Instruction for Ruth's "Readers"

* **Teach them strategies for reading less-predictable text**
* **Have them improve voice-print match by guiding them to attend to beginning, middle and end of words**

Ruth's readers take on leveled books.

Remember, both Mandy and Ruth had readers at the start of school! Ruth provided small-group guided reading for these five children. (Mandy sent her single, advanced reader to first grade for guided reading.) With the group of children I call "Readers," Ruth reinforced children's one-to-one voice-print match in conjunction with beginning and ending letters to help identify unfamiliar words.

Kindergarten Literacy Assessment
Class Record Sheet

Teacher __Ruth__   Date __Fall__

School _____

Ruth's readers can read leveled books

Student Name	Letters: Name	Sound	D'Nealian	Phonological Awareness: Rhyme	Beginning Sounds	Print Concepts	Spelling: List 1	List 2	Word Reading: List 1	List 2	List 3	Word Writing	Memory	Own Writing	Guided Reading: A	B	C	D	Drawing & Random	Copied & Letter-like Forms	Name	Words	Sentence	Text
Maddy	50	26		7	12	9	0		10			1					X				N			
Rose	49	23		8	12	7	5		2			3			X							W		
Walt	49	14		6	8	8	11		2			3			X						N			
Don	45	24		8	10	8	13		2			2			X							W		
Emma	41	14		7	8	10	0		0			3			X							W		

Gradually, she upped the ante by providing leveled readers with more words on the page and less predictable sentence patterns.

Instruction for Ruth's "Almost Readers"

Teach them strategies to:

* **write and read back writing**
* **apply early reading strategies to predictable books**

Ruth created a second group of seven students from among the high letter-knowledge children, all of whom were "pretend" reading familiar books from memory. I call students at their level "Almost Readers." To develop the insight that words are invariant, that is, they maintain the same sequence of letters from one context to another, she asked them to "quick draw" and caption their responses to the whole-group anthology during their small-group time. Demonstrating for the group, then conferencing with individuals, Ruth helped children sound-stretch words to map phonemes to letters and modeled the use of word wall words in personal writing and daily news (see page 211 for more about these practices). These seven children read their captioned drawings to one another, pointing to each word as they spoke it. Ruth introduced level-A books and emphasized left-to-right directionality, reading the spaces between words, one-to-one voice-print match, and locating one or two known words in the line of print to anchor the reading. Ruth taught the children to scan the line of print for unknown words and use first letters to "get their mouths ready" to say the word.

Almost all readers know many letters and sounds

Kindergarten Literacy Assessment
Class Record Sheet

Teacher __Ruth__   Date __Fall__
School _____

Student Name	Letters — Name	Sound	D'Nealian	Phonological Awareness — Rhyme	Beginning Sounds	Print Concepts	Spelling List 1	List 2	Word Reading List 1	List 2	List 3	Word Writing	Memory	Own Writing	Guided Reading A	B	C	D	Drawing & Letter-like Forms	Copied & Random	Name	Words	Sentence	Text
Allen	51	13		10	12	5	10		4			6	M								N			
Lea	49	25		9	12	9	5		8			4	M								N			
Zack	48	19		7	4	8	4		4			5	M								N			
Olivia	47	21		9	12	4	1		2			3	M								N			
Mike	44	5		4	8	8	7		2			3	M								N			
Greg	38	17		4	8	8	7		2			3	M								N			
April	37	1		10	12	10	6		2			2	M								N			

Instruction for Ruth's "Sounds" Kids

Teach strategies to:

* **associate sounds with letters**
* **notice and remember letter patterns**
* **stretch sounds to spell words**

Modeling word reading strategies

Another group of five students demonstrated inconsistent knowledge of letters, sounds, phonological aware-ness and print concepts. One common element across all of their beginning-of-the-year assessments, however, was that they knew little about the sounds of the letters. For these "Sounds Kids," and one student—Ashley—from the Almost Readers group who joined them for work on let-ter sounds, Ruth developed their associations between letters and sounds through picture and letter sorts, spelling sorts, and making and breaking wall words. Students kept a word study notebook that they archived to keep track of the letters that represented particular sounds and words they found that were spelled with that letter or letter pattern.

Ruth's Sounds Kids know some letters and a few sounds.

They can write their names and pretend read a book.

Kindergarten Literacy Assessment
Class Record Sheet

Teacher __Ruth__

School_____

Date __Fall__

Student Name	Letters			Phonological Awareness			Print Concepts	Spelling		Word Reading			Word Writing	Memory	Own Writing	Reading Text Level Guided Reading				Writing Text Level				
	Name	Sound	D'Nealian	Rhyme	Beginning Sounds			List 1	List 2	List 1	List 2	List 3				A	B	C	D	Drawing & Letter-like Forms	Copied & Random	Name	Words	Sentence	Text
Sy	34	4		10	12	8	3	0		1	M										N			
Charles	28	24		4	4	3	2	0		0	M										N			
Caden	25	5		7	10	9	0	1		1	M										N			
Jake	16	1		10	12	10	6	2		2	M										N			
Blair	13	5		10	12	10	5	4		6	M										N			
Ashley	3	0		0	0	6	0	0		1										D				

Kindergarten Literacy

Ruth's Letters & Sounds Kids know a few letters.

Kindergarten Literacy Assessment
Class Record Sheet

Teacher __Ruth__

School_____

Date __Fall__

Student Name	Letters			Phonological Awareness		Print Concepts	Spelling		Word Reading			Word Writing	Memory	Own Writing	Reading Text Level — Guided Reading				Writing Text Level					
	Name	Sound	D'Nealian	Rhyme	Beginning Sounds		List 1	List 2	List 1	List 2	List 3				A	B	C	D	Drawing & Letter-like Forms	Copied & Random	Name	Words	Sentence	Text
Jack	7	0		4	0	4	0		0			0	M						D					
Ashley	3	0		0	0	6	0		0					1					D					
Luke	2	0		9	0	6	0		0					1							N			
Sam	1	0		0	0	6	0		0					1							N			

Instruction for Ruth's "Letters & Sounds" Kids

Teach strategies to:

* **notice letter features**
* **associate letters with sounds**
* **use personal alphabet books and handwriting models**

The four kindergartners who identified fewer than ten letter names in the fall assessment and no letter sounds formed another group. The group, called "Letters & Sounds Group," had not yet developed the ability to notice rhyme or match pictures with the same beginning sound and did not yet map sound to any letters in the spelling task. On the print concepts task they did not track the print with their finger. For this group, Ruth concentrated on both letter identification and association of the letters with sounds. Because letter names carry information about sounds, she thought it was important to consolidate their knowledge of the alphabet. Each child used a personal alphabet chart for reference, and in their small

Matching pictures with beginning sounds

group, Ruth reread alphabet books from whole-class read-alouds, pointing out the different themes around which authors have composed alphabet books. With her assistance, each member of the Letters & Sounds Group created his or her own alphabet book and read and reread to partners. Like the alphabet charts, the books served as a personal reference.

Handwriting practice

Ruth designed instruction using letter font sorts, such as those I describe on pages 53–55, to match upper- to lowercase and to develop children's familiarity with the different fonts that appear in print. She also created picture-sound sorts to develop children's ability to discriminate among letter sounds and picture-sound-letter sorts with white board spelling to associate sounds with letters and support sound-letter mapping and handwriting. Because at least two of the children could not write any letters at the beginning of the year when asked to do so but instead drew pictures and made letterlike forms, Ruth provided explicit instruction in the formation of letters in D'Nealian script and gave each child a personal handwriting model for reference.

Instruction for Mandy's "Almost Readers"

Teach strategies to:

* **Read back writing**
* **Identify known words in writing**
* **Use initial letters to read words in predictable books**

After sending Tom, her precocious reader off to a first-grade reading group, Mandy created an "Almost Readers" group of five students. They knew most letter sounds, could identify rhyme and match pictures with the same beginning sounds, represented some phonemes with letters in the spelling task, and used their fingers to track print. Like Ruth's

Almost-Readers group, these kindergartners did not yet know how to read conventionally, but they could "pretend read" familiar text with book language and information from the pictures.

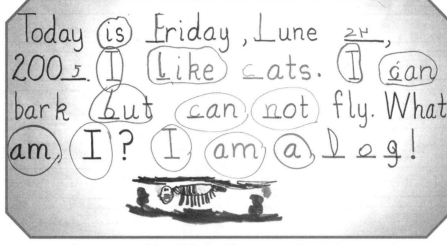

A morning message with a riddle provides opportunities for letter-sound matches and practice reading sight words.

As Ruth did, Mandy used purposeful writing activities to move these children forward with their reading. For example, during whole-class morning message, she emphasized one-to-one voice match, asking children to reread the message and circle and read known words. In small-group work with these five kids, Mandy introduced level-A readers, explicitly modeling for children how to picture walk for a sense of the book as a whole and for clues about the print on the page. She taught them to read the spaces between words, to locate known words as anchors, and to attend to initial letters for letter-sound mapping.

Instruction for Mandy's "Sounds" Kids

Teach strategies to:

* **distinguish sounds in rhymes and pictures**
* **associate sounds with letters**
* **stretch sounds to spell words**

Thirteen of Mandy's kindergartners—the majority of her class—provided sounds for five or fewer letters, and six did not provide any letter sounds. With one exception, the children were not yet able to map a phoneme, or sound, to letters on the spelling task; they were unsure of the concept of rhyme and did not match pictures that "sound the same at the beginning." Mandy offered this group, her "Sounds" group, instruction that developed awareness of the sounds of oral language, such as rhyme and beginning phonemes. In order to call attention to the sounds of language, Mandy reread the songs,

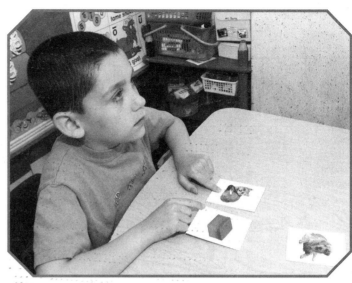

For Sounds Kids, offer picture sorts that emphasize rhyme.

chants, and poems from the anthology and used them for small-group shared reading. She explained rhyme, modeled attention to rhyme, and designed picture sorts that emphasized rhyme. Similarly, Mandy modeled attention to beginning phonemes.

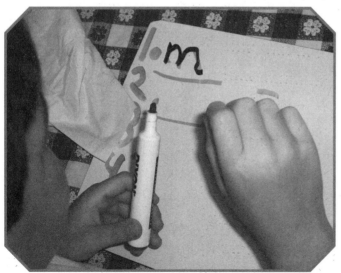

Sounds Kids spell the beginning sounds of words they have sorted.

She used picture sorts to help children listen to and distinguish sounds at the beginnings of words and match the pictures that had the same sound at the beginning. Once children were able to differentiate beginning sounds and put pictures with like sounds together, Mandy put the alphabet letter that represented that sound as a header for the sorts. Children took turns with partners, spelling (and checking) the letters that represented the beginning sounds on white boards. As always, using sorts instead of workbook pages gives children the opportunity to manipulate and problem-solve as they say, listen to, and categorize sounds. Inviting children to spell on white boards provides opportunities for partner practice in listening to and spelling the letters that represent the phonemes being studied.

Instruction for Mandy's "Letters & Sounds" Kids

Teaching strategies to:

* ✳ **notice letters and letter patterns in names**
* ✳ **notice features of letters**
* ✳ **associate letters with sounds**

Two children in Mandy's class, Dalton and Harry, needed intensive instruction in identifying the letters of the alphabet. Although most of her kindergarten had difficulty with some tricky letters, these two children could name only a couple of letters, not nearly enough to provide a foundation for the literacy work ahead. Unlike the students in Ruth's Letters & Sounds Group, Mandy's students were able to print their names.

Building on what they knew—their names—Mandy taught the students the letters in their names, making and breaking the names, cutting them apart, naming the letters, then rebuilding them, and then moved on to the names of their friends in the class.

Once the students had learned to recognize their own names and those of their friends and were able to name the letters in each, Mandy introduced sorts. The students first sorted like letters, then matched upper-

Letters & Sounds kids manipulate letters to make and break their names and those of their friends.

Adams Twelve Five Star Schools
Rocky Mountain Elementary School

and lowercase letters, then letters represented by different fonts. At the same time they were engaged in intensive study of the letters in names, the students were also continuing to participate in the activities of the larger group—the Sounds Group—because the activities of listening to and categorizing sounds would support the learning of letter names.

Meaningful letters and words are good starting points for instruction.

Students' Midyear Literacy Class Profiles

Kindergartners in both Mandy's and Ruth's classes made amazing progress by midyear, as you can see from their class charts on pages 148 and 149.

Many were reading conventional text:
* More than half of Mandy's students had reached proficiency, that is, were able to read level-A text, including several children who knew no letter sounds at all in the fall.
* All but one of Ruth's kindergartners read level-A text, and he began the school year with little phonological awareness and few print concepts.

Most children demonstrated alphabetic and phonological mastery:
* They could identify all the letters of the alphabet and most letter sounds.
* They could match pictures that rhyme or begin with the same sound.

* They were able to represent beginning and ending consonants and the medial short vowel in spelling three-letter words.

The majority of children were able to match voice to print:
* They tracked words with their fingers.
* They understood left-to-right directionality and return sweep while reading text.

Print concepts:
* By midyear all children understood what we mean by the labels we assign to literacy concepts—letters, sounds, words, sentences—labels that are essential for understanding the vocabulary of instruction in reading and writing.

Reading and writing vocabulary:
* The majority of children had developed at least a small repertoire of words that they recognized immediately—sight words.
* They could write quickly and accurately spell a small number of words.

Writing:
* All but three children in Ruth's class were able to write at least a sentence.
* Nine kindergartners in Mandy's class were able to independently write a sentence.

Predictable Gains, Pleasant Surprises

Generally, the children who started kindergarten knowing a lot of letter names progressed quickly, just as the district norms would predict. Nonetheless, there were children in both classes who surprised us. Sam, in Ruth's class, knew only one letter and no letter sounds in the fall. Yet, by midyear, Sam was reading level-A text independently! Dalton, in Mandy's kindergarten, knew just five letters at the start of school, but he, too, was reading level-A text by December!

Mandy's and Ruth's Midyear "Readers"

Mandy's single reader at the start of school was well into first-grade books by midyear; Ruth's five readers moved to level C (four students) and level D (one student).

Ruth's Almost Readers became readers, as did all of her students who were learning to identify letter sounds (five students from the Sounds Group), and three of the students who had limited letter-name knowledge in the fall (Letters & Sounds Group). All together, Ruth had 20 readers by midyear, levels A through C, and one level-D reader.

Small-Group Practice

Although these kindergartners had mastered the alphabetic and phonological assessments, and

Ruth has one Almost Reader who can read back her writing. →

Kindergarten Literacy Assessment
Class Record Sheet

Teacher: **Ruth** School: _____ Date: **Midyear**

Student Name	Letters Name	Letters Sound	Letters D'Nealian	Phon. Aware. Rhyme	Phon. Aware. Beginning Sounds	Print Concepts	Spelling List 1	Spelling List 2	Word Reading List 1	Word Reading List 2	Word Reading List 3	Word Writing	Memory	Own Writing	Guided Reading A	Guided Reading B	Guided Reading C	Guided Reading D	Drawing & Letter-like Forms	Copied & Random	Name	Words	Sentence	Text
Allen	51	25		10	12	13	19	0	16	7		16				82							S	
Maddy	54	26		10	12	14	20	12	16	10		29						96					S	
Rose	54	26		8	12	14	20	12	16	4		23					91							T
Walt	50	25		9	12	14	20	13	16	5		17					91							T
Lea	54	25		10	12	14	20	12	16	6		26					94						S	
Zack	50	23		10	12	13	20	8	16	7		10				91							S	
Olivia	54	26		10	12	14	20	15	16	16	13	21					100							T
Don	54	26		10	12	14	20	13	16	5		15				97							S	
Mike	50	22		10	12	14	15	0	16	0		14			100								S	
Emma	52	24		10	12	14	20	13	16	2		23					94							T
Greg	53	25		7	12	14	18	0	16	5		16					91							T
April	51	26		10	12	14	20	12	16	4		24					91						S	
Sy	48	21		10	12	13	19	0	16	4		17				94							S	
Charles	48	22		8	12	14	20	9	15	0		21				91							S	
Caden	51	23		10	12	13	20	12	16	4		24				82							S	
Jake	50	20		10	12	13	18	0	16	0		13			100								S	
Blair	53	22		10	10	13	18	0	11	0		12			100								S	
Jack	41	10		7	1	13	4	0	9	0		2			87							W		
Ashley	29	15		6	9	11	5	0	4	0		5		W									S	
Luke	50	24		5	12	12	15	0	4	0		4			100							W		
Sam	50	18		10	12	13	17	0	12	0		8			100							W		

Ruth's Readers at midyear are also mostly writing sentences and text. ──

Kindergarten Literacy Assessment
Class Record Sheet

Teacher __Mandy__   Date __Midyear__

School _____

Student Name	Letters Name	Sound	D'Nealian	Rhyme	Beginning Sounds	Print Concepts	Spelling List 1	List 2	Word Reading List 1	List 2	List 3	Word Writing	Memory	Own Writing	Guided Reading A	B	C	D	Drawing & Letter-like Forms	Copied & Random	Name	Words	Sentence	Text
Tom	54	26		10	12	14	20	12	16	16		18						above					S	
Jeremy	52	26		10	12	13	19		16	8		7				97							S	
Harriet	53	26		10	12	14	20	13	16	5		13					94						S	
Ellen	52	22		10	12	13	20	13	16	4		14			88								S	
Mary	51	26		10	12	13	20	13	16	5		13					94						S	
Wes	52	26		10	12	14	18		16	4		3			88								S	
Sherry	51	26		0	12	10	19		16	3		5		W								W		
Kelly	40	19		0	0	5	1		3			1		W						C				
Kara	41	11		10	12	9	5		8			6		W								W		
Diane																								
Nancy	50	26		9	12	12	18		16	4		9			87								S	
Terry	47	18		8	12	10	6		9			4	M								N			
Rachel	45	23		10	12	12	11		14			2	M									W		
Arthur	48	23		10	12	9	19		16	8		7				97							S	
Sarah	35	9		10	12	12	4		4			2		W							N			
Caroline	40	11		6	0	9	2		8			1	M							C				
Josh	52	22		10	12	12	18		15	4					93								S	
Dalton	33	14		10	12	12	12		14	4		4			87							W		
Harry	43	22		0	12	10	4		15	4		6		W								W		
Meghan	39	21		0	12	10	6		9			4									N			

At midyear, Mandy has ten Readers. Most of them are also writing sentences.

three-letter words with short-vowel spelling patterns, they were still beginning readers who were "using but confusing" within-word long-vowel patterns and some blends and digraphs.

In order to build fluency in reading and writing, they needed experience reading easy text and support decoding more challenging books with less predictable language. Using leveled readers within the core program and extra resources provided by the district, Mandy and Ruth organized their readers into small groups, meeting to consolidate and practice the decoding and word recognition skills they had learned by rereading previously read books independently and meeting for guided support in decoding and spelling within-word patterns. Mandy and Ruth used prompts to scaffold the children's reading as they moved from text that was fully supported by picture rebuses or illustrations and predictable language patterns to text that was decodable. Besides prompting students to read the spaces and look at the first letters, the teachers prompted them to "Look inside words for a part you know" or asked, "What do you know about that word that can help you?" When students needed more explicit support, the teachers provided known words with the pattern, often in a think-aloud as in the following example, modeling for students the use of the pattern in a known word to decode an unfamiliar word:

> RUTH: Hmmm. I'm not sure about this word (_autumn_), but I see a part of the word that I know. The letters _A-U_ are at the beginning of _Audrey_, so I think the first part of the word starts like the first part of _Audrey_.

Working the Word Wall

During small-group as well as whole-class routines, both teachers made extensive use of word walls, modeling for students the use of names, high-frequency words, and phonetically regular words to spell and decode other words with the same pattern. To develop "word consciousness," the teachers initiated word hunts, giving recognition to children who found and recorded words with particular patterns in books they were reading or in the school environment.

Midyear "Almost Readers": Now Reading Back Their Own Writing

Ruth had a single Almost Reader at the time of midyear assessment, and he was able to read back his own writing but had not yet developed a bank of sight words or enough knowledge of the way sounds map to letters to enable him to read level-A books. Mandy had five Almost Readers who also could read back their own writing but could not accurately read level-A books. Children in this group practiced writing high-frequency word wall words to fluency on white boards, conducted partner "spelling tests" of wall words or other sources of high-frequency words, and played high-frequency word games like "I Spy" during center work. Just as the teachers had supported the Almost Readers in the fall, Mandy and Ruth modeled and prompted the use of one or two known words in a line of text to anchor students' reading of level-A books, and they modeled and prompted attention to first letters as clues to recognizing unfamiliar words. Because the Almost Readers could read back their own writing, Mandy and Ruth used the writing composed interactively in morning message or daily news as texts for these students to reread in small groups, circling the word wall words or words with regular phonetic patterns or word families.

Almost Readers develop fluency by spelling high-frequency words.

Midyear "Sounds" Kids: Now Able to Represent Sounds With Letters

By midyear, all but seven of Mandy's Sounds Group (of 13 students) had achieved proficiency and were readers. Nonetheless, these seven students had made a great deal of progress: they had mastered letter names and sounds, they matched rhyming pictures and beginning sounds, and they had developed important understandings of print conventions. Although they were not yet able to spell three-letter words with short vowels conventionally, they were able to represent some sounds with letters. Because they were still grappling with the way sounds map onto letters, they were not able to write many words in the writing tasks beyond their names.

Three of these students were still "pretend reading," meaning that they had not grasped the concept that words—including their names—are the same, regardless of the context in which they are read. Mandy introduced short-vowel sorts with this group of students, beginning with the *-at* word family. As I explain in the section on word sorts (p. 190), the best way to introduce word families is by harvesting words with the pattern from familiar books, list the words, and make and break the words using tiles, magnetic letters, or reading rods, and white boards for writing. Besides focused word study, Mandy emphasized the writing connection to reading. Taking high-frequency wall words that were previously taught in the context of a shared reading chart or story—for example, *can* or *like*—Mandy asked each student to draw what he can do or what he likes, and write a caption underneath the drawing that expresses that idea. These captioned drawings

Making and breaking words with a short *a* word family sort.

became texts that students in the Sounds Group read and reread to each other, copied onto sentence strips, cut up into words, and then reconstructed.

Midyear: Intervention Students

At midyear, all of the children in Mandy's and Ruth's kindergartens recognized most of the letters of the alphabet, although both teachers had children that they thought needed extra tutorial support. Because the district dismissed kindergarten children early, Mandy and Ruth were able to keep six of these students at the end of the kindergarten day for extra support. They team-taught the six students and planned the instruction together, carefully targeting just what each child needed. I present here one of the students— Jackson, the kindergartner from Ruth's class who made phenomenal progress in Ruth and Mandy's after-hours intervention.

Jackson: Ruth's Case Study Student

As I described in an earlier section, teachers volunteered to participate in a Tennessee Higher Education Commission Teacher Quality (THECTQ) grant at the University of Tennessee that combined experience teaching struggling readers with graduate study. Ruth and Mandy were participants in the project. At the culmination of the first term of the project, teachers selected one student as a case study and presented the case study to the group. In that way, teachers learned from each other about the range of development represented in the kindergartners who participated, the progress that occurred, and the teaching that moved the children forward. Jackson participated in the after-hours intervention for approximately eight weeks; each session was an hour and a half long and focused on reading, writing, and word study. Both Ruth and Mandy taught Jackson— they planned each day's instruction for all six children based on the previous day's observations, arranging tutorials and conferencing, conducting small-group instruction, or providing independent and partner practice. The teachers identified each child's strengths and weaknesses based on the children's profile on the midyear kindergarten literacy assessments and the children's responses to instruction day-by-day during the intervention. At midyear, Jackson still had difficulty with phonological skills—he identified sounds for only ten letters and could not match beginning sounds that were alike or represent sounds (phonemes) with appropriate letters. He wrote only two words—his name and *I*. Ruth identified Jackson's strengths and weaknesses:

Strengths:
* Understands print concepts
* Tracks print while reading
* Good behavior and open to learning

Weaknesses:
* Difficulty identifying letter names/sounds
* Difficulty identifying rhymes
* Difficulty identifying beginning sounds
* Difficulty in spelling, reading, and writing

Ruth and Mandy assembled lots of materials for Jackson to manipulate as he discovered the properties of words and the way phonemes map to letters. With support from his teachers, Jackson noticed the different ways that the alphabet letters can be represented by fonts—uppercase, lowercase, D'Nealian, and the various typefaces in printed materials. He learned to categorize the different features of letters and the orientation of each in space, for example, what makes *W* different from a *V* or *U* in upper- and lowercase, or what makes an *l* an *l* and not an *i*. Similarly, Mandy and Ruth organized the reading rods and magnetic letters so that Jackson and his peers could easily manipulate them for sorting by either picture or letter or both. Each student had his or her own box of magnetic letters, reading rods, a lap white board, a lined notebook and an unlined notebook for word study and sentence writing.

The teachers provided students with sentence strips and word strips and large chart paper for sentence writing and illustrating. There were bins of high-frequency sight-word readers, emergent leveled books A through D, and rebus readers that accompanied the core reading program.

Materials to develop letter and sound associations, phonological awareness, and spelling:
* Letter cards/picture flash cards/alphabet cards
* Magnetic letters to sort and build word families
* Magnetic boards
* Reading rods with letters, pictures, word families
* Decodable word-family readers
* White boards—lap size and bigger ones
* Word study notebooks
* Phonics games

Activities for Letter-Sound Associations

Jackson sorted letters by font—uppercase, lowercase—and matched them with pictures representing the sounds. He identified the first letter of the picture sorts and checked his work with a partner. By the end of the year, Jackson identified all upper- and lowercase letters and provided the appropriate sounds for 23/26 letters—an awesome achievement for a child who, in the fall, knew no sounds and only a few letters.

Activities to develop letter/sound associations:

✴ Upper- and lowercase font sorts

✴ Letter and sound picture sorts

✴ Spelling first letters of picture sorts

Activities for Rhyme

To develop the ability to distinguish rhyme, Jackson first sorted pictures by sound, for rhyme. He used reading rods with letters to make and break word-family words, starting with the *-at* word family. After learning other short-*a* word families, e.g., *-an*, he sorted by word family, used reading rods and magnetic letters to make and break the words, spelled the words on white board, and read them to partners. Jackson read and reread easily decodable word-family books. He hunted for rhyming words and words with word families, wrote them in his word study notebook under the appropriate header, and read them to partners. Although Jackson made much progress during the year on matching pictures that rhyme, he still has some difficulty hearing rhyme.

Activities to distinguish rhyme and spell word families:

✴ Picture sorts for rhyme

✴ Making and breaking word-family words

✴ Spelling word-family words

✴ Reading decodable books

Jackson is using magnetic letters to build *–en* family words.

Jackson uses reading rods to make words and then changes the beginning letter to make a new word.

* Hunts for word-family words
* Copying words in word study notebook
* Reading words to a partner

Activities for Beginning Sounds and Spelling

At midyear, Jackson could not match pictures that had the same beginning sound. To help him distinguish beginning sounds, map sounds to letters, and to develop the concept of onset and rime as a way to build new words, Jackson first sorted pictures according to the initial sound. He spelled the first letter of the words and checked with his partner for corrections. Jackson sound-stretched the words and used magnetic letters and reading rods to represent the initial sounds and word family. He spelled the words on white board, carefully stretching out the sounds, and checked with a partner for accuracy. Next, he changed the initial consonants and spelled the new words on a white board, and read the words to a partner. By the end of the year, Jackson had mastered beginning sounds.

Activities to develop phonological awareness of beginning sounds and spelling with onsets and rime:
* Picture sorts
* Spelling first letters
* Sound stretching
* Spelling word-family words on white board
* Initial consonant substitution
* Spelling new words on white board

Activities for Word Writing and Word Reading

Jackson wrote only two words on his midyear assessment, but by the end of the year he wrote 14 words and read them back to Ruth. During the intervention, Jackson wrote high-frequency wall words to fluency using the white board and marker. He and his partners gave each other "spelling tests" on the words. He copied wall words onto small sentence strips, cut them up, and reassembled them. Once he was able to read and assemble a high-frequency word, he wrote it in his "personal word wall folder," for reference when writing.

Activities to develop word writing and reading fluency:

✳ Spelling words

✳ Cutting up and reconstructing wall words

✳ Personal word wall folders

Activities for Writing Sentences and Stories

At midyear, Jackson was writing just a word or two in response to a writing prompt. During intervention, Ruth and Mandy emphasized writing sentences. Jackson often responded to books he read or listened to by drawing his favorite part of the book and writing a sentence about it. He was an eager participant in shared reading activities that involved writing. Jackson noted the punctuation and capitalization used in the book and he consistently spaced his words, punctuated, and capitalized appropriately. In addition, Ruth or Mandy would frequently read a story and develop a chart with predictable sentences related to the story. Jackson, along with his peers, would copy a sentence from the chart, cut it into words, and reassemble the sentence. He often illustrated the sentence and pasted the cut-up words onto the illustration, creating a text that he and his peers reread many times. Jackson wrote the title, best part, and new words of each book he read in his book log.

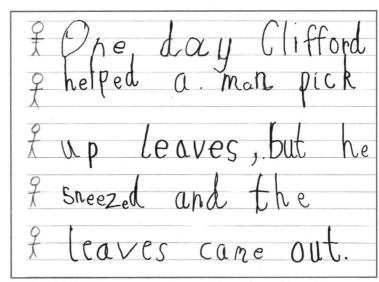

By spring, Jackson was writing Clifford stories that perfectly captured Clifford's character.

Activities to develop sentence writing and reading:

* Sentence writing and illustrating
* Cut-up sentences
* Book logs

By the end of the after-hours intervention, Jackson was writing one to three sentences, as Ruth noted, "without much help. He seems to enjoy writing and he is beginning to be a confident writer." Jackson's sentences became more complex, and as you see from the writing sample on the previous page, Jackson had some good stories to tell. After hearing a number of Clifford stories, Jackson wrote his own story about Clifford. He captured the character of Clifford perfectly: "One day Clifford helped a man pick up leaves, but he sneezed and the leaves came out."

Activities for Developing Reading Accuracy

Jackson read daily during the after-hours intervention. He read and reread the high-frequency sight-word readers to develop fluency and control over the reading vocabulary. Jackson read back the sentences that he composed daily as well. At midyear Jackson was able to read back his own writing. When reading text, he used the illustrations for support and was able to track the print with his fingers.

As Ruth wrote in her case-study report: "Our writing activities required Jackson to write sentences and read them back to us. I think Jackson's reading has improved because of his ability to write and read back what he writes. The word-building activities also enabled him to sound out words that he did not know and helped him improve his reading. At the beginning of intervention, Jackson mainly used pictures to help him decipher words, but by the end of the intervention, he was sounding out words on his own. Jackson is now at a level-A reading level, with 100 percent accuracy at 24 Words Correct Per Minute."

Activities to develop text-reading accuracy and fluency:

* Reading high-frequency sight-word readers
* Using fingers and pointers to track print

End-of-Year Literacy Profiles of Students

Except for two children—whose profiles were strikingly similar—all of Mandy's kindergartners were reading and writing text by the end of the school year. Mandy's readers were reading books at levels A through F with the exception of one very advanced child who was reading beyond second-grade level. Two of the children were not yet reading conventionally, but they were able to read back their own writing, a sign that they would make good progress next year in first grade. The two children were quite limited in the writing that they were able to do at this point in time—one child was able to write his name, but the other child only copied words. Future support clearly needs to emphasize writing for these two children.

Kindergarten Literacy Assessment
Class Record Sheet

Teacher Mandy   **Date** Spring

School _____

All Mandy students write one or more sentences and read at least level A books except Kelly.

Student Name	Name	Sound	D'Nealian	Rhyme	Beginning Sounds	Print Concepts	List 1	List 2	List 1	List 2	List 3	Word Writing	Memory	Own Writing	A	B	C	D	Drawing & Letter-like Forms	Copied & Random	Name	Words	Sentence	Text
	Letters			Phonological Awareness			Spelling		Word Reading						Reading Text Level				Writing Text Level					
															Guided Reading									
Tom	54	26		10	12	14	20	15	16	16	16	31						above F						T
Jeremy	54	26		10	12	14	20	13	16	15	13	12						F						T
Harriet	54	26		10	12	14	20	15	16	8	11	19						F						T
Ellen	53	26		10	12	14	17		16	12	12	27						96						T
Mary	54	26		10	12	14	20	15	16	18	11	19						F						T
Wes	53	26		10	12	14	19		16	13	11	4					88							T
Sherry	54	26		7	12	13	19		16	10	12	9		100									S	
➤ Kelly	46	20		1	0	6	2		2			1		(W)	A								(N)	
Kara	52	24		10	12	12	20	9	14	6		12		A										T
Diane																								
Nancy	54	26		10	12	14	20	12	16	9	8	21		87										T
Terry	52	24		10	12	12	14		16	17		9		94									S	
Rachel	54	26		10	12	12	18		16	4		4		100									S	
Arthur	54	26		10	12	13	20	13	16	12	8	8					100						S	
Sarah	49	26		10	12	12	15		10	3		5		100									S	
➤ Caroline	49	26		10	6	11	4		13			1		(W)							(C)			
Josh	54	26		10	12	14	20	12	16	12	10	9					94							T
Dalton	53	26		10	12	14	20	12	16	9	9	8				91							S	
Harry	54	26		9	12	11	17		16	10	8	16		100										T
Meghan	53	26		3	12	14	19		16	12	10	27					91							T

Kelly and Caroline learned most letters and sounds and can read back their writing. Good foundation for first grade.

Kelly and Caroline may need extra support in first grade.

Kindergarten Literacy Assessment
Class Record Sheet

Teacher __Ruth__   Date __Spring__

School _____

Student Name	Letters			Phonological Awareness		Print Concepts	Spelling		Word Reading			Word Writing	Memory	Own Writing	Reading Text Level				Writing Text Level					
	Name	Sound	D'Neelian	Rhyme	Beginning Sounds		List 1	List 2	List 1	List 2	List 3				A	B	C	D	Drawing & Letter-like Forms	Copied & Random	Name	Words	Sentence	Text
Allen	54	26		10	12	14	20	15	16	13	14	14						X						T
Maddy	54	26		10	12	14	20	15	16	16	15	30						F						T
Rose	54	26		10	12	14	20	15	16	16	15	42						X						T
Walt	54	26		10	12	14	20	14	16	14	11	19						X						T
Lea	54	26		10	12	14	20	14	16	16	16	27						X						T
Zack	54	26		10	12	14	20	11	16	16	15	26						E						T
Olivia	54	26		10	12	14	20	18	16	16	16	41						F						T
Don	54	26		10	12	14	20	17	16	16	15	12						D						T
Mike	54	26		10	12	14	19	13	16	15	12	22				X							S	
Emma	54	26		10	12	14	20	13	16	16	16	38						F						T
Greg	54	26		10	12	14	20	16	16	15	10	34						E						T
April	54	26		10	12	14	20	16	16	16	16	30					X							T
Sy	54	26		10	12	13	19	15	16	14	10	12					X						S	
Charles	54	26		8	12	14	20	10	16	14	14	40				X							S	
Caden	54	26		10	12	14	20	14	16	15	14	25						X						T
Jake	54	26		10	12	14	20	15	16	13	11	26			X								S	
Blair	54	26		10	12	14	20	13	16	15	12	17			X								S	
Jack	54	23		10	12	13	15	12	16	11	10	14			X								S	
Ashley	52	22		7	12	12	11	0	11	10	8	19			X								S	
Luke	54	26		8	12	14	20	14	16	11	6	10			X								S	
Sam	52	25		10	12	13	18	14	16	8	10	7			X								S	

Kindergartners who entered knowing only four letters are now reading and will make good progress in first grade.

All of Ruth's children were reading at least level-A books by the end of the school year; two were reading level-E, and three level-F books. Altogether, 15 were reading at highly proficient levels. All were able to write sentences, and 12 were writing text, and all were able to spell conventionally.

Part Four

Literacy Practices for Developing Readers and Writers

When asked to draw a picture of himself and write his name, 6-year-old Henry drew a picture of a motorcycle, a redheaded boy, and H.D. in capital letters. "Wow," his teacher commented as she knelt down beside his desk. "Tell me about this." The boy said that his parents were teenagers when he was born and that they loved their motorcycle. He said his parents wanted a name for their baby that was both gentle and strong and that would have the initials H and D—for Harley Davidson. So his parents named him Henry David. Henry beamed as he told the story. His teacher beamed too.

Chapter Five

Teaching the Alphabet, Names, and Words

What can you learn from Brianna's picture?

Children's names are their most prized possessions. Their names tell them, and us, who they are and where they came from. Not every child is so colorfully named after a beloved motorcycle, but most children's names carry powerful stories—and powerful clues to their literacy.

The story of H.D. also serves as an apt opener to this section on literacy routines within a kindergarten framework; the image of H.D.'s proud expression reminds us that in every teaching move we make, we must continually build from the known to the new in order to help our kindergartners advance.

Earlier in the book, I shared a framework for Kindergarten Literacy. It's displayed below, too, as I am now going to describe in more detail the routines and strategies outlined in it. These practices support the learner no matter his stage of literacy development.

FRAMEWORK FOR KINDERGARTEN LITERACY

Systematic Assessment of Literacy Development

Work samples
* Writing and spelling drafts
* Oral reading records

Observed behaviors
* Sorts
* Word reading and writing fluency
* Print and book-handling concepts
* Voice-print match

Reading Support Provided by Teacher

Classroom routines
* Read-alouds
* Shared reading
* Guided reading
* Reading and discussion groups
* Independent reading

Teaching Strategies
* Reading aloud
* Thinking aloud
* Prompting
* Linking reading to writing

Writing Support Provided by Teacher

Classroom routines
* Read-alouds
* Dictated writing
* Shared writing
* Interactive writing
* Writing workshop and conferences
* Independent writing

Teaching strategies
* Thinking aloud
* Prompting
* Linking writing to reading

Word Study Embedded in Reading and Writing

Classroom routines
* Name work
* Wall words work
* Sorting
* Hunting

Teaching strategies
* Sound-stretching
* Thinking aloud
* Prompting

Inquiry-based Content Study
* Family and community knowledge
* Thematic units and integrated curricula

Noticing Features of Names: Teaching Routines and Strategies

Okay, back to the power of names. By carefully examining how children write their names, we learn what children already know about print, and push these emerging concepts toward a greater grasp of the alphabet and the relationship of sounds to letters. In other words, beginning instruction with children's names isn't just a sweet ice-breaker activity. Research shows that knowing how to read and write one's name is a watershed event for young children, and that teachers can craft much beginning-of-the-year instruction once they know which kindergartners can—and cannot yet—pen their John Hancock. For example, Janet Bloodgood (1999) tracked the name-recognition and name-writing abilities of 3-,4-, and 5-year-olds for a year. She administered fall and spring assessments of name recognition and writing, letter recognition and writing, spelling, word reading, word tracking, phonological awareness, and writing production (writing samples). Being able to write one's name correlated with alphabet knowledge, word recognition, and voice-to-print matching among 4- and 5-year-olds. Letters that appeared in students' names represented 40 percent of the random letters produced by the children!

But Segmenting Sound Is Another Story

Children do not all learn how to segment sound by learning to write their names, however. Some children learn to write their names as "logograms" or pictures. This may be that they were taught to memorize the way the name looked as a whole rather than to know each letter of it. Some well-meaning parents and caregivers hand out dot-to-dot worksheets and ask children to trace the letters of the names, but don't do enough to teach children the names of the letters. This leads children to know letters in ways that won't be useful to them. For example, calling an *n* the "up-and-down letter" won't allow a child to tap into the sound knowledge that letter *n* carries or apply its sound to spelling other words.

To get those kids beyond this logogram crutch, it's crucial to show kids explicitly the similarities and differences across and between letter features, letters in names, letters in names that are also in other words, and the sounds that we associate with letters in each of these contexts. Let's look now at how to build this explicit teaching into the day's activities.

So how do we build on a child's name knowledge? We can take a visual route, asking kids, "What letters look the same as the letters in your name?" And we can take an auditory route: "What sounds are the same as the letters in your name?" And then, naturally, we can branch out. We can link their letter names to the names of classmates and friends, so that more letters and sounds are familiar to them. We can model the use of word wall names and sound stretching to read and spell words that are unfamiliar so that children's bank of familiar words grows. Bloodgood, the early literacy researcher cited earlier, suggests that "letter and name knowledge tend to grow in a reiterative pattern, reinforcing one another and leading to new understandings and growing automaticity" (p. 364). I agree that letter identification and children's names support each other, but I also believe that letter and name knowledge support children's emerging awareness of the phonology, or sound system of our language. When we demonstrate the way sound maps onto letters in children's names, we develop the insight that ultimately leads to decoding.

Offer a 10- to 15-minute Lesson Each Day

Children need to know what is important to notice about words. Point out each and every feature of names, letters, sounds, letter clusters, or patterns that you want children to notice. Often in these lessons you will be using the think-aloud technique (see next page) but not always. For example, you might read-aloud a book about names, such as Kevin Henkes' *Chrysanthemum*, to point out that some names are unusual, but each name is special. *Chrysanthemum* relates the plight of a child who has to learn to write a really long first name, an excellent segue into counting the number of letters in each kindergartner's name.

Create Visual Supports with Children

As many of the photos in this book show, there are myriad creative ways to "work the room," creating interactive wall charts to support children all day long. Lists of high-frequency words, character names and other words from books, and words embedded in environmental print, such as McDonalds, can be posted with appropriate fanfare in interactive wall charts. For the name work, work with children to put their first names in alphabetical order on a chart.

Use Think-Alouds

As proficient readers, we know that reading is actually thinking and it goes on inside our heads, not as we say the words on the page. A think-aloud is simply talking out loud about the thinking we do as we read. Think-alouds give voice to that thinking. By thinking out loud, we make what we're doing accessible to the emergent reader. Although think-alouds are usually taught in the context of comprehension instruction, thinking aloud is a powerful procedure that we can use to demonstrate to kindergartners any cognitive or "inside the head" work that we do. I provide an example of a think-aloud on page 169.

Follow With Guided Practice

After your lesson, you want your students to literally hold the letters of the alphabet in their hands! By manipulating letters, these abstract language symbols become more tangible for kids. After demonstrating how to build names with letters, gather the children in a small group, or with partners. By having the children close at hand you can monitor and support their manipulation of letters to create names and evaluate their understanding of key concepts like "letter," "word," "sound," and "first, last." You can guide their

In Maggie's first attempt at writing her name, it looks like *W* and *E* and some letter-like forms. Through successive approximations over time, Maggie mastered both the upper- and lowercase letters in her name, demonstrated her growing knowledge that letter names carry sound, and finally, she figured out how to orient that tricky *gg*—almost!

eyes to notice the orientation of letters in space—what makes a letter "upside down," for example, and features like "crosses" that differentiate say, a capital *A* from a capital *V*. Kindergartners need guided practice in writing the letters in their name.

If children need to copy and match the sequence of letters in their name from a model, you are there to provide it. By naming the letters you reinforce the association between the visual and auditory for any child who needs it. By saying the alphabet as you point to each letter in a posted ABC chart, you are once again demonstrating how children, on their own, can recall the names of the letters in their names if they have forgotten them. Children's performance in guided practice should be accurate and successful—you are there to step in and provide the help to make it so.

Tap the Power of Literacy Centers

Whether you call them play stations, activity centers, or literacy centers, here is where children go to do peer practice and independent work. Professional books like *Reading and Writing in Kindergarten* (Franzese, 2002) and *The Literacy Center* (Morrow, 2002) can provide you with further ideas for center setup and management. In brief, you'll need an alphabet chart, sorting trays, magnetic boards, wipe-off boards, dry-erase markers, letter picture cards, index cards, several sets of lowercase and uppercase letters, overhead projector, friends file or Rolodex with children's names and photos, pocket charts, and date stamps to start.

Keep the Center Tasks Open-Ended

Open-ended tasks are those in which children at different levels of development can participate and experience success. The most motivating tasks have a "just-right challenge," that is, not too easy and not too hard.

Children, like adults, want control over their work too—they feel more ownership and responsibility when they can exercise choice. In guided practice with the Wall Names tasks below, for example, allow children to choose one task for each day at the literacy center as long as over five days they complete all of them.

Sample Literacy Center Activities for Names

Day 1   Match classmates' names to photos of them

Day 2   Practice making names with cut-up letters or magnetic letters

Day 3   Copy the reconstructed names into a friend's file (like a Rolodex™)

Day 4   Group names that start with the same letter

Day 5   Group names that sound the same way at the beginning

Children, like adults, like to work collaboratively. Each of the wall names tasks lends itself to collaborative work. Children can sign up to work together on a task. (And have them sign off when they've completed the task).

SAMPLE THINK-ALOUD

Noticing Names With Same Initial Letter but Different Sound

After children have matched names to photos and arranged them alphabetically on a Wall Word chart, offer a lesson in which you categorize the names according to initial sound. Let's listen in as Shannon, a teacher in east Tennessee, puts voice to her thinking:

I'm looking at our Wall Names. I like the way we arranged them in ABC order—we put all the names that start with A's together, all the B's together, all the C's together. Hmmm. I'm looking at all the words that start with the letter C. We have Chelsey, Casey, C.J., Chase, Christopher.

Hmm. I notice that Ch-elsey and C-asey sound different at the beginning even though they start with

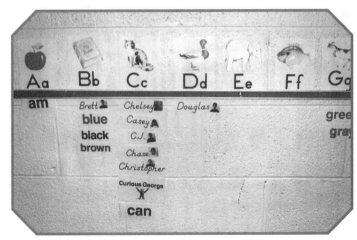

A Word Wall with children's names shows the different sounds represented by the letter C.

the letter C.

Hmm. C.J. C.J. /s/ That sound at the beginning is different from the beginning of /k/ Casey and /ch/ Chelsey.

Let me see what other sounds are at the beginning of our C names. Ch—ase. /ch/ Chase. Hmm. Ch-elsey, Ch-ase. They sound the same at the beginning.

Let's stretch and be sure— /ch/ Chelsey, /ch/ Chase. Yes, they sound the same at the beginning.

I'm going to put those two names together because they sound the same at the beginning. I notice that they start with the same two letters—ch. I wonder if all words that start with these letters sound like Chase and Chelsey at the beginning.

Christopher. /k/ Chr-istopher. Christopher starts with the same letters but does not sound the same at the beginning. It sounds like the /k/ at the beginning of Casey.

I see that the letter C can sound like /ch/—the beginning of Chase and Chelsey's names.

It can sound like /k/ like the beginning of Casey and Christopher.

It can sound like the /s/ at the beginning of C.J.

I am going to put together the C names that start with the same sound at the beginning.

Let's stretch the sounds in our names together.

Chelsey

Chase

They start with the same letters and sound the same. I'm putting Chelsey and Chase together.

C.J.

Hmm. C.J. doesn't sound like any of the other C names. I'm going to put it by itself.

Christopher

Casey

Hmm. Christopher and Casey sound the same at the beginning. I'm going to put them together for now even though they start differently—*Christopher* starts with *Ch* and *Casey* starts with *C*. There may be other words that start with the same letters as *Christopher* and sound the same at the beginning. Right now I'm going to put *Christopher* with *Casey* because they both sound /k/ at the beginning.

So I noticed three things about our *C* names. Even though they start with the letter *C*, they don't all sound the same at the beginning. So the letter *C* can have more than one sound. The letter *C* can sound like /k/ as in *Casey*, /ch/ as in *Chase*, or /s/ as in *C.J.* And the letters *Ch* can sound like the /k/ in *Casey*, as in the name *Christopher*, or /ch/ as in *Chase*. We also have *Curious George* under *Cc* on our Wall Word chart. Which name should we put *Curious George* with? [children respond] /k/ C-urious George. I agree. C-urious and C-asey sound the same at the beginning. *Curious George* should go with *Casey*. We also have the wall word *can*—a word we've been using in our writing. C-an—which name should we put *can* with? Let's stretch..../k/[children stretch the word *can*] I agree. *Can* sounds like *Casey* at the beginning."

◄ SAMPLE GUIDED PRACTICE ►

An "I Spy" Game for Names

In this example, small groups of children scan names for initial letters and look inside the names for letter patterns. You can adapt this game to "hunt" any words (see box, next page). To begin, offer children clues to the name you are thinking of: "I'm thinking of a name [*Chelsey*] that has six letters, sounds like *Chase* at the beginning and ends like *Casey*.

Each child in the group guesses to him or herself which word (name) fits the clues, writes it on the white board, raises his hand, and, if called on, reads the word. If someone correctly identifies the word, that person gets to choose the next word, give clues, and call on peers.

Recognizing Hard-to-Learn Letters

Children learn some letters of the alphabet without much trouble, but learning the tricky letters may require one-on-one help from a teacher.

Easy-to-learn letters have distinctive features that sets them apart from other letters. Because they are not visually similar to other letters, they are not easily confused. Easy-to-learn letters also have similar upper- and lowercase letters. Hard-to-learn letters share features. The most difficult letters to learn are lowercase *b, d, q*, and *p* because they share the exact same features. Only directionality, or the way the letter is oriented in space, distinguishes *b* from *d, q* from *p, b* from *q, q* from *d*, and so on. Even some second graders struggle to keep letters like lowercase *b, d, q*, and *p, i* and *j, l* and *I* straight. When upper- and lowercases look substantially different, for example, *A a, B b, D d, E e, G g, I i, L l, Q q*, and *R r*, remembering and writing the letters becomes even harder. Once children begin to look at and try to read alphabet books or easy leveled books, they see an even wider array of print fonts that may be

Activities for Guided Practice with Names

Remember, guided practice usually occurs in groups of three or four students, or in pairs. Trust your instincts on how long to give children. In my experience, 10–15 minutes is about right. Circulate from group to group to provide support.

Name Games

* Play name Lotto

* Play a memory name game (like Concentration)

Name Hunts

* Hunt for words/labels that start like names

* Hunt for names with particular letter clusters

* Hunt for names with particular numbers of letters

* Hunt for names according to particular clues ("I Spy")

Name Graphs

* Make a name graph according to number of letters

* Make a name graph according to number of syllables

Name Sorts

* Sort names that start the same way

* Sort names that end the same way

Activities for Guided Practice with Letter Recognition

Letter Sorts

* Letters in my name and not in my name
* Letters in alphabetic order
* Sort letters made out of different material
* Sort letters with tails (*g*)
* Letters with tunnels or mountains (*m*)
* Letters with circles (*d*)
* Letters with sticks (*l*)
* Letters that are tall (*l*)
* Letters that are short (*u*)
* Letters with crosses in them (*f*)
* Letters with slants (*x*)
* Letters with dots (*j*)
* Letters that are vowels
* Letters that are consonants
* Read and sing the alphabet chart
  * only the vowels
  * only the consonants

Font Sorts

* Match and pair upper- and lower-case letters that are the same
* Match and pair upper- and lower-case letters that are different

* Match and pair upper- and lower-case letters with different fonts

Making Letters

* "Rainbow trace" letters with each child writing over the same letter with a different colored marker on chart paper
* Write the letter in the air
* Write the letter on the rug
* Write the letter on a white board
* Write the letter on a chart
* Write the letter in a writing notebook or journal

Writing Names

* Write the name in all uppercase letters
* Write the name in all lowercase letters
* Write the name with the first letter uppercase and others lowercase
* Write the name on a white board
* Write the name on a chart
* Sign the name on the attendance sheet
* Sign the name on a message

different from those they learned. Font sorts, appropriately modeled, provide focused attention to the distinctive features of letters.

Let's listen to how Jennifer Glynn, a reading teacher in South Colonie, New York, helps Tyler. The "take-away" is: children appreciate it when you think aloud how you problem-solve.

Sorting letters from different print sources helps children identify letters regardless of font.

JENNIFER: "I can see why you are confused, Tyler. You are looking for an uppercase M to match with your lowercase m but you can't find one. Let's look at this one—(an uppercase W or M). This uppercase letter is a letter with mountains (runs finger along letter configuration) and slanted lines. Uppercase M and uppercase W have the same slanted lines so it's hard to tell them apart just by looking at the lines. It depends on whether we look at the letter this way (looks like a W) or whether we turn it upside down and look at it this way (looks like an M). We can make it either an M or a W (demonstrates). Now you make it a W."

Linking Read-Alouds to Word Study

There is nothing more appealing to children than listening to a good book read aloud. In addition to fostering engagement, reading aloud builds word knowledge and comprehension. Through read-alouds children experience the shape of stories, interesting vocabulary, and the sounds of language. They develop an ear for rhythm and rhyme, alliteration, prosody and intonation—all of which relate to reading skills. Thus, the read-aloud is a powerful literacy routine, and by selecting particular books to read aloud, you can emphasize rhyme, or initial sounds, or letter names, or all of the above!

Chants, Rhymes, and Songs

Read-aloud books that feature rhymes, alliteration, rhythm, number chants, and other rhythmic or patterned routines help develop children's knowledge of sounds and how sounds map to print. Nursery rhymes, chants, jingles, raps, and jump-rope and street rhymes are engaging oral language routines that can easily be written down for shared reading (see page 233 for more on shared reading and page 272 for a children's book list). Some books that are favorites:

* *Miss Mary Mack* adapted by Mary Ann Hoberman
* *Over in the Pink House: New Jump Rope Rhymes* by Rebecca Kai Dotlich
* *Who Took the Cookies From the Cookie Jar?* by Bonnie Lass and Philemon Sturges

Just think about all the engaging lessons about letters and words that can grow out of jump-rope rhymes like these:

Cinderella dressed in yellow
Went upstairs and kissed her fellow
How many kisses did she get?
1, 2, 3, 4. . .

Pancake Song
Hilda, Hilda, mix the batter.
Pour the pancakes. What's the matter?
Pour them perfect if you can—
silver dollars in the pan.
Sizzle, sizzle, flip them high.
Turn around and say good-bye.
　　　　　　—Rebecca Kai Dotlich

Flying Ninja! After listening to terse verse, Dom wrote his own rhyme: "Fly high."

The Power of Alphabet Books

Alphabet books are perfect books to read aloud to children at the earliest stages of literacy development. First, alphabet books render the study of the alphabet interesting to everyone. The illustrations and language in alphabet books usually dazzle the reader!

Second, reading aloud alphabet books not only develops children's ear for the intonation and prosody of written language but, with appropriate scaffolding, develops children's eyes for noticing the integration of drawing and print in text and the representation of the sounds of language with letters. Alphabet books support the nitty-gritty early reading work of noticing and remembering the forms and sounds of the letters of the alphabet. Immersing children in alphabet books provides repeated experiences with upper- and lowercase letters, myriad fonts and font sizes, and parallels precisely the kindergarten work of distinguishing letters and letter sounds.

Third, alphabet books are children's first introduction to the genre of informational text. By reading aloud alphabet books, we can show children how writers organize and display information on a wide range of topics using an alphabetic format. The alphabet book is itself a text genre—one that the emergent reader and writer can copy, adapt, and transform to create a personal alphabet book. In doing so, children see themselves as writers, and as they read back and interpret their personal alphabet book for their peers, they see themselves as real readers as well.

SAMPLE LESSON

Noticing the Features of Alphabet Books

Let's see how Shannon helps children notice important features of alphabet books.

> Hmm. I read *From Anne to Zack* yesterday and then found another
> alphabet book with names. It's called *My First ABC*.
> [Shannon holds up the new book so her class can see the cover.]
> *From Anne To Zack* has drawings of each person, and as I was reading I
> noticed that some words rhymed with the names.
> [Shannon reads from that text.]

Activities for Guided Practice with Alphabet Books

✳ Match letter cards to letters in alphabet books.

✳ Read aloud books, talk about how the writer represents the letters and sounds of the letters of the alphabet with children's names:

✳ Look in the library or online for alphabet books that offer a chance to explore:

— alphabet name rhymes (like Mary Jane Martin's *From Anne to Zach*

— a songbook format ("*A,* you're adorable," "...*B,* you're so beautiful...")

— alphabetical photos paired with children's names (*My First ABC* by Debbie MacKinnon and Anthea Sieveking opens with "Allison's apple, Brian's book...")

— alphabet riddles (for example, "You travel in this, it begins with an A. It starts on the ground, then flies up, up and away. What is it?")

— alphabetical labels and names (*All Around Kindergarten* by Christine Radow is one.)

— favorite themes and the alphabet (for example, there are ones on cars, farms, dinosaurs, monsters)

— another culture (*Folks in the Valley* by Jim Aylesworth explores the Pennsylvania Dutch)

— another language (*At the Beach* by Huy Voun Lee features a Chinese picture alphabet)

Some Other Teacher Favorites:

Alphabet City by Stephen T. Johnson which explores environmental print. For example, a streetlight makes an *E*)

Animalia by Graeme Base ("An armored armadillo avoiding an angry alligator")

Hurricane City by Sarah Weeks ("Hurricane Alvin swept through town...")

Tomorrow's Alphabet by Donald Crews ("*A* is for seed, tomorrow's apple...")

Into the A, B, Sea by Deborah Lee Rose ("Into the A, B, Sea where Anemones sting...")

I'm going to read *My First ABC* today because we're looking for ideas on making our own alphabet book using our names.

Hmm. I wonder how this book is different from *From Anne to Zack*. [Shannon opens book]. Right away I see that this book uses real photographs, not drawings, and it has another word that starts with the same letter. Hmm. I wonder if the other word also has the same sound. [Reads: "Allison's apple…"] /a/ *Allison*, /a/ *apple*. I believe that *Allison* and *apple* both have the same sound at the beginning. I wonder if the whole book has the same format.

[Shannon reads.] So I see a couple of ways we can make an alphabet book—draw a picture of the person and write the name underneath, and make up a sentence that rhymes with the person's name, we can take pictures with our camera and think of something that starts the same way and draw a picture of that. What are you thinking? Whisper your ideas for the alphabet book to the person sitting next to you.

Beyond Names: How Children Learn to Say, Read, and Write Words

In this next section, I'll explore classroom routines for further word study and wordplay, but before delving into the activities, here is a "refresher course" on how children develop their knowledge of letters, sounds, and words. This background helps anchor the activities in a developmental context.

At the simplest level, children learn that words are groups or clusters of letters that have white spaces to show the boundaries on either side. Children learn that words are invariant, that is, regardless of where the word appears—in reading materials, in writing—it is always spelled the same, with the same sequence of letters. Invented spellings often signal that children have acquired this insight. Observe, for example, Mike's whale text (opposite page). Mike spelled *of* the same: *-aav*. He spelled *water* the same: *wwdr*. Even though the spellings are not conventional, they indicate that Mike knows that words are invariant—regardless of the context, the sequence of letters is the same. Often called a *concept of word in text* (Morris, 1993; Clay, 1993), this insight allows children to match spo-

ken words with print. Once children are able to point to each word as they read, they notice the first and last letters in words, and, eventually, they scan the middles of words, leading to word memory and decoding.

Besides developing a concept of word in text, children also learn how letters in words represent sounds, or phonemes. Phonological awareness is an umbrella term that refers to a general ability on the part of children to notice the sounds of the language. *Phonemes* are the smallest sound units of speech. For example, the three phonemes of /c/a/t/ represent the word *cat*. Phonemic awareness refers to this knowledge—that words can be represented by a sequence of phonemes, as in the word *cat*. Children's awareness of *syllables*, the "pulses of language" (Temple, et al., p. 221), and onsets and rimes, are also part of phonological awareness. Children often clap to discover the number of parts, or syllables, in a word that may be analyzed for sound. The first part of a syllable, or onset, is usually a consonant or consonant cluster; the second part is the vowel and any consonants that follow; it's called the *rime*. By the end of kindergarten children typically demonstrate the following phonological knowledge: they can identify one-syllable words that rhyme; they can match rhyming words, and they can identify words that begin with the same consonant sound (Hall & Moats, 1999). These are all phonological skills that are measured on the literacy tasks.

The alphabetic principle refers to the knowledge that phonemes or sounds can be represented in print by letters. The system of rules governing these relationships is loosely referred to as *phonics*. By examining words closely, children begin to notice that letters are arranged in particular patterns or sequences within words.

The Stages of Word Recognition

Researchers have proposed four stages of word-recognition development (Ehri, 1991):

1. Pre-alphabetic

In this first stage, children remember words as logographs or pictures. They create a visual context to remember words—the letter *y* is a tail on *monkey* or the letter *g* is a tail on *big*,—but they can't yet remember or differentiate words with similar visual characteristics. For example, children at this stage would not be able to distinguish between the words *big* and *leg*.

2. Partial alphabetic

Children in this stage know some letter-sound correspondences and can segment at least initial sounds. They memorize words by noticing connections between some letters and corresponding sounds. For example, children at this stage can guess words using context and partial letter information. In an easy book, children may identify the word *jump* by looking at the illustration and the letter *j*.

3. Full alphabetic

Children notice all the letters and connect them to corresponding sounds. They are able to distinguish between similar words. What they are still developing is knowledge of how words are comprised of common sequences of letters. For example, children in this stage would be able to read and remember *jump* without the illustration.

4. Consolidated alphabetic

Children now notice common letter sequences and store these sequences in memory as chunks. Chunking enables children to recognize words rapidly and automatically. Early on, children can quickly identify onset and rime for short-vowel sounds, as in word families. Returning to the example of *jump*, children in this stage would be able to recognize other words with *-ump*, such as *pump*, *bump*, and *lump*.

Spelling Acquisition: What Children Do—and Why

The term *spelling* conjures images of spelling bees, of acing—or missing—the spelling of *Mississippi*! Linguists think of spelling as the understanding of the way the 26 sounds of the English language map onto letters and letter patterns. They use the term *orthography*, from the Latin, *orthos*, meaning straight, correct, right. It's important to remember that spelling is complex, and that kids' acquisition of it is full of three-steps-forward, one-step-back movement, as their desire to communicate outpaces their grasp of conventions. When children attempt to spell, they use sight, sound, and touch. First, children notice that letters have a name and next, that letters have a sound. Children use the names of the letters to help them spell words. In addition, children use the way their tongues, teeth, lips, and palate feel when they say the names of the letters. So children use both what they *hear* when they say the name of the letter and what they *feel* when they say the name of the letter. Often, children use a single letter to represent words in this stage of development, for example *G* for *jeep*. Sometimes the name of the letter leads students to spell the word unconventionally. For example, children may spell the word *wish* with a *Y* because the letter *Y* and the word *wish* are articulated in the same way.

So the way words feel when spoken may mislead children in their spelling. For example, affricates (*ch, dr, tr, g, j,* and the name of the letter *h*), which are made by pushing air by the roof of the mouth, and voiced and unvoiced consonants (*v* and *f*), feel similar. Children may spell *van* as *FN* and *drive* as *JRV* and *train* as *CHRAN*. Long vowels pretty much follow the rule that "the long vowel says its name." For short vowels, however, there are no letter names that help children to spell. Instead, children use the alphabet letter name that is closest to the place of articulation, or the way the sound feels, when they are trying to represent the short-vowel sound in words.

Invented Spelling			Logical Vowel Substitution		
BAT	for	*bat*	No substitution; short *a* is close to the letter-name *A*		
BAT	for	*bet*	*A*	for	short *e*
BET	for	*bit*	*E*	for	short *I*
PIT	for	*pot*	*I*	for	short *o*
POT	for	*put*	*O*	for	short *u*
Source: Bear, Invernizzi, Templeton, & Johnston, 2000; p. 146					

Spelling Stages: A Brief Review

As I described in more detail in Part Two (p. 73), the earliest stage of spelling development is the *emergent stage*, followed by the *letter-name stage*, and then the *within-word stage*. There are two more stages, the *syllable-juncture stage* and the *derivational stage*, for children reading fluently, beyond the early literacy level.

1. Children in the *emergent stage* confuse drawing and writing; they may use drawing, letter-like forms, and numbers to "write." They are likely "pretend readers" who can use book language to re-create a memorized or familiar story, but they do not attend to print.

2. Children in the *letter-name stage* use the names of the letters of the alphabet and the way the names feel as they speak them to match sounds to letters. Early in the stage, children spell words with a single letter, usually a consonant. As they learn to segment all of the sounds in short, three-letter words, children begin to represent the middle sound with vowels. By the end of the stage, children accurately represent most short vowels in three-letter CVC words (that is, consonant-vowel-consonant words), and they are "using but confusing" the letter patterns that represent long-vowel sounds.

3. Children in the *within-word stage* "use but confuse" long-vowel spelling patterns, such as, consonant-vowel-vowel-consonant words (CVVC) and consonant-vowel-consonant-silent *e* patterns (CVCe). They have moved beyond a sound-by-sound spelling strategy, and instead they are noticing and using letter patterns to spell. They understand that more than one letter can represent a single sound.

4. In the *syllable juncture stage* children spell longer, multisyllabic words. They "use but confuse" doubling consonant patterns at syllable junctures, for example, adding inflections such as *-ing* and *-ed*, and affixes such as *-tion*.

5. Children in the *derivational spelling stage* note the meaning-carrying properties of roots and affixes. Having mastered the ways that sounds map onto letter patterns, children in the last two stages—*syllable juncture* and *derivational*—attend to the ways that meaning maps onto spelling patterns. Children in these stages are already fluent readers and writers.

Purposeful Puzzling: Open-ended Word Study Routines

Kindergartners need lots of practice reading, writing, and spelling high-frequency words so that they can read and write them automatically. And the practice needs to be active, tactile, and purposeful, not unlike how toddlers "work" in a sandbox. They need to manipulate letters in familiar words to make new words. Word study routines, such as working with word wall words, word hunts, letter font sorts; sorts for beginning consonants, rhyme, and word families; beginning consonant, rhyme, and word family sorts give them this chance to manhandle words. Through this play—and with your guidance—they discover patterns in words so that known words can be used to decode and spell unfamiliar words. What do I mean by guidance? Modeling, modeling, modeling. As you read a book aloud, or write on the chalkboard, or sit by a child's side reading his work, always give voice to your process of connecting new knowledge to familiar, how you search for patterns within and across words, how you use word knowledge to read and write.

Think aloud while you:

* Demonstrate directionality and linearity in shared reading with big books; point to each word and emphasize the left-to-right sweep of the line of print.
* Point out the spaces between words, the first letter or spelling of high-frequency words, rhyme, or word family patterns.
* Decode and spell unfamiliar words.
* Link unknown words and word parts to familiar words, like names.
* Use wall charts to help remember letters, letter patterns, and words.

Activities for Patterned Charts

Patterned charts, which are structured responses to read-alouds or shared reading, help the emergent reader develop a concept of word in text as well as the early reading strategies of voice-print match, left-to-right and return-sweep directionality, and locating one or two known words in the text. After reading a text aloud, or through shared reading, construct a patterned chart:

* Write a story on chart paper with sentences that are predictable, using high-frequency words from the story. It might be a prequel or a sequel to the story.

* Practice reading the sentences.

* Cut off a sentence and hand it to each student. (This sentence strip provides the child with a handy refer-ence as he or she works with

Create a patterned chart to use in sentence-building activities.

the words and letters.) Ask each student to copy the sentence on a sentence strip, and then cut it apart and rearrange it in the correct sequence.

* Have children partner-read their rearranged sentences. Or you might invite them to sort the words in their two sentences according to particular criteria, for exam-ple, words that start the same way.

* Have each child choose one high-frequency word to cut apart and rearrange in the correct sequence.

* Have each child write the word on an envelope and put the cut-up word inside.

* Have children trade their envelopes and repeat the activity with the new word.

Improvise other renditions of these ideas for children to do independently or with a partner in a literacy center. Any patterned story (or it might be a message, a patterned letter to parents, and so forth) can be cut up and harvested in myriad ways. For example, children can write the cut-up words to fluency on white boards. They can also add them to their word banks or word rings and write them in their personal word wall folders.

Sound Stretching and Blending Activities

Sound stretching and blending are teaching strategies that develop awareness that words are composed of a sequence of phonemes. Sound stretching refers to the strategy of elongating or segmenting or breaking up words to help children notice the different phonemes or sounds that make up a particular word. Sound stretchers are visual supports for children, such as boxes or rubber bands or "turtles." Another visual support for sound segmentation is the use of Elkonin boxes, which are also called sound boxes. Children say the word slowly, stretching and segmenting the sounds. The children then push tokens, one for each sound, into boxes that represent the phonemes in each word. After the children are able to hear and segment the sounds in the word, the children write letters in the boxes to represent the phonemes in the word. Children can also use magnetic letters or letter tiles to represent the phonemes in words.

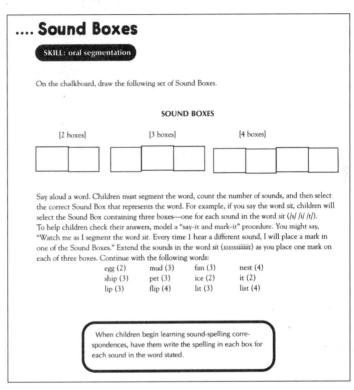

.... Sound Boxes

SKILL: oral segmentation

On the chalkboard, draw the following set of Sound Boxes.

SOUND BOXES

[2 boxes]   [3 boxes]   [4 boxes]

Say aloud a word. Children must segment the word, count the number of sounds, and then select the correct Sound Box that represents the word. For example, if you say the word *sit*, children will select the Sound Box containing three boxes—one for each sound in the word *sit* (/s/ /i/ /t/). To help children check their answers, model a "say-it and mark-it" procedure. You might say, "Watch me as I segment the word *sit*. Every time I hear a different sound, I will place a mark in one of the Sound Boxes." Extend the sounds in the word *sit* (ssssssiiiiiit) as you place one mark on each of three boxes. Continue with the following words:

egg (2)	mud (3)	fan (3)	nest (4)
ship (3)	pet (3)	ice (2)	it (2)
lip (3)	flip (4)	lit (3)	list (4)

> When children begin learning sound-spelling correspondences, have them write the spelling in each box for each sound in the word stated.

Before children use sound boxes independently, draw them on a white board and model their use in a class activity like the one shown here by Wiley Blevins, author of *Phonemic Awareness Activities for Early Reading Success*.

Sound stretching breaks or segments words into phonemes. Blending requires combining the individual sounds or phonemes into words. Stretching and blending helps children develop phonemic awareness and spelling. By stretching and blending sounds as we write or assist them, we make more visible to children the way we segment words into sounds and match sounds to letters.

Word Wall Activities

Word walls (Cunningham, 2000) are a collection of words displayed alphabetically on a wall or on some other highly visible place in the classroom. Tips for using them include:

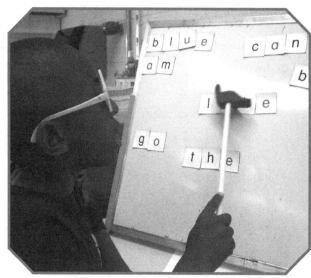

* Select wall words that are memorable (children's names), frequent (*the*) and/or phonemically regular (*at*).
* Start with just a few words.
* Identify "key words"—words that are helpful in decoding and spelling unfamiliar words.

After making and breaking high-frequency words, students can practice reading them "at sight" during center time.

Key words help children when they encounter unfamiliar words that share the same visual or sound patterns. By making explicit the use of analogy—comparing and contrasting visual or sound patterns across words—children can use key words to decode or spell unfamiliar words with the same patterns.

Jill used the following as prompts to remind children to look for patterns:

"Does it look like *at*? Then it must sound like *at* at the end of the word."

> or

"Does it sound like *at* at the end (rime)? Then it must be spelled like *at* at the end of the word."

Word walls help children become independent readers and writers by making the patterns within and across words more apparent to them. The words are displayed for easy reference so that children can use these words and word patterns to help them read and write.

Most children can recognize at least four or five words at the beginning of kindergarten (for example, *mom*, *dad*, *love*, *no*, their own names, some names for colors). By the end of kindergarten, children should know at least 25 high-utility words. "High-utility"

Kindergarten Literacy

words are words that appear often in easy-to-read books and words that have patterns that are helpful in decoding and spelling other words. High-utility words can be displayed in an alphabetically arranged chart of "Words I Use When I Write" or on a class word wall, a class word bank, or "I spy" pocket chart, and practiced to fluency on white boards. (See p. 192 for more about these word resources.)

Consonant Sorts

Sorting is a process of categorizing pictures and words into groups based on similarities and differences. Children compare and contrast words and pictures looking for letter patterns or listening for sound patterns.

Picture sorts have no words on them—children listen for sound patterns. They use cards with simple pictures that represent words with particular sound patterns.

Children look for letter patterns in word sorts. Word sorts use words from children's reading and writing. Word sort words should represent patterns that are frequent and phonetically regular or patterns that children "use but confuse" in their decoding and spelling. Both picture sorts and word sorts use familiar "key pictures" or "key words" to cue children.

"Open" sorts are sorts that children do on their own, putting together the words or pictures that go together. In "closed" sorts, the teacher determines the category for matching, as in the following example of a closed sort to distinguish between pictures with an initial /m/ sound and those without that sound.

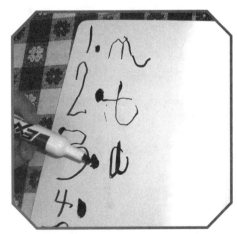

Sort 1: Pictures That Sound Like Man at the Beginning

In this sort there are two categories of pictures— those that sound like "man" at the beginning and those that do not. You will need five or six pictures representing /m/ and five or six pictures that do not. First, name the picture cards. Next, demonstrate what to

Spelling the first sounds heard in a beginning consonant picture sort.

notice about the sound patterns by thinking aloud:

Teacher: "Let's put all the pictures together that sound like *man* at the beginning. *Mat, man.* When I stretch /mm/at and /mm/an I hear the same sound at the beginning. I'm putting the picture of the mat under the picture of the man. *Sun.* /sss/un, /mmm/man. *Sun* does not sound like *man* at the beginning. I'm putting the picture of the sun in the other pile...."

Sort 2: Pictures That Sound the Same at the Beginning

Again, you need five or six pictures representing the beginning sounds of each of the consonant sounds you wish to compare. In this example, the consonants are *b*, *m*, and *s*. You will start with two categories—those pictures that sound like /b/ at the beginning and those that sound like /m/ at the beginning. You will add a third category—those that sound like /s/ at the beginning.

* First, name the *b* and *m* picture cards.
* Next, designate two known picture cards, one /b/ picture (*ball*) and one /m/ picture (*mop*), as "key pictures."
* Place key pictures faceup.
* Shuffle the other pictures together and place facedown in a deck.
* Model the procedure for doing the sort and for categorizing the sound pattern

  "I am going to put together the pictures that sound the same at the beginning. Some of these pictures sound like *ball* at the beginning and some sound like *mop* at the beginning. I am going to say the name of each picture and put it under (next to) *ball* if it sounds like *ball* at the beginning or under (next to) *mop* if it sounds like *mop* at the beginning. I'm going to listen carefully as I say each picture."
* Pick up one of the picture cards from the deck and put it under the appropriate key picture.
* Repeat the names of the pictures, stretching the initial sounds.

  "*Bike. Ball.* /bbb/ike. /bbb/all. Hmm. I'm going to put *bike* under *ball* because they sound alike at the beginning."

Once students are able to distinguish between /b/ and /m/ at the beginning of words, add a third consonant to contrast with the first two. In this case, the third sound is /s/. The procedure is the same.

* When children are able to hear the similarities and difference in the sounds of /b/ /m/ and /s/ at the beginning of words represented in picture sorts, place a letter above the key picture card.

* Explain that the letters represent the sound heard at the beginning of those pictures.

* Name the pictures, and identify the letter that represents the sound:

  "The letter b stands for /b/, the first sound in ball. The letter m stands for /m/, the first sound in mop. The letter s stands for /s/, the first sound in sun."

Explain that they are going to sort or put together the pictures under the letters that represent the first sound they hear in the picture.

* Model:

  "Bike. Ball. /bbb/ike. /bbb/all. Bike goes under the letter b because /b/ stands for the first sound in ball."

* After the children are able to sort *m*, *b*, and *s* picture cards by letter and sound, ask the children to write the letter that represents the sounds at the beginning of those words. For example, say the names of three of the pictures (or more) and ask the children to write the letter that stands for the first sound in each one. The children can use the picture card sort with the letter above each column to help them remember how to form the letters.

* Other consonant sounds may be sorted in clusters by letter and sound in the sequence suggested by the work of scholars in the area of spelling development (see right).

Sequence of Consonant Letter and Sound Sorts

c, f, l

t, g, r

j, p, v

k, n, d

w, z, h

Word Family Sorts

The next category of word sorts is the short vowel rhyming category, starting with short *a* word family words or pictures. Short /a/ is the sound closest to the letter name *A*—try it: say /a/ as in *cat*. Say the letter name *A*. Notice that the point of articulation in your mouth is almost identical for /a/ as in *cat* and the letter *A*. In other words, the child, using what he or she knows—the names of the letters of the alphabet and how sounds "feel" when articulated or spoken—will likely be able to match the short-*a* phoneme to the letter (*A*) that represents it. It is the easiest of all short vowels to learn, and the best place to start teaching short-vowel sounds.

Francine Johnston (1999) suggests first reading a book, such as Brian Wildsmith's *Cat on the Mat*, and harvesting words from the story that have the *-at* rime at the end. At the end of the read-aloud or shared reading, write the words *cat*, *mat*, and *sat* on a white board or chart paper and ask children, "What do you notice?"

Word families are easy for children. It is harder for children to segment each sound, as in /c/ /a/ /t/, or to blend letter by letter from left to right, as in /ca/ /t/. Noticing the letter patterns in word families leads children to decode and spell words by analogy. In other words, children are likely to use what they know—the *-at* in *cat*, to read and spell other words with the *-at* rime, such as *mat*. Remember, a rime is the vowel, in this case, short *a*, and the consonants that follow. Johnston culled a list of 37 common rimes that children can use to build more than 500 words—a way to help children see the patterns in unfamiliar words.

The counterpart to rime, which is found at the end of a word or syllable, is onset, the consonant or consonant clusters that precede the vowel. Onset and rime can be applied to words that have more than one syllable by looking at syllabic chunks. In a one-syllable word like *cat*, the onset is the *c* and the rime is the *-at*.

Teaching -at Word Family

* Harvest –*at* words from a book
* List on white board or chart paper
    cat
    mat
    hat
* Segment onset from rime
    c-at   m-at
* Make and break listed word using letter cards in a pocket chart or reading rods
* Students spell each word on white boards

In a two-syllable word, like *matter*, the onset for the first syllabic chunk is *m* and the rime is *-at*. In the last syllabic chunk in the three-syllable word *acrobat*, *b* is the onset and *-at* is the rime. The onset and rime approach is the most sensible for beginning readers and writers not only because hearing rhymes is one of the first phonological distinctions that children make, but also because at this early stage the onset and rime approach negates the issue of dialect.

37 Common Rimes for Building 500 Words

-ack	-ail	-ain	-ake	-ale
-ame	-an	-ank	-ap	-ash
-at	-ate	-aw	-ay	-eat
-ell	-est	-ice	-ick	-ide
-ight	-ill	-in	-ine	-ing
-ink	-ip	-ir	-ock	-oke
-op	-ore	-or	-uck	-ug
-ump	-unk			

Source: Johnston, F., 1999

Dialect Variations

Let's digress for a moment and speak to an important issue—children's oral language patterns. Children come to school with speech variations that reflect the language spoken in their homes and communities. I cannot imagine anything worse than telling a child he doesn't have language because he pronounces *pin* and *pen* the same way, that is, as homophones, when standard English pronunciation would vary the vowel sounds. Pronouncing *pin* and *pen* as homophones is characteristic of African-American vernacular, as well as some Appalachian dialects. Some Midwestern dialects pronounce *marry* and *merry* as homophones; and Southern dialects may elongate the vowels in some words, pronouncing short *o* vowels in words like *dog* as /aw/. From an onset and rime perspective, it does not matter how children pronounce the vowels because they are stable within word families, that is, the sound remains the same across word families. Thus, the short *o* in *hog* and *dog* are both pronounced the same way in East Tennessee—as /aw/. Approaching the study of short-vowel sounds from the perspective of onset and rime, and making explicit the use of analogy to spell and decode unfamiliar words that share the same rime, circumvents the problem of dialect and renders moot the issue of children's variant word pronunciations.

Short Vowel Picture/Word Sorts

Sort 3: -at *Word Family*

Follow the same format as that for picture/letter sorts for consonants:

* First model how to match the word with the picture representing that word: "This is a picture of a mat—/mmm/aaa/t—the word *mat* has the letters that spell *mat*. The word, *mat* matches the picture of the mat. I am putting the word *mat* and the picture of the mat together."
* Students match each picture with the word that represents it.
* Next, take away the picture cards, leaving only the words.
* Model the reading of each word, and guide students to do the same.
* Replace the word cards with the picture cards.
* Model the spelling of each of the words represented by the picture, stretching the sounds as you write the letters.
* After this guided practice, the children make and break the *-at* words using letter cards and a pocket chart or reading rods.
* Finally, working with a partner, each child takes turns selecting a picture from the stack of picture cards and spells the word on individual white boards.
* Partners check the spelling by looking at letter-by-letter matches from the picture/word match in the pocket chart or with reading rods.

Encourage children to hunt and harvest more words with the *-at* rime by reading and rereading little phonics readers and writing these new words in their word study notebook or "words I use when I write" folder, or putting them on a personal word ring. A word study notebook is a little notebook tabbed with familiar word family patterns where students can list words found in familiar books under appropriate word family headers. A "words I use when I write" folder is an alphabetical list of taught words that have high utility for early writing. A personal word ring is like a word bank—it includes high-frequency words that each child is learning to read at sight and spell fluently and regular words that can be decoded and spelled by using a familiar word family word.

Sort 4: -an Word Family

After children are able to read -at words without picture support and spell -at words without word cards, they are ready to learn to read and spell words from the -an word family. The procedure is the same:

* Read a book with -an words, and then harvest or list the words.
* Note onset and rime.
* Make and break -an words using letter cards in a pocket chart or reading rods.
* Practice spelling each word on white boards.
* Guide students to match word cards with pictures representing -an words, to read words without pictures and to spell words from the picture alone.
* Have students independently or with partners make and break -an words using letter cards or reading rods and then take turns with partners spelling words from picture cards alone.
* Set up independent practice with picture/word sorts comparing and contrasting word families. Children can do these alone of with partners.

Independent Practice for -an and -at Families

* For picture sort practice, you need four picture cards to represent the sound of the -at family and four picture cards for the -an family. You may need to model the process before kids work alone.
* Follow the same procedures as in the beginning consonant picture sorts, sorting first by sound, then by the -at or -an word family patterns in words.
* Use key words that the children already know, for example, cat and man, as headers. If the children do not know how to read the key words, teach those words first or find others that the children can read.
* Explain that the six remaining words can be sorted under cat or under man.
* Demonstrate the concept of a sound sort by picking up the next card and saying, "Hat rhymes with cat so it goes together with cat."
* Put the word under the appropriate key word.

After children are able to read and spell -*at* and -*an* words, they will need much less time on the other short /a/ rimes (word families). The next step is to contrast short /a/ words with short /i/ words, followed by short /u/, short /o/, and short /e/ rimes. As a rule of thumb, always use familiar words as headers for the word sorts, so that children are able to return to the header for guidance on how to read or spell unfamiliar words. The use of familiar words as headers helps children to develop strategic word-recognition behavior, looking inside words for what is known, or familiar, to read and spell words they have not encountered before.

Sort 5: Other Short /a/ Word Families

As in the teaching of -*at* and -*an* families, guide children to categorize words according to rime:

* Compare and contrast within and across word families.
* Make explicit the relationships between letters and sounds that you want children to notice and generalize.
* Provide children with partner practice, and finally, individual practice, to consolidate children's application of known rimes to reading and spelling new words.

After students have completed picture and word sorts under your guidance, they need opportunities for continued word study practice. Concentration, making words, and spelling games provide such practice.

✳ Sequence of Short Vowel Sorts

a

i

o

u

e

Partner Word Sorts

Visual word sorts and sound sorts are two venues for word study practice. Once children understand that rimes are spelled the same, visual sorts (looking at words and placing them under headers with the same rime) are relatively easy for students to do. Partner work with visual sorts needs to include the reading back of the lists of words categorized according to the spelling of the rime. Sound sorts require that one partner read the word

Kindergarten Literacy

to the other without allowing her or him to look at the spelling of the word. The partner who is listening for the sounds of the rime either spells the word or indicates which header the word falls under.

Partner Concentration

In Concentration, the teacher places two key picture cards or key word cards for -*at* and -*an* word families (or beginning consonant sounds) face down along with the other six cards used in the sort. Each player picks up two cards, looking for a rhyme or word family match, which the player must read out loud. The game is played until all the cards have been picked up.

Push It, Say It, Spell It

Another word game is a Push It, Say It, Spell It game. Once students have completed the rhyme and word family sorts for a particular pattern, for example, short *a*, the teacher places tiles or magnetic letters for the two key words for the -*at* and -*an* word families faceup. The teacher or a peer dictates four new words, one at a time, and encourages the children to use the key words to help spell unfamiliar words, pushing the first letter out, replacing it with another, then saying and spelling the new word. The same procedure is repeated for the last letters of the key words.

Making Words

Making Words (Cunningham, 2000) from cut-up words or letters is a game that helps students use their knowledge of word patterns and word structure to write and read new words. Words can be culled from children's own reading and writing, from morning messages, class chart stories and/or wall words, word sorts, word study notebooks, and word banks. Children can work independently or with their peers at centers to create words or the teacher can tell them what to do:

* ✳ "Change one letter at the beginning to make a new three-letter word."
* ✳ "Change one letter at the end to make a new three-letter word."

Word Hunts

In a Word Hunt, children scan previously read material and/or their writing for words that have a certain pattern or feature.

* Children point, circle, and write in their word banks or word study notebooks, or cut and paste words found in word hunts.
* They may work alone, in groups, in pairs, in centers, at their desks.

Through word hunts children make connections between their work with words and their actual reading and writing. They practice using words that are familiar in order to read and write words that may not be as well-known or familiar. Use prompts such as:

* "Circle all of the words you can find that start the same way as _____."
* "Find all the words that sound like _____ in the middle."
* "Find all the words that rhyme with (or end like) _____."

Bringing It All Together

As I close this chapter, I can't emphasize enough that what holds kindergartners' attention to letters and sounds is their motivation! They want to do the "grown-up" reading that gives them access to storybooks and they want the power of writing a message that can be understood by others. At times we pull apart words to enable kindergartners to closely inspect the way sounds map to letters, as we've seen in this chapter, but what keeps kids engaged in the nitty-gritty work of spelling, decoding, and remembering words is the opportunity to successfully read and write. Next, I discuss literacy practices that support learning to write. As you use these practices on your own, remember to build on children's strengths, link new information to familiar, and make your instruction explicit and personal.

Chapter Six
Writing

The desire to write is powerful.

Children write for the same reasons we write. They have something to say that they want understood by another. Wanting to write motivates children to learn how print works. Learning to write often precedes learning to read.

Learning to write is an awesome task. Children must gain control over the conventions of print at many different levels, that of letters and words, sentences and paragraphs, and story and topic. In a sense, writing is talk—with an added twist. When we talk, we voice ideas in the interest of being heard (and in a sense, in the interest of getting our way, having our ideas affirmed.) When we write, the twist is, we must also choose a form in which to convey our ideas. We shape our ideas into particular forms, which is something even the youngest children tune into as they enjoy storybooks, videos, the family's shopping list, the funny Jack Prelutsky poem about pizza they learned in school, and so forth.

Marilyn Chapman (1994), a researcher who has studied children's development of narratives, proposed a definition of genre as ways of structuring discourse, "shaped by and in response to recurring situational contexts". The context might be a classroom, where writing reports takes place, or home with to-do lists. If we hang on to this idea of teaching kindergartners to see writing as a way of discourse, a way of organizing what we want to share, we'll be in good stead. Keep the reasons for writing in the foreground of writing instruction.

We also have to keep in mind what research has shown us about how children's writing develops. In the sections that follow, I define a continuum of writing development, one that reflects the fact that children learn many aspects of writing simultaneously, and that these concepts should thus be taught in tandem.

A Child's Understanding of Print Concepts

Letters: Recognizes that speech maps onto letters, not pictures

    The child can:

draw	copy letters
compose letterlike forms	write random letters

Words: Recognizes that letters make words In predictable ways

    The child can:

copy words	write memorized words
write name	recognize and use spelling patterns

Sentences: Recognizes that words make sentences In predictable ways

    The child can:

compose with linearity

compose with directionality

compose with appropriate spacing between words

punctuate writing with periods, capitals, and other conventions

---

A Sequence of Writing Development

Children need to be great pattern detectors as they learn to read and write. Much as they did as babies, when their random babbling became one-word utterances that approximated speech, children "babble" on the page, exploring writing with squiggles and lines, circles and sticks, as they gradually learn to approximate letters and letterlike forms, and develop their writing from there. They notice increasingly complex patterns, from, say, the pattern of a consonant blend to the pattern of narrative structure. So as you will see in the sections that follow, our role as teachers is to help our students continue to build from the simple to the complex, from the one to the many, from the random to the related. We teach them to build their knowledge from the one letter, to the one word, to one sentence, and beyond, until by year's end, our kindergartners are writing many sentences of sustained ideas.

Scribbles Become More Like Letters

Just as children need to differentiate drawing from print, their next job as pattern detectors is to notice the way letters are formed. Pencil in hand, they need to try out different orientations in space in order to differentiate one letter from another. Thus, their scribbles become more like letters, and their letters become more like words. Because children's names are so salient in their lives, it's often these letters that show up first in the random letter-writing that children do, for these are the letters they have copied and memorized.

By the time they reach kindergarten most children are able to write their names in some form, and as they reach for mastery there, and learn to write a "bank" of new words, they rely on the same technique of copy-and-memorize. With teacher support and an environment that motivates and affirms emerging literacy, they move beyond simple memorizing and begin to "invent" a system for mapping what they want to say onto written language. By using what they know—letter names and letter sounds—they create their first messages. Experience with print through shared reading and writing helps children notice regular sequences of letters, or spelling patterns, and that these letters follow in a linear, left to right progression to make words. They discover that words march left to right also, with spaces between them, to make sentences. They learn that sentences can be combined to make stories and other messages that inform and entertain us.

Children Explore More Complex Patterns

At this stage, children write more words and notice patterns that help them organize ideas. Children's sentences may be simple, that is, a single thought, or complex, with ideas and their relationships to one another made explicit by anaphora (pronouns), or prepositions (*in, on, to*), and conjunctions (*and, but, or, although, because*). In any kindergarten classroom midyear, you'll find some children writing a sentence such as:

IMAVPPLAGA ("I am at the playground.")

and others who are capable of writing a sentence such as this:

I LIF TO DUTX ("I like to do tricks")

As writing develops, children can compose more complex sentences, which are typically longer with more words, phrases, and clauses. Complexity may come from a central idea or topic with details or explanations embedded within the sentence—a sentence with "centered clauses"; from a series of related ideas connected as in a chain; or from only two related ideas coupled together—called a "couplet." For example,

i I IKETO PLAY ("I like to play.")

iLIKPLAY BLUE ("I like to play [with] Blue" [Blue is his dog.]

Paragraphs may be thought of as a number of "ordered" sentences, that is the order of the sentences cannot be mixed up because each sentence contributes in a particular way to the topic that is being developed. A paragraph is a pretty difficult concept for early writers to grasp, and you'll find that children may string six or seven beautifully articulated sentences together—but the sentences don't relate, as is shown at right.

This child writes a series of sentences that don't relate.

Through exposure to literature and having paragraph writing modeled to them many times, children gradually learn how to link their ideas into paragraphs, though it's a skill that continues to develop throughout the school years.

Similarly, stories, or narratives, and expository writing have organizational patterns that children learn through experience and instruction, just as they learn to decipher and, ultimately, to create, the spelling patterns of words and the syntax of sentences.

Children Notice Narrative Patterns

In order to describe in more detail what you can expect children's writing to look like over time, I turn again to the work of Marilyn Chapman and also the work of Thomas Newkirk. Chapman examined all the writing and drawings produced by a small number of young children, selected to represent delayed, average, and advanced development, over the course of a school year, looking for qualitative change and similarities and differences within and across children. She classified the writing into non-chronological and chronological categories. **Non-chronological writing** typically used verbs of attribution, such as *are*, *have*, *got*, or verbs of attitude, such as *like* and *want*, and usually was written in a generalized present tense. **Chronological writing** typically included action verbs, written in past or future tense, often with temporal connectives such as *then* or *next*, and temporal adverbials such as *yesterday*, *after school*, *in two days*, and so on.

Children write to tell stories. What we call "stories" are chronologies: they follow a time sequence. Besides being bounded by time, narratives are constructed according to a "story grammar." Well-formed narratives include not only characters and settings, but also a problem, a resolution of the problem, and often a moral or tying up of the central theme at the end. Children's first attempts at writing stories start with a simple sentence that records a single event or experience. Chapman calls this a *basic record*. Single events can be elaborated to include more events, and when children put these events into a time sequence, Chapman calls the composition a *recount*. Ultimately, with the addition of story elements, such as a problem and resolution, children's compositions evolve into actual narratives.

Early Concepts of Text Writing

Non-chronological Genres

Topic Organization
a label
a list
a couplet—two related details about topic
an attribute list—a series of details about topic
a hierarchical attribute list—clusters, subcategories of
  information about topic
a basic paragraph—three logically related sentences about topic
an ordered paragraph—an essay or an article about topic

Chronological Genres

Story Organization
a record of a single event or action
an expanded record—a series of events or actions
a recount of events described in sequence
a story—a series of events with characters, problem, and resolution

Children Notice Expository Patterns

Newkirk (1987) defined expository writing as any writing used to convey information in a non-chronological way. Expository writing is less predictable than narrative in that topics can be organized in a number of ways—question and answer, cause and effect, description, and classification, to name a few. Newkirk examined a cross-section of informational writing samples collected from the earliest grades through third grade. He discovered that children move developmentally from writing lists and labels to categorizing related phrases and sentences into topics and subtopics. The earliest forms of informational writing are *labels*, then *lists* of labels. Next, children organize phrases or sentences together around a central topic and the attributes or details about the topic; this type of structure is called an *attribute series*. Or, at a more advanced level, children may identify subtopics or clusters of information within a topic and organize sentences accordingly; this type of topic organization is called a *hierarchy*.

Because most youngsters in Newkirk's sample first wrote labels, captions, and lists, not stories, Newkirk challenged the assumption that the easiest form of writing for children is narrative. He claimed that children develop competence in writing informational text by building upon early listing and labeling rather than moving from stories to expository writing. This finding that children write first to convey information should not surprise us, given that most of the writing children are exposed to in the home and outside of school is information-based.

Nell Duke and Susan Bennett-Armistad (2003) champion introducing informational reading and writing to young children as well. In *Reading & Writing Informational Text in the Primary Grades*, they share research that supports the benefits of working with expository text, including research that points out that we are an increasingly information-based society, and that it makes sense to prepare our children for the type of text that has the most relevance in the world. Duke and Bennett-Armistad, like Newkirk, remind us that some children prefer reading and writing informational text and that we have to give up our assumption that stories are more popular or appropriate.

But, as is true with most things, it's not an either/or situation: informational text, nonfiction narratives such as biographies, how-to texts, poetry, stories—these genres all have their place in the kindergarten classroom. Children need to learn how to write for different purposes and for different people. As kindergarten teachers, we can help them do this by setting up a classroom that is rich in literacy support and also a social community, where children, regardless of their level, can write, share and discuss their writings, and in doing so, entertain and inform their peers.

In the next section, let's look at some classroom practices that foster these ideals.

Writing Routines From Day One

Charles Temple describes Marilyn Snyder, a kindergarten teacher from Michigan, who from the opening of school helps children create writing from their talk: "She always calls [her early morning] activity 'writing' as opposed to sharing, drawing, or coloring, because she wants her children to understand that composition entails pulling together one's thoughts for others to interpret and enjoy" (1993, p. 208). So, too, did Angela Anderson, a kindergarten teacher from upstate New York with whom I worked. From day one, Angela's children write. On the very first day of school Angela shares the pen with her kindergartners, jointly composing with them a sentence about what they did on their first day of school:

We made new friends.

Dictated Writing: Teacher Writes, Children Observe

Dictated writing is writing done by teachers for children to observe. Acting as the children's scribe, you record the word-for-word oral texts that the children dictate. You can do this one-on-one or as a group. Invite children to write a message first. Children in the early stages of writing may scribble a script or use letterlike forms or single letters to represent their thoughts. After asking the children, "What did you write?" Record children's exact words above or below the children's writing. Interestingly, children may "read back" different messages for the same text. At the early stages of literacy development, children may not yet understand how writing works and they may also ask the teacher the same question, "What did I write?"

Dictated writing is a valuable transitional experience for children who come to kindergarten with little exposure to literacy, for they can see up close how their teacher orchestrates the use of letters, words, and punctuation to convey a message. It's of limited value for teaching children to read and write, however. Why? Children's oral language at this stage is way more sophisticated than any reading or writing that children can do on their own, so the texts that children can compose orally far outstrip their abilities to read them back. So it can be a kind of frustrating mismatch for them—they want to be able to read the message back, but can't.

Shared Writing: Teacher Writes, Children Read Back

Shared writing is writing that children can read. Shared writing is the kind of writing done early in the school year when few children are able to write. You stand in front of an easel of big chart paper, or a big white board, and you assume most of the responsibility for writing so that children can see how it is done. Many of the charts typically posted at the onset of the school year may be created through shared writing:

rules	labels
lists	directions
notes	schedules

Through shared writing, you can collaboratively compose:

daily news	learning logs and journals
science diagrams	weather charts
rhymes	recipes

"star of the week" and "about me" stories

story maps and summaries

thank you letters, welcome letters, and so on

Think Aloud as You Compose

Think aloud about the process of writing, sharing your process of choosing an idea and elaborating on it, or pondering what to write next, or thinking about your audience, or choosing words, and so on. Other teaching strategies to use:

* structure the message so that it will be easy for children to remember and read
* invite children to contribute what they know
* call children's attention to capitalization and punctuation
* note spaces
* use different colored markers, Post-it tape, masking pointers, and other tools to highlight words, letters, and punctuation
* reread the whole text each time you add a new word
* point to each word as you read
* use known letter patterns and refer to wall words to spell unfamiliar words
* harvest words from your shared writing message and use them for word study, just as you do in shared reading

Reread the shared writing text many times as a shared reading activity. It eventually becomes a text that is posted and children can read independently when they "read the room," "write the room," or during center time.

Interactive Writing: Writing Done With Children

Interactive writing is writing with children. You "share the pen" with the children so they may write whatever words or letters or punctuation they are able to contribute. Through conversations with the children, invite them to participate in composing the text and support their attempts to do so. Ultimately, you shape the text so that it is easy for children to write and read back, but the children help plan what the text will say. Stretch words with children to help them segment the sounds that you jointly map onto letters or letter patterns. Make explicit the connections between what children already know— their names, the names and sounds of letters of the

Children write newly learned word patterns during shared writing.

alphabet, word wall words and other references, words and punctuation used in shared reading and shared writing—to what they want to write.

During interactive writing, use the following teaching strategies:

* invite children to plan what the writing will say
* stretch words jointly with children using visual aids, such as Elkonin boxes
* segment the sounds and demonstrate the sound's letter or letter pattern
* demonstrate for children how to use what they know, as well as use classroom resources such as word walls
* demonstrate how to find examples of punctuation and capitalization from shared reading to use in their writing

As in shared writing, support children's emerging concepts of print, holding them accountable for what they know, and providing for them letters, letter patterns, words and punctuation that they do not yet know. With support, children work on the "edge of development," increasing both the amount of writing that they are able to do on their own and the kind of writing they are able to do.

Interactive writing can take place in whole group, small groups, with pairs of children and in one-to-one conferences with children. Children can serve as knowledgeable peers for one another and support each other's development. However, children will be in different stages of development and it is important that you are selective in choosing children to share the pen and careful about what the children are asked to contribute in whole-group interactive writing. You should acknowledge partially correct responses and encourage risk-taking on the part of all students.

Interactive writing is writing that should be read and reread. Like shared writing, interactive writing can be posted for independent reading during "reading the room" (see page 264), "writing the room," and center time. Harvest words for word study from interactive writing.

In the example that follows, Tennessee teacher Cindy Ellison used the class pet, a hedgehog named Miss Irene, as the impetus for writing. Brief observations of Miss Irene provided kindergartners with many, many ideas for daily interactive writing. Cindy and her students reread each day's writing on the following day, reviewed the spelling patterns and conventions that were demonstrated and practiced, and then posted the chart on the wall for reading and writing the room.

Example 1: Daily Interactive Writing

Notice in the conversation that follows how much teaching occurs. For example, Cindy reviewed the digraph *sh*, used *sh* in the text that she and the class composed, and asked a student to circle it afterward. She demonstrated how to write two-syllable words by first clapping the parts, then sound spelling the parts one syllable at a time. For this demonstration she used a Magnadoodle divided in half vertically. Cindy shared the pen, but first wrote the letters representing the sounds in question on the Magnadoodle for the students to see before asking individual children to come up to the chart to write. Besides stretching out words with regular spellings, Cindy directed students to the word wall for *has*, a high-frequency word. She emphasized the concepts of left-to-right directionality and starting to write on the far left side of the paper; she scaffolded students' ability to match speech to print by printing a small dot under each word. She taught students that the first letter of proper names must be capitalized.

> She has four short legs.

TEACHER: [Cindy reviews the previous day's writing] Let's read what we wrote yesterday about Irene: She has four short legs. Remember we talked about this sound. [Cindy points to the circled *sh*]. Two letters go together to make the /sh/ sound. S-H

We used the word *she* because the word *Irene* was getting kind of tired, wasn't it? We needed to use a different word for Irene.

Converse about writing

[Cindy looks at the class pet] She's snuggling down.

What is a way we can write about her quills and tell it to somebody who might not know what a hedgehog's quills are like? What can we say about them?

STUDENT: Miss Irene has quills.

TEACHER: That is a wonderful sentence.

STUDENT: Miss Irene has sharp quills.

TEACHER: Sharp. Yes, sharp—that is a good word. Now do you see something in your mind when you hear the words *sharp quills*? Can you see in your mind the edges and can you almost feel those sharp quills?

STUDENT: She has two ears.

TEACHER: Yes she does have two ears. What else can we say?

STUDENT: She has prickly quills.

TEACHER: That's another good word that describes the quills.

STUDENT: She has white quills.

TEACHER: Can we say "Irene has sharp and white quills"?

STUDENT: Irene has sharp, white quills.

TEACHER: I like that sentence even better. It's describing the quills, isn't it?

Share the pen

TEACHER: Let's write the first word in our sentence: Irene.

TEACHER: Let's clap that word. I-rene. How many parts do you hear? Let's clap it again. How many parts?

STUDENTS: Two.

TEACHER: Let's work on the first part. [Cindy uses a Magnadoodle and divides it into two parts] I—What letter is it? I—. It's an *I* isn't it? Is it capital or lowercase I?

STUDENT: Capital.

TEACHER: Why?

I	rene

STUDENTS: It's the beginning of the sentence.

TEACHER: Yes, it's the beginning of the sentence, and...?

STUDENT: It's the starting word.

TEACHER: Yes, it's the starting word.

STUDENT: It's the first letter of the starting word.

TEACHER: Yes, and it's her name. Your name starts with a capital. Names start with capitals.

[Cindy writes an uppercase *I* on the Magnadoodle]

[Student writes *I* on the chart paper]

TEACHER: What do you hear next? Don't tell me the name of the letter. Tell me the sound you hear. I-r-r-r-ee-nnne. Irene.

STUDENT: R.

[Cindy writes an *r* on the second part of the Magnadoodle]

TEACHER: John, come up and let's write a lowercase r. [John comes up and writes an *r* on the chart paper]

STUDENT: I have an r after my name.

TEACHER: Yes, you have an r after your first name. That is correct.

John, we don't need to use spaceman because it is the same word. Thank you. Ir-eee-nnne. What else are you hearing?

STUDENT: E.

TEACHER: Yes, E and what else do you hear? /n-n-n/

Emma, your name starts with an e—come up and let's write a lowercase e and you can finish our word by writing the sound you hear in I-r-e-nnne.

Good job! And you know what? There's a silent -e. [Cindy writes the final, silent *e* on the Magnadoodle and Emma adds the *e* to the letters she has written.]

TEACHER: And put a tiny dot under the word so we know where to begin reading. What was the next word in our sentence? *Irene*

STUDENT: Has s-h.

TEACHER: Well, there is an H and an S in it, but where could we find that word if we were having a little trouble?

STUDENTS: Word wall.

TEACHER: John, can you find *has* on the word wall for me? Can you spell it out for us? I know many of us already know how to spell *has*.

STUDENTS: H-a-s.

TEACHER: Yes. Let's see if John can find it. If you think the word *has* begins with an *h* sound, what letter would you look underneath?

STUDENTS: H.

TEACHER: Good. Do you see it, John?

> Irene has sharp,
> ● ● ●
> white quills
> ● ●

Dots under each word help students track print as they compose and reread the sentences.

Reread the writing

TEACHER: All right, pointer, are you ready?

Let's read it for the last time: *Irene has sharp, white quills.*

[Student points to each word using the tiny dot as a marker.]

TEACHER: Pat yourself on the back. Give yourself a little woo-hoo! Woo-hoo!

Revisit the spelling pattern

TEACHER: Who can circle the two letters that make the /sh/ sound?

[Student circles the *sh* in *sharp*.]

TEACHER: Did he circle the right letters? Give him a little woo-hoo! Woo-hoo!

Everyday Writing Routines

During everyday routines such as morning message, daily news, class letter, class message, class writing, writing every day, and writing workshop, model the writing process for emerging readers and writers and provide them with opportunities to discover and practice writing. Depending on the kind of support the children need, develop daily routines for shared writing, interactive writing, and independent writing. As you model what good writers do, think aloud, talking about why you are writing or how you are getting your ideas down. Show how to plan and draft writing, how to reread and proofread, and how to add to and revise writing. Demonstrate strategies for sound stretching and spelling, and demonstrate how to use resources, like the word wall, to remember the spellings of frequently written words. Through talk and modeling on the white board (or chart paper), make the purposes as well as the conventions of written language more visible and understandable to children.

Morning message and other daily writing routines provide opportunities for emerging readers and writers to learn and participate in the processes that lead to independent writing. With the support of the teacher, emerging readers and writers plan and make decisions about print conventions, stretch words and match sounds to letters, and actually create text by sharing the pen to write on the white board. You can extend children's learning during the everyday writing activities by asking children to hunt for and circle letters, patterns, words, or text features.

Everyday writing routines are a bridge to independent writing. For example:
* during center time, children can use words from the daily writing to independently write other words with the same beginning sounds or spelling patterns.
* children can write their own sentences using questions, periods or other punctuation from the daily writing.
* children can use the daily writing as a model to write their own labels, lists, letters, memos, logs, observations, responses, journals, or stories.

Linking Reading to Writing

It almost goes without saying that the books children love are fabulous springboards for writing. Mine your read-aloud books, big books, chart stories from shared reading, and even your leveled books for topics to teach. As you'll see in the sample lesson that follows, the arc of

your teaching moves from read-aloud to guided practice to independent practice, during which children write on individual white boards or paper. As you plan a lesson, here are a few questions to ponder:

As she reads aloud a leveled book, Debra showcases the words and word features she wants to emphasize.

1. What question(s) can I pose to get my students talking and thinking in the direction I want them to go? Is there a particular page of this text that I can use to open my lesson?

2. What do I want to model for students? Does this modeling and thinking aloud give them all they need to write [the sentence or whatever] on their own?

3. What writing strategies and skills might I model?

   Here are a few of the many writing strategies you can teach:

   Revision

   * Rereading text to see if it makes sense
   * Adding information
   * Staying on the topic
   * Sequencing the events or ideas
   * Adding endings
   * Choosing an appropriate title

Kindergarten Literacy

Editing

* Using upper- and lowercase letters appropriately
* Spacing between words
* Directionality
* Awareness of end-of-sentence punctuation (period, question mark, exclamation point)
* Correct formation of letters

Articulation

* Stretching words to hear sounds in order to spell
* Referencing classroom charts such as the vowel chart, the alphabet chart, the word wall

4. How might I extend the lesson? For example, what new word(s) from the text (or writing) can I harvest for a word wall or more focused word study?

Example 2: Link Writing to a Read-Aloud

Let's listen in on how Angela Anderson, a teacher in South Colonie, New York, orchestrated a writing lesson around Kevin Henke's *Owen*, a picture book about a little mouse who doesn't want to give up his fuzzy yellow blanket. Notice how she carefully embeds the concept of main character in her introduction, and invites kids to make personal associations with the story.

Introduce the Book

TEACHER: [pointing to the cover] This story is about a little mouse who drags around his blanket wherever he goes. And there's another mouse looking after him. She has her binoculars on. This little guy—his name is Owen. He's the main character of the story—that means that's who the story is mostly about.

TEACHER: In this story you're going to see Owen carry around a blanket—he just loves to carry it around everywhere. As you listen to the story, I want you to think if there is some thing that you love, maybe something you were given as a baby, maybe something you still have. Don't tell me now. Keep it in your head. Something you had when you were a baby and you still have it and you just love it so much and you can't give it away or throw it away—don't tell now—keep it in your head, keep it to your own self—what you have at your house.

[Teacher reads entire book aloud.]

Invite Children to Think-Pair-Share

Angela then invites children to share how the events of the story relate to their own experiences. Because 20-plus children cannot all share their experiences at the same time, she has them whisper information about their experiences to a peer—a Think-Pair-Share format for discussion:

> TEACHER: Raise your hand if you had a blanket or something at home like Owen did in the story.
>
> STUDENT: My blanket has my name on it.
>
> TEACHER: You still have it from when you were a baby? Do you sleep with it still?
>
> STUDENT: I have two blankets. . .
>
> STUDENT: I have a thumb. . .
>
> TEACHER: Whisper to the person next to you something you have at home that you wouldn't want to part with.

Make Connections With Other Books

One student says the story about Owen is like the Joseph story—a story they read earlier in the school year. He rummages through the browsing box to find the book and gives it to Angela. Angela immediately picks up on the opportunity to relate similar themes across books and makes the connection between books explicit for the children. She again calls attention to the structure of stories by helping children notice that the characters in both books were good problem-solvers.

> TEACHER: In this story, this little boy—his name was Joseph—he had a jacket he loved. His jacket was made from a blanket his grandfather made for him when

he grew out of his blanket that he wouldn't give up. Remember, his grandpa kept making different things—a jacket, vest, belt, tie—all kinds of things out of this blanket. . . . Remember the mice taking little snippings and making curtains and blankets? There are all kinds of things going on in the story. . . . How is the Grandpa in this story like Owen's mother? Grandpa was the problem-solver in this one. Who was the problem-solver in the Owen story?

Use the Personal Connection to Motivate Writing

Nine times out of ten, the most memorable teaching and learning is based on the personal connections children have made to whatever it is we are teaching. So milk it! Watch how Angela builds a sentence-writing lesson around cherished things:

TEACHER: We talked about our own lives, our own special things that we had at home, that we still have, like Owen.

We're going to write a sentence today about the story we read and how we feel about the things we have. Who can tell me some ideas about what we can write?

James, what do you think?

Student: I could write about my thumb.

TEACHER: James doesn't want to part with his thumb.

STUDENT: My blanket.

TEACHER: We could write about Alice's blanket.

STUDENT: I want to write about the blanket my mother gave me when I was born.

TEACHER: So we all have things we can't part with just like Owen. Could we say we want to write "We love our blankets as much as Owen"?

Do we all have blankets or does somebody have a stuffed animal?

[Students tell about the various stuffed animals they have.]

TEACHER: Can we say, "We love our toys and blankets as much as Owen does"? That would be a good sentence to go along with what we've been talking about today.

Engage in Interactive Writing

Now Angela moves on to interactive writing, when children have the opportunity to write meaningful text and develop writing strategies. Each child may have individual white boards with markers so that they can try writing what you or a child has added on the chart paper. Or, you can introduce the individual white boards once your children are familiar with interactive writing.

Angela and her kindergartners jointly write a response to the storybook *Owen*.

In the beginning of the year, children tend to write beginning sounds on their own, and the high-frequency words they know, and so the teacher helps them by writing middle and ending sounds of words on the chart paper. Gradually, children take ownership of the pen and write one and two sentences with little or no assistance.

The beauty of this strategy is that every child is able to participate. Let's see how it plays out as Angela's lesson continues. Previously, we saw how Angela ensured that the children had something to say. In the section that follows, Angela holds children accountable for the writing conventions they have learned and supplies those conventions they have not yet encountered. Angela supports children's practice of writing conventions such as: left-to-right directionality, capitalization of first words in the sentence, use of word wall words to support spelling, spacing between words, the spelling patterns *ou* and *oy* and corresponding sounds, sound stretching, the plural *s*, formation of the letters *s* and *b*.

TEACHER: Everyone take a deep breath. Breathe through your nose, out your mouth. Get your writing hand ready.

Our first word is going to be We. We love our toys and blankets just as Owen does. We. How do we spell *we*?

Mariah, you write *we*. Where does Mariah start to write? [Angela puts Mariah's finger on the far left side of the white board.]

What kind of *W* does Mariah need?

Kindergarten Literacy

STUDENTS: *Capital W*

TEACHER: *Capital W because it is the first word in the sentence.*

love. . . . /l/ /l/ /l/ How do we spell love?

STUDENTS: *L-o-v-e*

TEACHER: *We know how to spell love. That's one of our word wall words. We use love when we write to our family.*

> *James, write love.*

> *Remember to put the space between We and love.* [Angela demonstrates by putting her two fingers between the words on the white board]

> *Those of your who are not writing can spell it in the air.* [Teacher and students spell "love" in the air]

TEACHER: [Rereads text so far] *We love our. . . our—this is tricky. Does anyone know what two letters say /ou/? Like ouch, mouse, house. . . ?*

STUDENTS: *o-u*

TEACHER: *Meg! Come on up! Our has /ou/. Let's stretch it /o-u-r/.*

> *Ready?*

STUDENTS: *R.*

TEACHER: *Let's read what we have so far: We love our—toys—What do you think toys starts with? /t/ toys?*

STUDENTS: *T.*

TEACHER: *Good job! What do you need to remember between our and toys? Yes, a space. Jillian? Come up! Now this is kind of tricky—/oy/ It has an O and Y.* [Teacher writes.] *Some of us knew that.*

> *And it's more than one toy—what do we put at the end of toy to make more than one?*

STUDENTS: *An S.*

TEACHER: *Who can make an S for me? Let's practice in the air. Make sure the S is going in the right direction. Ss are tricky. Madhi has two of them in his last name. Since Madhi has them in his name, I figure he knew how to make them.*

> *Let's read what we have so far: We love our toys and-and*

> *I'm going to call on Amanda because she has and in her name. Excellent. How*

do you spell and *everybody?*

STUDENTS: *A-n-d.*

TEACHER: *And* is one of our word wall words.

Let's read our sentence so far: We love our toys and blankets—/b/ blankets. Let's make a b *in the air. That letter is a tricky one.*

Brendan, do you think you can make a lowercase b*? Brendan has an uppercase B in his name.* [Teacher coaches Brendan one-on-one on the formation of the letter *b*.] *Show me with your finger how the lowercase* b *will go. Good. Where will you start to write the* b*? Put your two fingers after* and *to help you remember to leave a space. Good. Start at the top and make a line down. Good. Which side will the circle be on? Show me with your finger first. Good.*]

This interactive writing lesson has given Angela's students lots of problem-solving strategies that they can put to use in subsequent group work and independent practice.

Interactive Writing After Guided Reading

Teachers often ask: Can we use guided reading books as a springboard for interactive writing? Sure. Although leveled books and other patterned books that are written for instructional programs are usually not as engaging as trade books suitable for read-aloud, they have their advantages. Their patterns and predictable sentences provide a highly supportive model for interactive writing. The words in these little books are usually high-frequency words that children should recognize automatically—many of which, children ought to be able to write fluently as well. So following a guided reading lesson with an interactive writing lesson can be an effective way to bring about the many additional exposures to these high-frequency words that kids need.

Organize With a Schedule-of-the-Day

Setting out the daily events of your day can help you organize and pace your teaching. I write out a detailed schedule of the day for myself and post a simplified version for the children. I write each activity on a sentence strip. Next to each I place a photo of the children engaged in that activity, or I draw a picture that represents that activity. My schedule might go something like this:

8:40–8:55	Unpack and sign-in
8:55–9:10	Morning Meeting—Morning Message, Power Name, Letter Strip
9:10–9:35	Song/Shared Reading
9:35–10:20	Guided Reading and Reading Stations
10:20–10:55	Word Study Activity/Class News using interactive writing with white boards
11:00–11:45	Lunch
11:50–12:10	Independent reading
12:10–12:50	Independent writing
12:50–1:30	Math
1:30–2:15	Prep (students attend specials, i.e. gym or music)
2:20–2:45	Read-aloud

Excerpted from *Reading and Writing in Kindergarten: A Practical Guide* by Rosalie Franzese (Scholastic, 2002)

Other Ideas for Daily Writing

As children become more sophisticated readers and writers, you can expand the writing genres you explore with them. Early in the year, their stories and articles may be just one or two lines—by the end of the year, move over, Dostoevsky! Here are some genres and writing formats to include in your shared writing, interactive writing, and writing mini-lessons. Again, the teaching arc is model, guided practice as a whole group or small group, and then independent practice.

Lists

* names of friends and family
* names and phone numbers
* address books
* birthday calendars
* things to do
* favorite things
* things to find out about
* things to write about
* favorite stories

Patterned Charts

* I can _____
* I can see _____
* I like _____
* I like to _____
* (Name) likes _____
* (Name) likes to _____
* "I like to _____," said (Name).
* I like kindergarten.
* I like to go to kindergarten.
* I like to go each day.
* I like to go to kindergarten.
* Hip-hip, hip-hip, hooray!
* I like to _____ in kindergarten.
* I like to _____each day.
* I like to _____ in kindergarten.
* Hip-hip, hip-hip, hooray!

Photo Books or "Instant Readers"

* Here is _____
* This is _____
* Where is _____ ?
* Mom is _____
* Dad is _____
* In winter, I _____
* In spring, I _____

Messages

* news (class news, school news, the weather, local news)
* notes
* memos
* letters
* cards
* postcards

Journals

* daily journals
* learning logs
* observation journals
* buddy journals
* dialogue journals

Captioned Books

* child-drawn pictures or photos cut out of magazines with labels and captions
* scrapbooks with special pictures or photos with labels and captions

Books Patterned on Literature

* Clifford books
* alphabet books
* counting books
* cumulative storybooks
* any favorite book, such as *If You Give a Moose a Cookie* by Laura Joffe Numeroff

Nonfiction Articles and Books

* how-to descriptions (e.g., how to eat an ice cream cone, how to care for a dog)
* nonfiction narratives or informational books on topics such as butterflies, cats, horses
* bar graphs
* interviews

Independent Writing Routines

Independent writing is where it all comes together. The cadences and conventions of read-aloud stories, the explicit modeling of writing children have seen their teachers do, the practice they've racked up during shared and interactive writing—all this understanding flows through children's heads and hearts and onto the page during independent writing time. It's powerful stuff. Have your kids write independently every day, between 10 and 15 minutes. Teachers usually schedule independent writing time to immediately follow a lesson in which they model writing, but, of course, children can also write on their own during center time, first thing in the morning, or whenever you find the opportunity.

For kindergartners, it's motivating to finish one piece of writing during writing time. And yes, early in the year, the piece might be as brief as a single picture and caption.

Mini-lessons. Through mini-lessons, you can model for children the recursive steps of the writing process: drawing, drafting, composing, revising, editing, and publishing (or just sharing). In time, children will be able to move through these phases with greater independence and ability to use resources and references such as writing charts, alphabet and vowel charts, and personal dictionaries. For more about mini-lessons, see professional books by Donald Graves, Lucy Calkins, and others.

Conferring. Talking with children about their work is instrumental to children's progress as writers, and to their sense of themselves as capable writers. As children write, walk around the room and chat with several children each day. Initiate the conversation with an open-ended question like "How are you coming along?" or invite the child to read her piece, and then simply say, "Wow, that's something. Tell me more." Carl Anderson's book, *How's It Going?* is a classic on the art of conferring, and Donald H. Graves' *A Fresh Look at Writing* brims with insights about mini-lessons and responding to children's writing. In the next chapter on reading, I share a part of Angela's conference with a young writer as she edits her story for publication (see p. 259).

✳

The Perks of Our Profession

Watching a kindergartner learn to write is like watching a morning glory unfurl in the morning sun. One minute the child is writing a faint scribble on the page, and the next time you turn around, the writing is in full bloom. What a thrill it is to see that full, bold color, and hear a new voice declaring itself to the world. And, oh, children have so much to say!

Chapter Seven

Reading

Partner reading—and enjoying—
a *No, David!* book

How a child changes from a "pretend reader" to a "real reader" seems like a miracle to most parents, and although teachers know the hard work it entails, we are often hard-pressed to identify exactly how it happened. A number of researchers have speculated about the trajectory from emergent to conventional reading as well. Phil Gough from the University of Texas contends that reading, or more precisely, reading comprehension, is the result of decoding plus listening comprehension and that these two elements are separate and distinct. In other words, there is no reading if either decoding or listening (oral language) comprehension is missing.

Recently, Grover Whitehurst and Chris Lonigan (2001) proposed a similar but more elaborated view. They posit that there are two constellations that "crosstalk" to enable a person to read (p. 13). One such constellation comprises information that is outside the printed word; the other constellation is information that is "inside" the word. "Outside-in" sources of information include concept or topic knowledge, genre knowledge, and vocabulary, and these sources all support children's construction of meaning. "Inside-in" sources of information support children's ability to decode, and include knowledge of letter names and sounds. Just how these interdependent domains of information "talk" to each other in the service of beginning reading is suggested by several other lines of research.

Early work by Richard Lomax and Lea McGee (1987) demonstrated the reciprocal nature of the different components of literacy development—knowledge about books, probably acquired through experience listening to books read aloud and "pretend-reading," contributes to children's knowledge about letters and sounds; likewise, letter and sound knowledge contributes to more elaborated understandings of print and book conventions. Another important finding by Lomax and McGee was that children do not have to "master" one component, for example, the names and sounds of all the letters, before learning to read words or before developing more sophisticated ideas about how reading works. Rather, knowing some letter names and a few anchor words (child's name, the word *the*) supports the development of the ability to "finger-point read" by matching speech to print. The ability to point to each word as it is read is a watershed insight—called the "concept of word in text"—that ultimately leads to decoding.

I discussed *concept of word* in the chapter on print concepts, but I want to briefly review its significance here. Darryl Morris, Janet Bloodgood, Richard Lomax, and Jan Perney (2003) suggested a developmental model in learning to read that gives further credence to the idea that print concepts and phonological awareness jointly support early reading. Let's look at the following sentence. See how noticing the spaces between words, a few sight words, and finger-point reading go hand-in-hand with knowledge about the way sounds map onto letters to help a kindergartner read "I ride my bike."

I xxxx my xxxx.
I rxxx my bxxx.
I rxdx my bxkx.
I ride my bike.

- First, the child notices the anchor words   *I, my*
- Then he notices the beginning consonants   *r* and *b*
- Next, the child develops finger-pointing reading
- Then he notices ending consonants   *d* and *k*

- Next, after the spaces around the word virtually "frame" the word for inspection by the child, he attends to the vowel patterns within the word.
- The last stage makes full phonemic segmentation possible—that is, isolating the sounds represented by spelling patterns, including the medial vowel.
- Finally, by analyzing the vowel patterns, the child is able to decode and recognize unknown words.

Knowledge of the "Outside In" Leads to Reading-to-Learn

It stands to reason that the more up-close experience children have with print, the more likely they are to develop insights that lead to decoding, word recognition, and comprehension. Children's proficiency with within-word domain knowledge, namely, letter and sound correspondences, predicts first and second grade achievement. But outside-in components—topic knowledge, syntax, vocabulary, and genre knowledge—likely enhances their understanding and recall of complicated text and sustains motivation to read. By the time children are fourth graders, the influence of these more global outside-in domains are evident. Vocabulary, content knowledge and the ability to parse complex sentences and connected text are critical elements in the "reading to learn" curricula of the upper elementary grades and beyond. In a classic study of "the fourth-grade slump," Jeanne Chall, Vicki Jacobs, and Luke Baldwin (1996) reported that word meaning—vocabulary that represents content knowledge—was the first skill to lag in the upper grades, but ultimately, other skills fall behind. A balanced reading program is one that develops children's proficiency in both domains.

As kindergarten teachers, we need to bear in mind that these domains are interdependent, not mutually exclusive. Certainly, we need to explicitly teach letter-sound correspondences to make the alphabetic principle accessible to all children, guide children's fingers to make speech match print, and model and prompt strategic reading and writing. By establishing certain predictable classroom routines—read-alouds, shared reading, guided reading, and independent and paired reading—we can support children at all levels.

Ira's story, on the next page, represents the intersection of popular culture in TV and movies, literary genres experienced through read-alouds, and personal identity.

Reading Routines: Read-Alouds

Read-aloud reading is reading done by the teacher or some other proficient adult reader. The books selected can be more complex in vocabulary or structure than the books selected for shared reading or guided reading. Reading aloud to children provides a rich "language input" in the use of words rarely heard in everyday conversations. Even though she was referring to preschoolers, Catherine Snow's (2003) observations about "non-immediate" talk of book interactions and its influence on vocabulary development hold for kindergartners too. Non-immediate talk is talk that goes beyond the here and now—it may relate the book to children's lives, or other books, or the world at large. According to Snow, non-immediate talk "creates opportunities for children to understand and use the somewhat more sophisticated vocabulary required for [making] evaluative reactions to the book, discussing characters' internal states, making predictions concerning the next episode, and so on. These kinds of talk inevitably introduce relatively complex vocabulary" (p. 21). Likewise, experience with book reading is related to advanced understanding of complex syntax (Chomsky, 1972), and the ability to understand and use linguistic markers of different kinds of text, informational text (Pappas, 1993) as well as narratives (McGee, 1993). During read-alouds, we help students notice the shape or structure of the text as well as the ideas presented and the vocabulary and conceptual framework that represent those ideas.

First Genres: Alphabet Books, Counting Books, Color Books

Alphabet books are a perfect example of how outside-in knowledge developed during book reading supports inside-out knowledge of letter-sound correspondences. As I

This is John Henry
and Wonder Woman.
By Ira.

Wonder Woman rescued
John Henry!

This is JOHN HENRY
Ad WLᴰ WMN
By Ira

WLᴾ WMN RCd
JOHN HENRY

Ira, an African-American kindergartner, loved
stories, whether they were Disney stories like Cinderella,
comic books like Wonder Woman, or classic children's
literature like Ezra Jack Keats' *John Henry*. She was
particularly moved by the plight of John Henry, who
worked so hard he died, and so, wrote her own story,
putting herself in the role of a "wonder woman" who
rescues the doomed African-American hero. Notice the
I—for Ira—on Wonder Woman's cape!

discussed in Chapter 5, knowing letter names gives children information about letter sounds—they are, after all, "letter-name spellers" at this point in time, meaning they spell by using letter names and points of articulation. Also, by attending to letters in the initial consonant position, children begin to analyze words and notice the boundaries marked by white space in a line of text.

Besides conveying particular letter-sound information, alphabet picture books, along with color books and number books, constitute a particular genre. By reading aloud and talking with your students about a variety of alphabet books (or counting or color books), you can help children notice features of the book and how one topic—the alphabet, or numbers, or colors—can be represented in many different ways, by many different authors and illustrators. Such read-aloud and discussion develops a framework for children to understand writers' and reader's purposes and may serve as a general introduction to the larger genre of nonfiction.

Into the Sea: A Sample Alphabet Book–Based Unit

Yvonne, a kindergarten teacher in an urban school in Florida, was especially concerned about keeping those students who struggled motivated to learn to read. As one of our teacher collaborators in a summer project for children who failed during the school year, Yvonne tried to match the books she selected to her students' interests, cultural and linguistic backgrounds, topic knowledge and developing reading abilities. Of course she selected more challenging texts to read aloud, and less challenging but related by topic or genre for shared and guided reading, depending on the level of children's skills. In many cases, the texts that children read were texts that the children themselves created, as in the patterned chart stories that she developed jointly with children from read-alouds, or the sentences that the whole class or small groups created through interactive writing. By the end of the year, children were able to write three-part stories, as in the Clifford stories that I describe at the end of the chapter. In the beginning of the school year, and particularly in summer, Yvonne was careful to select books that her children could relate to.

She chose an alphabet book, *Into the A, B, Sea* (Rose, 2003), because her community is located near the ocean, and children have great interest in the ocean as a habitat for living things. Many of the sea creatures illustrated in the book were unfamiliar, however, so Yvonne not only read the book aloud, as one of a number of books about the sea—a text set she developed—she also used a big book version of *Into the A, B, Sea* as shared reading, to be read and reread many times.

Demarkus captioned his drawing of a sea urchin as part of a class picture glossary on sea creatures.

Through interactive writing, she and her kindergartners jointly created a Post-it picture glossary of sea creatures, divided into fish and shellfish, displayed for all to read. Children drew and labeled their own favorite sea creature, identified it as having a shell or not, and in many cases wrote something to describe it. Demarkus, in the example above, captioned his drawing of a sea urchin with "Sea urchins sting people" to help his classmates remember a salient fact about his favorite sea creature.

The big book, with its colorful illustrations and rhyme, helped the children to visualize the creatures and to make the names of the sea creatures more memorable and available as mnemonics for the letters of the alphabet and the sounds that represent them. Besides the obvious use of the big book to enable meaningful exposures to alphabet letters, the rhythm and rhyme of the text help children develop awareness of the sounds of language—phonemic awareness—a precursor to more subtle, but important distinctions among sounds:

> Swim the oceans waves with me and dive into the A, B, Sea where anemones sting, where sea stars grab and barnacles cling, where crabs crawl in and dolphins spin. . . . (p. 1)

Developing Concepts

Like many quality trade books, the alphabet book *Into the A, B, Sea* uses "rare" words, like *anemones* and *barnacles*, and *sea urchins*, and unusual verbs, such as *cling*—vocabulary that's unlikely to crop up in kindergartners' everyday talk. And so by combining the alphabet read-aloud with other books on the topic of ocean life, Yvonne was able to develop not only vocabulary but also rudimentary concepts about ocean life as a habitat and distinctions between crustaceans and fish.

Another teacher, Kathy, also from an ocean community, used a read-aloud text set on ocean life as a springboard for children to independently write a flip book with other categories of information about a favorite sea creature: each book included a freehand diagram of the creature with labeled body parts, a list of what the sea creature eats, and an interesting fact about the creature. A flip book is an example of a template or pattern that may be used to scaffold children's earliest nonfiction writing. Besides drawing-to-learn tools such as labeled diagrams, captioned drawings, cutaways, Post-it picture glossaries, and flip books, other kinds of templates include "foldables" and predictable charts.

Labels or **captions** provide extra information about the drawing, sometimes with a single word or phrase; other times with a complete sentence, as in the "sea urchin" example. **Fact boxes** or **dialogue boxes** show at-a-glance details about the subject (see example, next page). Stephen's excellent drawing of an underwater scene includes dialogue boxes: "A deep sea hatchet fish is hunting" and "A dune fish is hunting in seaweed" with arrows to appropriate fish. **Annotations** point out features of an illustration—a simple annotation is one like Stephen's "seaweed" with an arrow to the seaweed. **Flow charts** show ideas linked in sequence or chronology, such as life cycles and other patterns such as food

Some Drawing-to-Learn Ideas

Invite your kindergartners to:
* write a caption for a magazine or book photo, or caption their own drawing
* draw a diagram and label it or annotate it
* add dialogue or a fact box to an image
* make a cutaway diagram
* make a scale drawing
* make a flow chart or tree chart
* make a time line

chain, or a series of events that can be used to build a narrative.

A **tree diagram** is similar to a flow chart in that it represents a sequence, but, like a tree, it has branches and twigs suggesting a hierarchy. It is important to note that drawings, diagrams, and illustrations typically are not to scale but interpretations. An exception is the scale drawing, as in the scale drawing comparing the cookie cutter shark with Adi's little brother ("The cookie cutter shark is as small as my little brother"), a comparison elicited by Florida teacher Colleen Croft in a multi-text readaloud unit on ocean life. **Cutaways**, another type of diagram, show

Above: Adi shows the size of a cookie cutter shark by comparing it to his little brother in a scale drawing. Below: Stephen uses dialogue boxes to describe hatchet fish and dune fish.

what something is like on the inside. A shark cutaway for example, shows the vertebrae, dorsal fins, cartilage, jaw muscle, swimming muscles, nostril, gills, heart, liver, and developing baby sharks.

Children's drawing and writing may be revisited many times—as an occasion for discussion and conceptual development, as in idea circles (Gambrell, et al., 2000), or as a way to develop print and word knowledge as in cut-up sentences and words harvested from predictable charts. (We'll look at idea circles in more detail on p. 238.)

Example 3: Noticing Title, Illustrations, and Making Connections

Besides developing vocabulary and content knowledge, the books you use in your lessons can develop children's awareness of how readers choose and use books for enjoyment and to learn new things about the world. Let's now listen in on Yvonne's think-aloud lesson based on *I Love My Hair* (Tarley, 2001):

YVONNE: I love my hair! I chose this book because I was wondering why she was so happy on the cover. Obviously, by the title she's talking about her hair. . . so I love my hair. [She turns to the first-page illustration of mom brushing girl's hair and girl's face all scrunched up. She reads aloud the text.] 'When mama gets to especially tangled places I try my hardest not to cry, sucking in my breath and pressing my hands together till they're red. . .'

Hmm. I wonder what's going to happen next? I'm wondering if she's going to start crying because I know I would. It hurts! I have very vivid memories of my mom brushing my hair. I had very, very long hair. I know what she's going through! I remember when my mom used to brush my hair. . . the fights and how I behaved! She cut my hair! She had had it with me! No more! So I wonder what's going to happen next. Did she cry? Look at her little face. What will happen?

A typical next step would be to engage children in a conversation about the book. Depending on Yvonne's goals for the lesson, she could think aloud during another point in the story, modeling for the children a strategy like prediction, or relating events in the narrative to lived experiences. Children could partner think-aloud, demonstrating for each other personal strategy use.

Another option, depending on the purpose of the read-aloud and how it fits into content area inquiry, is to read another text about hair or faces or families, and develop a conceptual framework for developing a local or state social studies standard such as "understanding the uniqueness of individuals."

Shared Reading

Shared reading is read-along reading. The teacher does most of the reading and the children read along with the teacher, contributing words they know. Shared reading is typically a whole-group activity, led by the teacher. The materials used are usually those that can be seen by all children, and the texts range far beyond big books!

Shared Reading Texts

* Big books or poems
* Weather charts
* Calendar charts
* Predictable charts
* Drawings with captions
* Diagrams with labels
* Maps
* Songs
* Rhymes
* Chants and other enlarged or copied texts on chart paper
* Dictated, interactive, and shared writing
* Individual or class books
* Children's murals or collaboratively made murals

In shared reading, fully support children's attempts to read by modeling the process:
* Show the students how to read from left to right, the return sweep, and voice-to-print match by pointing to each word.
* Point out title and author, punctuation, capitalization, and other conventions of written language.
* Model how to predict and search for information, such as pictures and beginning letters, to read unfamiliar words.
* Explain unknown vocabulary or sentence or text structures, always relating the familiar to the unknown, helping children learn to make those connections for themselves.

By frequently rereading shared texts, children consolidate emerging reading strategies. During these repeated readings of the same chart, book, or text, you can informally assess the children's developing knowledge of reading by asking individual children to locate familiar words, letters, or word parts. Children often memorize the texts that are used in shared reading and reread them independently in "reading the room" or other center activities. If you take or harvest words for word study from the charts, poems, songs, chants, books, and dictated and interactive writing materials used for shared reading, children will always have a model of those words "in context" to return to again and again.

Developing a Shared Reading Text

In Cindy Ellison's Tennessee classroom, the texts for shared reading were all homegrown in interactive writing. Cindy and her students read these texts over and over for shared reading, and ultimately, for independent work like reading or writing the room.

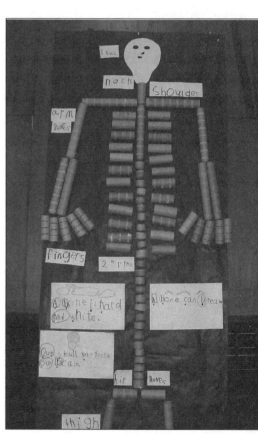

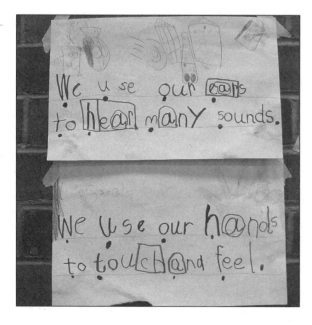

Cindy and her kindergartners built this floor-to-ceiling model of the human skeleton out of toilet paper rolls. The kids drew, labeled, and captioned each body part, thus putting to use their science words like *skeleton* and *bones* as well as high-frequency sight words like *is* and *can*. Cindy put a dot under each word in the captions to guide little fingers as they match voice to print.

Kindergarten Literacy

Theme-Driven Shared Reading Texts

Besides the model of the skeleton, Cindy developed similar shared reading texts on food groups, the life cycle of plants, the five senses, and other topics that typically comprise the science curricula of kindergarten. Cindy gathered and read aloud many informational books related to the topic she selected; she talked through and charted the concepts presented in the books. During interactive writing, children created texts, often diagrams or flow charts, and a brief caption, around the knowledge gained by inquiring into these topics. Notice in the pumpkin sample at right that the text includes a flow chart illustrating the changing colors of a pumpkin as it reaches maturity.

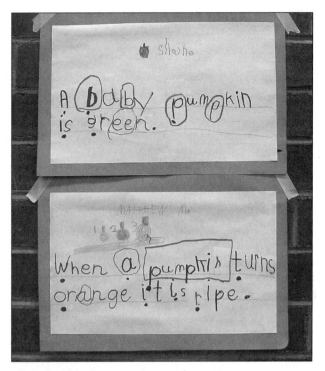

Notice in this and other samples that the teacher circled and outlined features of print she wanted to teach—beginning consonants, high-frequency words, letter patterns, and the one-to-one match of sound patterns to words.

Small Group Routines: Guided Reading, Inquiry Circles

Effective instruction is intensive as well as personal. To maximize the attention we give to each child, we group. And we group for different purposes. As our analysis of Mandy and Ruth's class assessment scores demonstrated, children vary in their knowledge about literacy, even within the same school community, and they vary in interest, background, and motivation. Small groups help personalize instruction.

Forming Guided Reading Groups

In guided reading, we group children by reading ability in order to teach at children's instructional level. Guided reading is reading done by children but supported with a teacher's modeling and prompts. During guided reading children read leveled books or other instructional-level materials—materials that are not too easy or too hard but are challenging enough that children will learn from each new reading experience. (See Fountas & Pinnell, 1996, and Schulman & Payne, 2000, for a fuller discussion of guided reading.) To set up guided reading groups, review children's reading assessments. Using children's performance on the literacy assessments, including the letter names and sounds assessments, word writing and reading, phonological sorts, and spelling assessments, select students for three or four flexible, tentative, homogeneous groups. Identify teaching points for focus and select materials for instruction.

While you work with guided reading groups, the other students will be engaged in independent, partner, or center work. Make sure these other working groups are heterogeneous, or mixed ability. Assign the mixed-achievement groups to particular independent activities on a rotating basis, similar to center work, or allow self-selected independent work. Choose one or two students from each mixed-ability group to participate in guided reading instruction. To facilitate management, you may want to use a system of icons and work boards, as described in Fountas & Pinnell's *Guided Reading* (1996).

Guided reading presents many opportunities to point out words with newly learned or tricky letter patterns like digraphs.

The Guided Reading Lesson Plan

1. First, introduce the story. Use questions to activate children's prior knowledge about the topic and help them make connections between the topic and their own lives.
   * Introduce the title and author.
   * Ask children to predict the story.
   * Summarize the plot for the children.
2. Take children on a picture walk through the book, making sure to use any unfamiliar or "book" language patterns in conversation about the pictures.
3. Explain vocabulary likely to be unknown, call attention to words likely to be difficult to decode.
4. Ask children to find those words in the text.
5. Next, children whisper-read the entire book, and the teacher listens to the oral reading and prompts children as needed. Examples of prompts that are helpful to emerging readers follow:
   * Point to each word as you read.
   * Read that again (or: Try that again).
   * Look at the picture.
   * What is the first sound?
   * Get your mouth ready to say a word that starts with that sound.
   * Does it match?
   * Does it sound right?
   * Does it make sense?
6. Listen to children's responses to the book and let these responses guide the next teaching moves.
7. After reading, revisit parts of the text that posed problems for the readers, emphasizing successful strategies and rereading tricky parts that readers were unable to work through on their own, prompting as above.
   * Try that again. Does it make sense? Does it sound right? Does it look right?
   * What do you know about that word that can help you?
   * I like the way you figured that out.
8. Acknowledge partially correct responses, as emerging readers try to use visual clues, meaning, and syntax to help them read unfamiliar words.

Source: Adapted from *Guided Reading: Good First Teaching for All Children* by Irene Fountas & Gay Su Pinnell (Heinemann, 1996).

Forming Inquiry Circles

Inquiry circles and idea circles are small heterogeneous reading groups, that is, mixed ability and collaborative; they focus on a single topic but multiple books. Idea circles and inquiry circles have much in common with literature circles. (For a fuller discussion of literature circles, see Linda Gambrell & Janet Almasi, 1996; Harvey Daniels, 2002; for idea circles, see Guthrie & McCann, 1996.) To set up inquiry circles or idea circles, first select a topic for inquiry—a character in a series book; a particular genre of book, like mystery; or a science or social studies topic, such as bugs. Gather multiple levels of text on the topic. For series books, for example, Clifford, be sure to include the easiest levels (*Clifford Can*) as well as the unabridged books (*Clifford, the Big, Red Dog*). For content area topics, for example, bugs, include not only challenging field guides but also text at easy guided reading levels. Much of the knowledge-building during inquiry circles is done by the teacher through read-alouds, although children should have access to books they can read on the topic. As in guided reading, model and prompt strategic reading of different genres, and demonstrate drawing-to-learn and appropriate writing and discussion responses. In inquiry circles, teachers often facilitate, rather than direct, interaction, as in guided reading.

Children who develop expertise in one area, for example, animal alphabet books, or a certain kind of bug, can then regroup, or jigsaw, and share that information with members of other groups who researched other bugs or composed alphabet books based on other topics. The children's work shown here are two

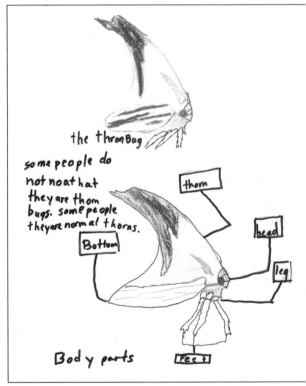

Andrew writes an "amazing fact" annotation about thorn bugs, saying that they can fool people into thinking they are normal thorns.

examples of drawing-to-learn. The inquiry topic was bugs, and Florida summer-school teacher Kathy asked children to draw the body parts for the bug they chose to study. As children shared their work, Kathy wanted them to draw conclusions about common body parts in insects and specific information on eating, habitats, and at least one amazing fact.

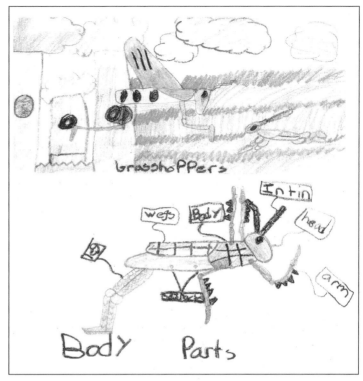

Stephen, an excellent artist, shows grasshoppers camouflaged in the grass, and below that, he labels the parts of a grasshopper's body.

Finding "Just Right" Books

A "just right" book is the book the child wants to read and can read. What makes a book easy or difficult depends not only on features of the text, that is, the number of words in the sentences and number of syllables in the words, but also on what the child brings to the text—interest, motivation, background knowledge. When I was in graduate school, we called a strict focus on the text, a "bottom-up" approach to reading; a strict focus on the reader, a "top-down" approach. An "interactionist" approach looked at factors both "inside the reader's head" and "inside the text," meaning that the ability to read and understand is an interaction between the reader and the text. A "just right" book takes into account both what the reader brings to the book in terms of interest and prior knowledge and what kinds of challenges the book presents, such as vocabulary, complex language, and genre. Certainly, deep background knowledge and the ready assistance of a parent, peer, or teacher will help the early reader read and understand books that might otherwise be too hard.

Different Purposes, Different Levels

The reader's purpose is also important—why is the reader reading the book? Often informational texts are constructed like field guides, as a reference for the reader, not a book to read from cover to cover. The early reader with a great deal of firsthand information on snakes, for example, may be able to scan, peruse, and dip into a challenging informational text on reptiles to find just what he needs to describe a particular snake's penchant for preying on the unsuspecting rodent or ability to camouflage. Likewise, the early reader with firsthand experience watching Clifford or Scooby Doo on television already knows a great deal about the characters and the kinds of problems they encounter and resolve, the settings, and the slew of secondary players who participate with Scooby and Clifford in one predictable story after another. Background knowledge and motivation make series books more accessible to the beginning reader than we would otherwise expect if we looked at the readability alone.

Also, books that are too hard for early readers to read on their own but highly motivating, like series books or informational books, are good choices for read-alouds. Read-aloud immersion in a particular series, like Clifford, or topic, like reptiles, provides the grist for children to talk about, draw, write, and share their own texts. Almost Readers, as we learned from

Inquiry Circles: Step by Step

* Teacher selects a topic or series
* Teacher immerses students in a topic or series
* Teacher reads many books aloud
* Books are topic- or concept-centered
* Books are multi-level
* Students respond to read-alouds by drawing or writing, or mixing drawing and writing
* Students' responses (drawings, writings) are springboard for discussion
* Students use Post-its to bookmark what they want to share
* Teacher models and facilitates
* Students lead, asking questions, predicting, summarizing, noting funny spots, noting amazing facts, compare books in a series, compare information within topics

Kindergarten Literacy

Mandy's and Ruth's kindergartens, learn to read conventionally by reading back their own writing, like a Clifford-inspired story or an amazing fact about some bug. Children still working on letters and sounds benefit from cut-up sentences and words harvested from predictable chart stories based on read-alouds.

"Just right" books vary, depending on the purpose, background of the readers or listeners, in the case of read-alouds, and the reading ability of the readers. So the "just right" book for an inquiry circle may not be the same difficulty level as the "just right" book for guided reading. The "just right" book for independent reading is likely the easiest, most familiar book of all.

"Just Right" for Guided Reading: The Leveled Text

The "just right" level for teaching guided reading is at children's "instructional level." It is the level of book that the child can read with at least 90 percent accuracy. If the child's accuracy rate is below 90 percent, then the child probably needs an easier book or more supported instruction so that the child is not frustrated. You can determine children's accuracy rate by dividing the number of words read correctly by the number of words in the book. Or, alternately, you can select a book or passage from a book that is 100 words long. If the child makes fewer than ten errors, the book is appropriate. For example, if the child made three errors in a 100-word passage, the accuracy rate would be 97 percent (97 words read correctly/100 total words). For a 50-word passage, instructional level is fewer than five words; for a 25-word passage, fewer than two or three words.

If the purpose of the oral reading record (similar to a running record and also referred to as oral reading checks) is to find an appropriate book and place the child in the reading group, the child should be reading a new leveled book—one that the child has not read or seen before. If the purpose of the oral reading record is to observe children's reading behaviors, that is, the strategies that children use while reading, then children should be reading a familiar leveled book, for example, the book that they read the day before. Books that are too difficult will frustrate the reader. Easy books are appropriate for independent or partner reading but may not be challenging enough to be used for instruction.

Instructional level books present the reader with opportunities to use problem-solving strategies but do not overwhelm the reader with too many unknown words. Besides the number of unfamiliar words, books vary in other features that make them harder or easier for emerging readers.

Example 1: A Snapshot of Guided Reading Levels A–D

At Guided Reading levels A–C, the text is simple. The same high-frequency words are repeatedly used. The text consists of one or two sentence patterns that are repeated. Let's look at some examples. The book *Hats* by Catherine Peters, with illustrations by Shari Halpern, is composed of a single sentence pattern "I like ___ ___ hats." The words that change on the first page, *big, purple*, can be determined by looking at the illustrations. Each subsequent page, until the last page, has the same sentence pattern and the same high support from the illustrations for the words that vary from page to page. On the second page the text reads, "I like little red hats." The last page has a slightly different pattern—it has two sentences, and four words that are different from the previous patterns: "Hats, hats, hats. We like all kinds of hats." The language used is natural, similar to oral language (not literary or "book" language).

The topic or contents of the books at levels A–D are familiar to children. The illustrations provide a high level of support; that is, the pictures can help the reader identify unfamiliar words. The format is uncluttered with consistent placement of print and large spaces.

As texts become more difficult, there are more unfamiliar words, longer sentences, and more print on each page. Sentences are less predictable, and opening and closing sentences may be different from the early patterns. *Green, Green* by Kana Riley, with illustrations by Rene King Moreno (Houghton Mifflin) is a guided reading level-D book. Instead of a single sentence, the book repeats parts of a two-sentence pattern. The ending is a bit more complex with one sentence continuing over two pages. Illustrations still support the reader, especially since color words are used in the text: "I can paint the green, green grass (p. 2). I give the grass a green, green tree (p. 3)."

Example 2: A Snapshot of Guided Reading Level-F

Illustrations in *I Love Cats* by Catherine Matthias, with illustrations by Tom Dunnington (Children's Press) and *Itchy, Itchy Chicken Pox* by Grace Maccarone, with illustrations by Betsy Lewin (Scholastic), both guided reading level-F books, offer much less support to the reader. In both books there is repetitive rhyme that supports the decoding of words with particular letter patterns although the sentence structures vary. In *I Love Cats*, a single sentence can run over several pages or a single page can have a long, complicated sentence: "I like pigs, both small and big, and ducks and geese and goats and sheep (p. 14). I like them all a great big heap (p. 15)." *Itchy, Itchy Chicken Pox* presents text with similar patterns of rhyme and variation in length and complexity: "Don't rub, don't scratch. Oh no! Another batch!" Note the more challenging vocabulary in both books at level F—the words *heap* and *batch*.

Dialogue and other "book" language adds difficulty; language becomes more literary with narrative and expository structures, vocabulary becomes more complex and specialized, and illustrations provide less support. *The Dog* by John Burningham (Candlewick), a guided reading level-F book, is a case in point. The book opens with narrative language: "One day a dog we know was left at our house for a visit." The text is a chronology, unlike easier levels, and has a narrative structure—the dog was left with the boy, the dog did many things that got him into trouble, and at the end, the owner came to pick up the dog. One of the most difficult things about this particular book is that the reader has to infer the ending from the illustrations. The text reads: "I wish the dog could stay with me," but the drawing is of a man with the dog waving goodbye to the boy. At the earliest levels the reader often has to make inferences from the illustrations in order to construct a coherent text.

Example 3: A Snapshot of Guided Reading Levels H–K

A close look at the text structures of books at levels H–K makes clear that children need to notice not only the patterns within words, but also the patterns within texts. *Animal Builders* by Jon Mudge, with illustrations by Bill Pappas (ScottForesman), level H, has the same expository text pattern on each page:

"Who builds a house of clay?

[illustration]

Ovenbirds do.

Ovenbirds use clay to make nests.

Their nests look like little ovens." (p. 4)

"Who builds a house of leaves?

[illustration]

Tailorbirds do.

They use leaves to make nests.

They sew leaves together with spider silk." (p. 5)

Although the format is predictable, the vocabulary is specialized, and the information is presented as a series of attributes about a particular category of animals. *This Is the Seed* by Alan Trussell-Cullen, with illustrations by Kelly Riley (ScottForesman) presents another genre of text that may be unfamiliar to children—the cumulative story. So although there is a clear, cumulative pattern ("This is the boy who ate the slice that was cut from the bread. . ."), it is unlikely that children have encountered this structure prior to this level. Yet another structure is the fable, difficult not only because the organization of the text is a particular kind of narrative, but also because fables are fantasy, not representative of real life. I list *Mr. Sun and Mr. Sea*, by Andrea Butler, with illustrations by Lily Toy Hong, (Good Year Books) an African legend, because the language of the text is so literary—the heart of the legend is the personification of the sun and the sea, that is, making them flesh-and-blood people who talk, negotiate, and get jealous.

"Just Right" Books for Inquiry Circles

The series book is an important genre in early literacy development. Researcher Dina Feitelson and her colleagues (Rosenhouse, Feitelson, Kita, & Goldstein, 1997) found that listening to series books in the early grades—kindergarten and first grade—was the most effective way to motivate children to read voluntarily. Experience with series books increased book borrowing, book buying, and book reading. Most important, children who listened to series books "took on" the language of books, using language with more complexity than those without the experience and constructed more cohesive oral and written narratives. In terms of achievement outcomes for children, those who experienced the series books scored significantly higher on measures of decoding and comprehension. Although the actual words themselves are not predictable in series books, as in easy leveled books, the characters, the plots, the settings are all familiar to beginning readers, providing them a level of comfort and control. I am thinking here about *Clifford the Big, Red, Dog*, a much-loved dog and a much-loved story that kindergartners adore. (For more discussion of series books, see page 252.)

Another kind of "just right" book is one on a topic that the beginning reader knows well. In earlier sections of the chapter, I described the multi-text experiences that many teachers provide on particular topics or genres—ocean life or alphabet books, for example. Through read-alouds or shared reading, children develop familiarity with the vocabulary particular to that topic or genre as well as familiarity with the way writers organize information on that topic or in that genre. Extensive experience with series books enables children to construct more cohesive narratives and more well-developed resolutions and codas (morals) than children without such experience. It is likely that extensive experience with particular content topics confers similar benefits on children—the more they know about something, for example, ocean life, the easier it is for them to read an informational book on ocean life.

Example 4: Multi-Level Text Set on Bugs

The heart of inquiry is knowledge building. Using small field guides is a perfect way to introduce children to the domain of insects or bugs and the way a scientific classification system works. Three field guides for children that we really like are the *National Audubon Society First Field Guide: Insects* (Wilsdon, 1998), *National Geographic Society My First Pocket Guide: Insects* (Bickel, 1996), and *Popular Science Miniguide: Bugs* (Setford, 2001). Of course, you need to model the use of a field guide and informational books in general, then support children through read-alouds and vocabulary study as they build and organize domain knowledge. Once you select a topic for inquiry, the next step is gathering the books. By scanning the list of levels and titles on the text sets on bugs and the following one on Clifford stories, you can see at a glance the wide range of levels available for inquiry circles. Remember, children are immersed in the topic—through read-alouds, partner reading, and collaborative work—so they can often stretch themselves to read books at higher levels.

Bug Text Set

Bugs, Bugs, Bugs!	Mary Reid	Bugs	Scholastic		A
Spider Names	Susan Canizares	Bugs	Scholastic		A
What Do Insects Do?	Susan Canizares	Bugs	Scholastic		A
What Is an Insect?	Susan Canizares	Bugs	Scholastic		A
Butterfly	Susan Canizares	Bugs	Scholastic		B
Frightened	Joy Cowley	Bugs	Wright Group		B
Beautiful Bugs	Maria Fleming	Bugs	Scholastic		C
Bugs!	P. & F. McKissack	Bugs	Scholastic	1.4	C
The Busy Mosquito	Helen Depree	Bugs	Wright Group		C
Beetles	Cheryl Coughlan	Bugs	Pebble Books	1.3	D
Crickets	Cheryl Coughlan	Bugs	Pebble Books	1.3	D
Honey Bees	Lola M. Schaefer	Bugs	Pebble Books		D
The Big Bug Dug	Mary Serfozo	Bugs	Scholastic		D
Where Do Insects Live?	Susan Canizares	Bugs	Scholastic		D
Honey Bees and Hives	Lola M. Schaefer	Bugs	Pebble Books		E
Mosquitoes	Cheryl Coughlan	Bugs	Gail Saunders-Smith	3	E
The Bug Club		Bugs	Barron's	1.3	E
Are You a Ladybug?	Brian & Jill Cutting	Bugs	Wright Group		F
Cicadas	Helen Frost	Bugs	Pebble Books		F
Flies	Cheryl Coughlan	Bugs	Pebble Books	1.4	F
Grasshoppers	Cheryl Coughlan	Bugs	Pebble Books	1.4	F
Honey Bees and Honey	Lola M. Schaefer	Bugs	Pebble Books		F
It's a Good Thing There Are Insects	Allan Fowler	Bugs	Children's Press		F
Praying Mantises	Helen Frost	Bugs	Pebble Books		F
Water Bugs	Helen Frost	Bugs	Pebble Books		F
What Is an Insect?	Lola M. Schaefer	Bugs	Pebble Books		F
Ants	Christine Young	Bugs	Wright Group		G
Find the Insect	Cate Foley	Bugs	Children's Press	1.2	G
Spiders Are Not Insects	Allan Fowler	Bugs	Children's Press		G

Kindergarten Literacy

Spinning a Web	Lisa Trumbauer	Bugs	Newbridge		G
Flies Are Fascinating	Valerie Wilkinson	Bugs	Children's Press		H
From Caterpillar to Moth	Jan Kottke	Bugs	Scholastic		H
I Love Spiders	Rita Parkinson	Bugs	Scholastic	1.6	H
Insects	Sara O'Neill	Bugs	Sundance		H
Inside an Ant Colony	Allan Fowler	Bugs	Children's Press		H
Sir Small & the Dragonfly	Jane O'Connor	Bugs	Random House		H
A House Spider's Life	John Himmelman	Bugs	Children's Press		I
Animal Builders	M. Clyne & R. Griffiths	Bugs	Sundance		I
Busy, Buzzy Bees	Allan Fowler	Bugs	Children's Press		I
Butterflies	Karen Shapiro	Bugs	Scholastic		I
From Hive to Home	Isabella Jose	Bugs	National Geographic	Pre–2	I
Spiders Spin Silk	Bronwyn Tainui	Bugs	National Geographic		I
Staying Alive	Jenny Feely	Bugs	Sundance		I
A Monarch Butterfly's Life	John Himmelman	Bugs	Children's Press		J
Bugs! Bugs! Bugs!	Barner	Bugs		2.8	J

Observing Behavior in Small Groups

In order to teach effectively, we must observe children reading orally. In order to know what to teach next, we must identify what children already know about print and what kinds of information they are using to decode words and make sense of print. Remember, as P. Johnston said, the expert teacher notices patterns in children's literacy development—patterns that include strengths as well as weaknesses. Observing children while they read familiar leveled books will tell us what children already know how to do, that is, strategies they are using, and what they need to learn. For the emergent reader, notice the directional movement of the child's finger and whether there is a one-to-one voice-to-print match. Asking the beginning reader to locate with his finger

Purposes of Observing Oral Reading

* To place children in flexible reading groups
* To select books that are appropriate
* To note strategy use
* To identify patterns in word recognition errors
* To keep track of reading progress
* To report to parents, other teachers, administrators

Clifford Text Set

Clifford's Word Book	Bridwell	Clifford Series	Scholastic	1.6	G
Clifford to the Rescue	Bridwell	Clifford Series	Scholastic	1.3	I
Clifford Goes to Hollywood	Bridwell	Clifford Series	Scholastic	1.5	J
Clifford Keeps Cool	Bridwell	Clifford Series	Scholastic	2.6	J
Clifford Takes a Trip	Bridwell	Clifford Series	Scholastic	1.9	J
Clifford's Birthday Party	Bridwell	Clifford Series	Scholastic	1.7	J
Clifford's First Autumn	Bridwell	Clifford Series	Scholastic	2.2	J
Clifford's First Valentine's Day	Bridwell	Clifford Series	Scholastic	2.8	J
The Big Leaf Pile	Bridwell	Clifford Series	Scholastic		J
The Dog Who Cried "Woof!"	Bridwell	Clifford Series	Scholastic		J
The Show and Tell Surprise	Bridwell	Clifford Series	Scholastic		J
The Stormy Day Rescue	Bridwell	Clifford Series	Scholastic	2.1	J
Clifford and the Big Storm	Bridwell	Clifford Series	Scholastic	2.1	K
Clifford at the Circus	Bridwell	Clifford Series	Scholastic	1.9	K
Clifford Grows Up	Bridwell	Clifford Series	Scholastic	2.1	K
Clifford the Small Red Puppy	Bridwell	Clifford Series	Scholastic	1.5	K
Clifford's First School Day	Bridwell	Clifford Series	Scholastic	2.1	K
Clifford's Kitten	Bridwell	Clifford Series	Scholastic	1.5	K
Clifford's Manners	Bridwell	Clifford Series	Scholastic	1.9	K
Clifford's Puppy Days	Bridwell	Clifford Series	Scholastic	1.8	K
Clifford's Spring Clean-Up	Bridwell	Clifford Series	Scholastic	2.2	K
Clifford and the Big Parade	Bridwell	Clifford Series	Scholastic	2.7	K
Clifford's Best Friend	Bridwell	Clifford Series	Scholastic	1.9	K
Clifford's First Halloween	Bridwell	Clifford Series	Scholastic	1.9	K
Clifford's Sports Day	Bridwell	Clifford Series	Scholastic	2.2	K
Clifford's Family	Bridwell	Clifford Series	Scholastic	1.5	K
The Runaway Rabbit	Bridwell	Clifford Series	Scholastic		

one or two known or "anchor" words, such as *the*, and one or two unknown words allows us to observe the strategies he is using. Taking an oral reading record for one or two children before or after guided reading groups, and probing for strategy use, will provide enough information to guide instruction. For beginning readers it is important to listen in on children's reading and take oral reading records very frequently.

A common system for noting and recording children's errors enables teachers to collect and share their oral reading records. Irene Fountas and Gay Su Pinnell (1996) suggest that teachers record everything—accurately read words, substitution errors, words omitted or added, repetitions, attempts to read words, words told by the teacher, and self-corrections. I based the notational system presented in Part Two on that developed by Clay (1993) and adapted for use by teachers in core reading programs and popular informal reading inventories. It is the same notational system I included in the Guided Reading protocols (see pp. 110, 113). To become adept at using this assessment tool, please see Marie Clay's *An Observation Survey* (1993). I share an outline of it here, but encourage you to read more about using this instrument.

Prosody and intonation are two other areas to notice in children's oral reading. We do want children to "make reading sound like talking" but, as Marie Clay pointed out, some dysfluency in the oral reading of brand-new readers may not be cause for concern, but

Notes for Recording Oral Reading Errors

Errors	Notes
Correct words	Put check or no mark
Substitutions	Substitution Text word
Attempts to read	(Note phonetically what the child said)
Added words	Added word ------ OR Inserted word^
Omitted words	------ Text word OR Circle omitted word
Words told by the teacher	T (Next to the text word or substitution or attempted word)

Problem-solving strategies—Not errors

Repetitions	R (To the beginning of the repetition)
Self-corrections	SC (Next to the substitution or attempt)

instead, evidence of problem-solving strategies. Self-corrections, hesitations, and repetitions are all problem-solving strategies and should be noted, but not counted as errors.

There are other reading behaviors besides oral reading that are worth observing. Children develop in their ability to interact socially. Surely, one of the most important behaviors that kindergarten teachers teach is how to get along in the classroom, and the behaviors that are appropriate for different social contexts. For example, peer-led small-group discussion is a particular kind of social context with particular kinds of interactions that are appropriate. It is critical for children to learn how to participate in small-group, peer-led discussions in order to establish inquiry circles in the classroom. Social behaviors as well as thinking behaviors are important to observe and document. Being able to participate in the group discussion in an orderly way, listening to and building on the responses of peers, and negotiating disagreements are as important as being able to justify and revise thinking (see p. 253).

Oral Reading Strategies	Observational Notes
Match voice-to-print	Note tracking and whether child "runs out of words"
Read high-frequency words	Note and record words not known at sight
Use meaning to read	Note whether child substitutes words or self-corrects words in order to make sense
Use language or sentence structure (syntax)	Note whether child substitutes words that "sound right" in the sentence (same part of speech)
Use familiar words or word parts and regular spelling patterns to decode unfamiliar words	Note whether child substitutes words that share the same initial letters or spelling patterns as the unknown words
Cross-check visual, meaning, and syntax clues	Note whether child rereads tricky spots
	Note whether child uses multiple sources of information to figure out unknown words (initial letters, spelling patterns, illustrations, sounds right, makes sense)
	Note whether child self-corrects errors

Modeling Reading Strategies

Whether teaching guided reading groups or building students' knowledge through inquiry circles, you need an instructional focus. Select texts or tasks at appropriate levels of difficulty to address that instructional focus. Mark the text pages that you will use to model particular strategies, write out the language you will use to make your thinking visible, and post it on the marked text pages.

Readers at different stages of literacy development need different kinds of prompts and varying levels of support from the teacher. Different texts, including informational text, have different formats and organizational patterns as well as varying levels of complexity. At the beginning stages of development, model strategic reading and prompt children to use all sources of information—pictures, beginning letters, familiar words and word parts, and sentence and story sense. The easiest texts, those at guided reading levels A–D, have very few words, presenting a particular challenge for the beginning reader. The beginning reader has to infer what the text is about based on the illustrations. In other words, in order to make sense of the text, the beginning reader has to construct a context within which the words can be understood. I will illustrate what I mean with an example from a guided reading level-A book, *In the Woods* (Gibson, 2002) and a level-D book, *Hide and Seek* (Brown & Carey, 1994).

Example 5: Developing Inferences From Illustrations

In the Woods has only 37 words, 18 unique words. The same sentences, "What can you see? I can see a ___" are repeated several times. But in order to understand the story, the reader has to infer that a conversation is taking place between two mice. For the beginning reader, we need to model the process of making that inference. Katie Solic, a University of Tennessee graduate student, demonstrated how to make that inference with a think-aloud: *"Hmmm. I see two mice in the picture. Their mouths are open and they're looking at each other. I wonder if they are talking to each other. I'm going to read to find out."*

In the second book, *Hide and Seek*, the reader has to infer that the characters in the story are playing the game of hide and seek and what the game entails. A think-aloud might go like this: *"Hmmm. I wonder if the story will be about playing hide and seek. I know in hide and seek someone is 'it.' That person has to hide his eyes and count to 100. Everyone else hides. Then he looks for everyone in all the hiding places. If he can't find everyone, he gives up. I'm going to go on a picture walk to see if I'm right and it's about playing the game of hide and seek.*" In order to recognize several hard words, for example, "ready," and "closet," the reader would have to think about the word within the context of the hide-and-seek game as well as the illustrations.

Returning to the words *heap* and *batch* from the guided reading level-F books that I discussed earlier, how can we make those words and word meanings accessible to the beginning reader? By modeling the strategies we use—as proficient readers—we can show the beginning reader what to do. In *Itchy, Itchy Chicken Pox*, a think-aloud might go like this: [Reads text] "Don't rub. Don't scratch. Oh, no. Another …. *Hmmm. I see that the word ends the same way as* scratch. *It must sound like* scratch—batch! *But what does* batch *mean? I know when my mom makes a batch of cookies—it means a bunch of cookies. I wonder if* bunch *would make sense in that sentence? Another* bunch *of chicken pox? I think that is what* batch *means—another bunch of chicken pox. Hmm. I looked inside the word. I read around the word. I tried another word to see if it made sense.*"

Linking Reading to Writing With Series Books

Curious George, Chrysanthemum, Clifford—there is no better way to link reading and writing in children's heads and hearts than by exploiting series books. Why? Children's knowledge of the characters in series books helps to build a natural redundancy into the plots of the stories, creating a comfortable framework that children can appropriate for their own storytelling. As I pointed out in an early *Reading Teacher* article, "children who get hooked on series books may make reading discoveries on their own and begin to feel at home with some of the rules for reading [and writing] fiction. Becoming involved with books, getting to know some story worlds well, feeling comfortable with a few old fictional friends and familiar . . . language will surely help" develop interest and motivation to read (1993, p. 426). We know from the research by Dina Feitelson and her colleagues that children learn a great deal about the language of stories by listening to series books. Children can also learn how to read and write words.

Early work by Mary Anne Richek and Becky McTague (1988), for example, used words and phrases from the Curious George series books to teach struggling primary grade children to read. Rosenhouse, Feitelson, Kita, and Goldstein (1997) discovered that kindergarten and first graders who listened to series books improved decoding skills as well as comprehension. Thinking back on Mandy and Ruth's classroom, I remember that children became "real" readers by writing and reading back their own writing. This is not surprising. In writing, children use high-frequency words over and over; they sound stretch and spell unfamiliar words, using the letter patterns in words they already know to help them spell new words; they use drawings to help them rehearse and compose what they want to write, and then, after they have written a story, the drawing helps them remember the words they wrote. The whole story, or the sentences or captions, becomes a text for shared reading, to which students can return again and again. By harvesting words from writing for word study, we likely tap useful words for children to know.

Social Behaviors

* Look at and listen to the person speaking
* Yield and take the floor
* Challenge and disagree
* Build on previous responses

Thinking Behaviors

* Link ideas to text
* Link ideas to personal experience
* Revise thinking in light of disconfirming evidence
* Draw or write to learn and remember

Prep Tips for Success

Whether teaching guided reading groups or building students' knowledge through inquiry circles, you need an instructional focus. Select texts or tasks at appropriate levels of difficulty to address that instructional focus. Mark the text pages that you will use to model particular strategies, write out the language you will use to make your thinking visible, and post it on the marked text pages.

Building Print Knowledge From Clifford Stories

Let's see how listening, talking, writing and reading can all be linked. Upstate New York teachers Jill McClement and Angela Anderson developed an integrated approach based on Clifford stories. By immersing children in Clifford stories, kindergartners develop schemata for the bare bones of narrative structure. Clifford is a big red dog who often gets into trouble by "trying to be helpful" as one kindergartner put it. Clifford's problems vary, depending on the particular story, but he always manages to solve the problem, much to the relief of Emily Elizabeth, the friend who loves him dearly. Over the course of several weeks in spring of the kindergarten year, Jill and Angela's kindergartners develop Clifford stories in five phases, ultimately leading to publication and sharing.

Phase 1: Read Aloud, Talk, Teach "Clifford" Words

1. **Talk.** Jill and Angela engage the children in talk about Clifford—comparing one story to another and identifying characteristics that describe Clifford. Such talk creates a community of readers with shared knowledge and interest—everyone can participate because everyone can listen to the stories and everyone can watch Clifford on television.

2. **Share the pen.** Jill and Angela write each child's observations about Clifford on chart paper in a predictable story format, color-coding each sentence:

   Clifford is big.

   Clifford is red.

   Clifford is kind.

   Clifford is funny.

   Clifford is a good dancer.

3. **Read back the predictable chart story.** Reread it as shared reading.

4. **Cut-up and reconstruct sentences.** Jill asks each child to choose a sentence to copy on color-coded sentence strips (one color for each sentence). Children read the sentence, tracking the print with their fingers, and then cut up each sentence into words. They reconstruct the cut-up sentences from the words, rereading and check-

ing for accuracy against the predictable chart. Jill puts the cut-up sentence into an envelope for center activity. The color-coding helps the children still working on letters and sounds (Mandy and Ruth's Sounds & Letters Kids) find the sentence on the chart and use that as a model.

Angela models how to write the beginning of the story.

Phase 2: Draw a Clifford Story With Beginning, Middle, End

The next step in composing Clifford stories is to revisit the genre and brainstorm possible Clifford stories. Jill asks her kindergartners, "Do you remember all those Clifford stories? What kinds of things happen to Clifford?" She asks children to think about what kind of story about Clifford each of them would write or, "If you were in that story, what would you do?" Jill writes ideas on chart paper. Angela asks her kindergartners to close their eyes and imagine a Clifford story, then, "Whisper that story to a friend." Both teachers model the construction of a three-part narrative by creating a class story about Clifford. Jill's class typically creates a three-part mural for in-class display and Angela's composes a three-part story with each part on a single page of chart paper, which she hangs.

Students construct a three-part narrative by drawing three pictures to represent the beginning or start of the story; the middle of the story, where something happens; and the ending, where everything usually works out.

1st picture — "How are you going to begin your story?"

2nd picture — "What happens?"

3rd picture — "How does it turn out?"

Phase 3: Compose the Words

Once children have composed a story with three pictures, they need support—some more than others—to write a sentence to go with each picture. By talking and listening to the children, and sharing the pen, help each child compose a predictable sentence to go with each picture. Children "draft" the sentence on a "work sheet," stretching out the sounds in each word, and using wall words, alphabet and vowel strips, and other words that they already know to help them spell unfamiliar words. In the example I provide of an individual conference (p. 259), you can see what a child's work sheet might look like and how Angela supports Rosa.

Building on Story to Develop Print Knowledge: Making a Class Story

Read Aloud and Share the Pen

* Immerse children in the genre—read aloud books
* Talk about the read-aloud books
* Write children's observations down on chart paper
* Read back written observations as shared reading
* Write each observation on color-coded sentence strips
* Read back, match to print, and cut up sentence strips into words
* Put cut-up sentence in envelope for center activity

Compose the Story

* Revisit the genre ("Remember all those Clifford stories...?")
* Connect the genre to children's lives ("What kind of Clifford story would you write?" or "If you were in that story, what would you do?....")
* Brainstorm and discuss possibilities on chart paper
* Model the process of writing a three-part narrative by making a class story
* Children compose a story by drawing three pictures—an introduction ("How are you going to begin your story?"), a problem ("What happens?"), and an ending ("How does it turn out?")

Phase 4: Publish and Share With an Audience

After conferring, the children copy the conventionally spelled sentence onto sentence strips. They read back the sentence, pointing to each word and matching to print. They cut up the sentences, reconstruct the sentences on story paper, and read them back to you, tracking print with their fingers, and checking to be sure the words are rearranged correctly. Finally, they arrange the drawings and cut-up words into a three-part sequence, and glue them onto the pages of the book. After writing the story title, the author, and a drawing an illustration for the cover, children read their stories to an audience of their

Conference
* Talk and listen to the child talk about the pictures
* Help structure a predictable sentence to go with each picture, building on what the child knows and what he/she has drawn
* Ask the child to try the spelling for each word
* Stretch out the sounds to unfamiliar words with the child
* Model the use of the word wall, alphabet strips, known words or word patterns

Publish and Share
* Children copy the conventionally spelled sentences onto sentence strips
* Children read back the sentence, pointing to each word and matching to print
* Children cut up the sentences, reconstruct the sentences on their story paper, read back, match to print, check, and glue with their drawings
* Children arrange the pages in a book, make a cover
* Children read their books aloud to classmates
* Put books in class library for shared and independent reading

Harvest Words to Study
* Children reread stories, match words, hunt words, make words, do word sorts based on patterns identified as important
* Make word matches, hunts, and sorts based on children's work

peers. Each individual reading of a Clifford story becomes a shared reading for the class—the child points to each word, tracking the print from left to right, locating known or anchor words to support the oral reading of each sentence, and using the drawings to make unfamiliar words memorable.

Phase 5: Harvest Words for Word Study

Not only do Clifford stories provide opportunities for children to manipulate words into sentences, and sentences and ideas into narratives, but Clifford stories also provide supportive contexts for learning more about words. Once the Clifford stories are written, read, and published, Jill and Angela harvest words for word study. Jill uses the words in published stories for two purposes—to help strugglers develop beginning reading strategies and to focus the spotlight on high-utility words that kindergartners actually use when they write. To support kindergartners still struggling to match voice to print, Jill provides color-coded sentence strips for them to copy each sentence from their story, cut-up into words, and place in an envelope that is attached to the back cover with Velcro. Because the sentences are color-coded, struggling kindergartners can find the appropriate page in the book, rearrange the words into sentences, noting initial letters, and matching word-by-word to the model. For other children, or the class as a group, Jill and Angela both identify words with particular patterns or high-utility words from class Clifford stories and post them as wall words, stomp them, clap them, and make and break them to form new words. Some kindergartners may add particular words to their individual word wall or "Words I Use When I Write" folders.

In Rosa's case (see p. 259 for her conference with Angela), Angela might ask her to hunt for other *-ing* words in the Clifford stories composed by her classmates and to write these in her word study notebook. Or, if other children were "using but confusing" two-syllable words, like *going* or *into*, Angela might clap out the syllables in two-syllable wall words or names and teach a mini-lesson. Or, perhaps Angela would identify past-tense markers, like *-ed*, or inflections, like *-ing* words for word study. Certainly by the end of kindergarten, Jill and Angela expect most children to fluently read and spell many high-frequency words like *to, is, and,* (see list on p. 118). For those who do not, they harvest high-frequency words from Clifford stories for children to manipulate during center as cut-up words to be reconstructed or spelled on white board for fluency building.

Side-by-Side Teaching: Angela's Conference with Rosa

Let's listen in as Angela meets with Rosa. At this point Rosa has composed her three-part story by drawing pictures to represent the introduction, Clifford's problem, and the ending, or how Clifford works things out. Rosa drafted three sentences, one for each picture (shown here).

Angela met earlier with Rosa on sentences two and three, helping her to conventionally spell all the words. Angela sound stretched the words with

"Clifford is going to Florida."

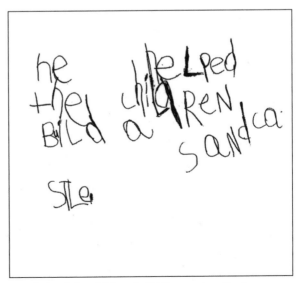

Clifford knocked over the sand castle."

"He helped the children build the sand castle."

Rosa, modeling the use of wall words and known spelling patterns to spell the words. For especially tricky words, Angela used "letter lines" rather than Elkonin boxes to segment and represent sounds with letters. Because she wanted Rosa to represent not only the sounds she heard but also conventional spelling patterns—including silent letters and vowels in unstressed syllables—Angela used a line to stand for each letter in the word. Rosa, with Angela's support, edited her sound spellings to spell each word conventionally. At a later point, Angela may harvest words from Rosa's draft writing for class mini-lessons, as I suggested earlier.

Being privy to Angela's conversation with Rosa is wonderful! It is testimony to all the good teaching that can take place in a one-to-one interaction. Not surprisingly, the most effective classroom teachers are those who spend at least a third of the time engaged in side-by-side teaching (Taylor et al., 2000). In the first segment of the conversation Angela is scaffolding Rosa's spelling of *Clifford*:

ANGELA: Are you all finished? [Rosa shakes her head "yes."]
  Can you read the last part to me? Let's read and point the whole sentence.
ROSA: [reads back her third sentence] He helped the children build a sand castle.
ANGELA: Great. Excellent job. Excellent pointing.
ANGELA: You're all finished with that part of your story! [Rosa shakes her head "yes."]
  Do you have the first two parts? Let's read the first two parts.
ROSA: [reads back her first sentence] Clifford is going to Florida.
ANGELA: Good job. Let's read it one more time.
ROSA: [reads] Clifford is going to Florida
  Let's read the word C-l-i-f-f-or-d [Angela stretches Clifford]
TOGETHER: C-l-i-f-f-or-d.
  Let's stretch it really slow. Ready?
TOGETHER: C-l-i-i-i-fford.
ROSA: I—it's an i.
ANGELA: Where do you think the *i* goes?
ROSA: In the front.
ANGELA: Let's listen again. C-l-l-l-iford.
ROSA: After the C.

ANGELA: Let's put the letter lines on paper [writes a line for each letter in Clifford].

— — — — — — — —

Clifford is a long word, isn't it?

Let's see. What's the first sound in Clifford?

ROSA: *C* [writes on the letter line].

<u>C</u> — — — — — — —

ANGELA: *What's the next sound?*

ROSA: *L* [writes].

<u>C</u> <u>l</u> — — — — — —

ANGELA: *Let's think before you write the next sound. i-i-i-f.*

Do you know how to spell if?

ROSA: No.

ANGELA: *Let's sound it out. i-i-i-f.*

ROSA: *I* [writes].

<u>C</u> <u>l</u> <u>i</u> — — — — —

ANGELA: *Let's stretch it from the beginning. Cl i-i-i-fford.*

Let's stretch it again. Cli-ffff-ord.

ROSA: *F-F* [writes].

<u>C</u> <u>l</u> <u>i</u> <u>f</u> <u>f</u> — — —

ANGELA: *How did you know there were two f's?*

ROSA: From what I wrote there [points to her paper]

ANGELA: *How did you know to write two f's there?*

Did you remember that from the stories we read and our own story we wrote?

[Rosa nods head "yes."]

ANGELA: *Now or*

ROSA: *O-R* [writes].

<u>C</u> <u>l</u> <u>i</u> <u>f</u> <u>f</u> <u>o</u> <u>r</u> —

ANGELA: *Let's read it from the beginning. Cliffor-d.* [Emphasizes *d*.]

Angela stretches the sounds in words to support Rosa's spelling.

Rosa: *D* [writes].

<u>C</u> <u>l</u> <u>i</u> <u>f</u> <u>f</u> <u>o</u> <u>r</u> <u>d</u>

Angela: Excellent. *Clifford.* Super duper.

In the next segment, Angela helps Rosa realize that *going* is one word, *go + ing*, with two syllables. She also models using what is known—in this case, the letter pattern in the names of two of Rosa's friends—to spell an unfamiliar word, *Florida*.

Angela: Let's reread.

Rosa: [reads] Clifford is going to Florida.

Angela: You have all the letters. [She points to *go-ing*.] You have all those sounds. In your good copy…we'll put the two words together. You have the *go* and the *-ing*. It's one word.

Rosa: Yeah, because it would be like *go-* and *-ing*.

Angela: *Flor- iii-da* [stretches the i].

Rosa: *I* [writes the *i* before the *r*—*Floird*].

    The vowels are tricky [points to vowel strip]. You can hear them when we stretch them out. Where does the *i* go? Stretch it again.

Rosa: *Flor-i-i-i-da* [erases the *i*—puts it between the *r* and the *d*—*Florid*].

Angela: What do you think should go at the end?

Rosa: A period [writes a large period].

Angela: You have a period but you're missing a letter in *Florida.*

    Let me think who has a name that ends like Florida. . . Isabella and Bria! What letter is at the end of their name? *Florida* ends the same as *Isabella* and *Bria*.

Rosa: A.

Angela: Yes! *Isabella* and *Bria* have an *a.*

Rosa: I definitely know how to spell Isabella's name.

Angela: Is she one of your best friends? [Rosa nods her head "yes."] You must write to them a lot.

Celebrating Authorship:
Shared Reading of Student-Made Books

At this point, it's Author's Day, and Angela's students share their Clifford sequels. As Lucy Calkins and her colleagues at Teachers' College Reading and Writing Project remind us, celebration is part of the "rhythm of a writing classroom." Calkins recommends that we establish Authors' Days, scheduled frequently and predictably, "to harness the teaching power of publication" (p. 267). To make it work, you will have to facilitate each step of the way. Scaffold children's reading aloud, guide the class by modeling appropriate ways to discuss the story, naming the narrative elements ("Where does the story take place—the setting?"), and fostering early comprehension strategies ("Who can predict the ending?")

Display the child's book on the big book easel, and help the child read one page at a time. For the youngest authors, the occasion marks not only children's accomplishments as fiction writers but also children's accomplishments as readers. In order to read their texts to classmates, children must orchestrate a number of early reading strategies and use information from many sources: print and book concepts, left-to-right directionality, spaces between words, support from the illustrations, sentence and story sense, initial letters, spelling patterns, and high-frequency words, to name but a few.

Reading Workshop and Reading Center Routines

Independent reading is read-alone reading. Children read the material on their own, without the support of the teacher. Reading workshop—time when you work with small groups—or center work should involve reading that children can do independently. One reading activity that children can do independently is "reading the room" or "writing the room." During "reading the room," children, by themselves or side-by-side with friends, read, sing, rap, or chant.

Reading the room. When children read the room, they should read with a pointer as a reminder that their speech must match each word of print, developing the important print concept of one-to-one match. Reading the room provides much needed practice so that children can have many experiences with words and opportunities to try out reading strategies on their own—strategies that have been modeled again and again during shared reading and read alouds. Writing the room provides opportunities for rereading text, matching voice to print, noticing the features within words, and developing fluency in the recognition of high-frequency words.

Try to keep children accountable for workshop or center time. Kindergartners can sign in and out of work centers or tasks; partners can sign off on partner spelling, word study, or buddy reading; making and breaking words can be recorded in word study notebooks; books read can be recorded in a book log. My book logs are simple—a place for the date, title, good part of the book and new words. For kindergartners just learning to form letters and numbers, a stamp is perfect for the date. Typically, kindergartners will draw a picture to represent the "good part" of the book, and often draw a picture to label the "new word" as well.

> ✳
> ### Independent Reading: What to Read?
>
> * Alphabet chart
> * I Spy word pocket chart
> * Labels, word banks, & word study notebooks
> * Calendar chart
> * Weather chart
> * Names & friends' file
> * Number charts
> * Color word charts
> * Word walls
> * Poems, rhymes, songs
> * Murals & class books
> * Science diagrams & drawings
> * Social studies diagrams & drawings
> * Story diagrams & drawings
> * Star of the week & other charts posted
> * Shared reading books
> * Browsing box books

The Comfort of Routines

Routines create comfort and predictability. Teaching strategies make the process of reading and writing visible and accessible to the young learner. Routines, and the tasks embedded

Toward Independent Reading:

Purposes of read-alouds
* Develop knowledge of topic, language, or genre
* Model decoding, vocabulary or comprehension strategy with appropriate text
* Model responses to narrative or informational texts
* Build shared understandings about important topics

Purposes of shared or partner reading
* Encourage participation in strategic reading at different levels
* Provide opportunity to observe peer strategies
* Provide authentic venues for fluency

Purposes of small-group reading
* Model decoding, vocabulary, or comprehension strategy
* Observe students' use of decoding, vocabulary, or comprehension strategies
* Document observations with anecdotal records
* Support students' reading with prompts or background knowledge
* Identify teaching points for on-the-run instruction or mini-lessons for whole class

Purposes of independent reading
* Engage students in literacy
* Create a community of readers
* Consolidate strategic reading skills

within, all support the same goal for kindergartners—to read and write independently. Read-alouds create community and shared understandings about important topics; listening to books enriches the language we hear and use. Shared reading provides children models of how reading works. Guided practice presents opportunities for us to observe and prompt strategic reading and writing. Independent and partner work consolidates kindergartners' skills and provides a venue for collaboration and talk.

Match Instruction to Students' Needs

The literacy assessments help us learn about the children we teach—what they know, so we can build on that knowledge, what they still need to learn, so we can look ahead and plan our teaching. Looking across studies of emergent literacy, Lea McGee and Victoria Purcell-Gates identified one common thread: "Children learn to read and write successfully if their teachers accommodate their instruction to the children, and they struggle if they do not" (1997, p. 312). By matching assessment and instruction, we can accommodate the needs of all learners.

Now that you're familiar with the assessments and practices that support learners at many developmental levels, in the Afterword I introduce you to collaborative talk, an idea developed by Rhonda Nowak (2005) in her dissertation study of coaching interactions. It is a form of professional study, but with more depth than typically takes place within grade-level meetings in a school. Kindergarten teachers across classrooms share data from the literacy assessments with a focus on particular children and their responses to instruction. By putting the concerns and questions of colleagues at the forefront, teachers use these discussions to extend and build new knowledge about teaching literacy.

Using Assessment Data for Teacher-to-Teacher Learning

Collaborative professional study—study by teachers with other teachers—can transform our thinking. Teachers engaged in such study learn together and support each other's learning through their talk. We call it *collaborative dialogue*. University of Hawaii professor Rhonda Nowak (2005) studied the discourse between coaches and teachers and developed ways to analyze that talk and make it more productive. She defines coaching that empowers teachers as *intentional talk*. It's a quality of exchange that supports reflection and leads to informed action.

In our University of Tennessee Teacher Quality kindergarten project, Rhonda helped us apply her analysis to peer discussions of video clips of our teaching. Rather than viewing professional development as a way to transmit expert advice from a coach to a teacher, we came to see it as collaborative study. We pursued inquiry grounded in real contexts; in our case, kindergartner's literacy development in actual classrooms. In our collaborative dialogues, all participants contribute to the discussion, and most important, the participants first address the ideas and questions of the teachers whose students are being observed. Together, the group builds new understandings, not only using research-based theory to improve instruction but also using their own experiences teaching kindergartners to build theory.

Rhonda refers to knowledge-building talk as *progressive discourse*. She emphasizes that progressive discourse—that is, talk that leads to progressively more nuanced understandings and new practices—must be exploratory:

> "Information is presented in such a way as to be open for discussion, rather than as indisputable statements of fact" (p. 3).

Prompts to Initiate and Sustain Collaborative Dialogue

Problem-posing ensures that participants address ideas and issues that are most important to them.

* What are your questions or concerns about teaching literacy in kindergarten?

Higher-level questioning helps focus the talk on building participants' knowledge.

* Generalizations: "What went well? Why?"
* Analysis: "Which part would you do differently? Why?"
* Predictions: "What do you think might happen if. . .?"

Counters are statements or questions that pose a different idea.

* "Have you considered. . .?"

Planning supports "next steps"—trying out a new teaching strategy or identifying the tools to evaluate the results of a teaching strategy, such as videos, students' work.

* "What will you do next as a result of. . .?"

Synthesizing supports participants as they search for common ground across students, teachers, and classrooms.

* "What themes emerge?"

Theorizing enables participants to pose tentative explanations of common elements or themes identified in the dialogue.

* "What do you know that helps to explain. . .?"

Source: Nowak, R. (2005). "Intentional Talk: Literacy Coaching That Empowers Teachers." Presented at IRA, San Antonio, TX, May, 2005.

What gives collaborative professional study its power, however, is the focus on children's development. This book, and its many assessments, makes possible teachers' research into children's development. It is my hope that teachers will gather information about children and use that information in ways that promote reflection and "optimal instruction for all children" (Johnston, 1987, p. 46).

The centerpiece of professional development in our Teacher Quality project is the teachers' case study presentations of struggling readers. By focusing intensely on a few children over time, teachers develop a deep knowledge of literacy, an expertise that they can call upon to teach all children. Specifically, teachers gather information on children's performance on the literacy assessments, video observations of classroom instruction, children's feelings toward reading and writing, their motivation, engagement, and any perceptions that other teachers or parents may have shared.

Case study presentations provide the context for teachers to learn from one another by:

* Reflecting on their own about how to teach each child and sharing ideas with colleagues
* Discussing what might be significant about each child's responses to the reading and writing he has experienced

The purpose of these case studies and observations is to help teachers use each other to improve diagnostic and teaching strategies and to experience firsthand the diversity of interactions and issues in teaching reading to children. Instructional decision-making in classrooms is mostly "on-the-run" and these collegial discussions provide opportunities for us to make our observations of children more expert and insightful.

Procedure for Conducting a Case Study

Our procedures for the case study can be summed up as: select, observe, gather, analyze, present, reflect, and act.

1. Select one struggling student from your class to serve as a focus student.
2. Develop a case study of the child based on your assessments and observations, both formal and informal, in after-hours intervention and in the classroom setting. Include:
   * results from Kindergarten Literacy Assessment tasks

* additional running records
* writing samples from a variety of tasks
* completed picture/word sorts
* anecdotal notes including post-lesson observations of child's participation and success

3. Interview information:
   * student
   * parent
   * classroom teacher, if other than yourself, about student's development as a reader and writer.

4. Videotape/Audiotape:
   Videotape or audiotape your case study student while he or she is participating in meaningful word study, reading, or writing.

5. Analyze and interpret your observations, assessments, interview, and video information.

6. Prepare handout for colleagues:
   * provide assessment results
   * highlight student's strengths, weaknesses, and instructional plan
   * document progress in these specific areas:
     ✓ letter/sound knowledge
     ✓ print concept knowledge
     ✓ voice/print matching
     ✓ word writing
     ✓ writing
     ✓ reading

7. Present your case study student during grade-level meetings.
   Case studies in the context of collaborative professional study require that you listen to your colleagues, reflect on their interpretations, and revise or affirm your own practices:
   * reflect
   * act

   Presentation Format:
   * Share several clips that highlight your case study student's strengths, weaknesses, and individual needs. Clips should include something your student can do well or

has shown tremendous growth in and something the student still needs support in.

* Provide a handout that includes a brief statement or two describing your student, information gathered from informal interviews, classroom observation, or your anecdotal notes. Describe your areas of focus for instruction. List at the bottom any questions you have for the group about your student or the intervention experience.

8. Reflective Response

After the case study presentation, write a reflection and submit it electronically to your colleagues. Address the following two parts:

* Based on ideas from your colleagues and the other case studies presented, what aspects of your instruction or observations about the child were affirmed; which are you questioning; what might you do differently; what aspect of literacy development and teaching do you want to learn more about?

* How will you adjust your teaching based on what you learned from the experience of working closely with struggling children, collaborating with colleagues, and professional study?

Final Thoughts

We must know children in order to teach them, as child advocate and MacArthur Fellow Lisa Delpit has reminded us many times over. Echoing that sentiment, Patricia Carini, an originator of case study inquiry and former director of the Prospect School in Bennington, Vermont, proposed: "To know one child well is to know all children better." Systematic observations of children's literacy development and reflections on our practice will help us know all children better and enable more personal and intensive teaching.

Children's Literature Cited

Base. G. (1987). *Animalia*. New York: Harry N. Abrams.

Bickel, D. J. (1996). *My First Pocket Guide: Insects*. Washington, DC: National Geographic Society.

Blevins, W. (2002). *Clifford Can*. New York: Scholastic.

Bridwell, N. (1985). *Clifford the Big Red Dog*. New York: Scholastic.

Butler, A. (1994). *Mr. Sun and Mr. Sea*. Glenview, IL: GoodYearBooks.

Bunting, J. (1999). *My First ABC Book*. Dorling Kindersley Publishing.

Brown, R. & Carey, S. (1994). *Hide and Seek*. New York: Scholastic.

Carter, J. (1999). *Hair*. New York: Newbridge.

Cowley, J. (nd.). *The Birthday Cake*. Bothell, WA: Wright Group/McGraw-Hill.

Cutting, J. (nd.). *The Barbeque*. Bothell, WA: Wright Group/McGraw-Hill.

Dotlich, R. (2004). *Over in the Pink House*. Honesdale, PA: Boyds Mills Press.

Forbes, C. (1993). *The Tree Stump*. Glenview, IL: Scott, Foresman and Company.

Gibson, A. (2002). *In the Woods*. New York: Scholastic.

Henkes, Kevin (1988). *Chrysanthemum*. New York: Greenwillow

Hoberman, M. A. & Wescott, N.B. (1998). *Miss Mary Mack*. Megan Tingley.

Johnson, S.T. (1995). *Alphabet City*. New York: Penguin.

Langer, S. (nd.). *My Butterfly Garden*. Glenview, IL: Addison-Wesley.

Maccarone, G. (1992). New York: Scholastic.

Matthias, C. (1983). *I Love Cats*. Canada: Regensteiner.

National Geographic. (2001). *My First Pocket Guide: Insects*. National Geographic.

Numeroff, Laura (1985). *If You Give a Mouse a Cookie*. New York: Harper and Row.

Packard, D. (1993). *The Ball Game*. New York: Scholastic.

Peters, C. (1995). *Hats*. Boston, MA: Houghton Mifflin.

Riley. (1995). *Green, Green*. Boston, MA: Houghton Mifflin.

Rose, D. L. & Jenkins, S. (2000). *Into the A, B, Sea*. New York: Scholastic.

Seuss, Dr. (1960). *Green Eggs and Ham*. New York: Random House.

Shannon, D. (1998). *No, David!* New York: Scholastic.

Shannon, G. (1996). *Tomorrow's Alphabet*. New York: Greenwillow.

Stetford, S. (2001). *Popular Science Mini Guides: Bugs*. New York: Sterling.

Stewart, D. & Milne, S. (2002). *Animal Builders*. Franklin Watts.

Tafuri, N. (1984). *Have You Seen My Duckling*. New York: Scholastic.

Tarpley, Natasha Anatasia (1998). *I Love my Hair!*. Boston, MA: Little, Brown and Company

Trussell-Cullen. (1993). *This Is the Seed*. Glenview, IL: Little Celebrations.

Weeks, S. (1997). *Shoes*. Parsippany, NJ: Celebration Press.

Wilsdon, C. (1998). *National Audubon Society First Field Guide: Insects*. New York: Scholastic.

Works Cited

Anderson, C. (2000). *How's it Going? A Practical Guide to Conferring with Student Writers*. Portsmouth, NH: Heinemann.

Ballou, D., Sanders, W., & Wright, P. (2004). Controlling for student background in value-added assessment of teachers. *Journal of Educational and Behavioral Statistics*, 29 (1),

Bear, D., Invernizzi, M., Templeton, S., & Johnston, F. (2004). *Words their way: Word study for phonics, vocabulary, and spelling instruction, 3rd Ed.* Upper Saddle River, NJ: Pearson.

Beck, I., McKeown, M., & Kucan, L. (2002). *Bringing words to life: Robust vocabulary instruction*. New York: Guilford.

Beck, I., McKeown, M., & Kucan, L. (Spring, 2003). Taking delight in words: Using oral language to build young children's vocabularies. *American Educator*, 27 (1), 36-41, 45-46.

Biemiller, A. (Spring, 2003). Oral comprehension sets the ceiling on reading comprehension. *American Educator*, 27 (1), 23, 44.

Blevins, W. (1997). *Phonemic Awareness Activities for Early Reading Success*. New York: Scholastic.

Bloodgood, J. W. (1999). What's in a name? Children's name writing and literacy acquisition. *Reading Research Quarterly*, 34 (3), 342-367.

Brown, R. (1973). *A first language*. Cambridge:MIT.

Bruner, J. (1986). *Actual minds, possible worlds*. Cambridge, MA: Harvard University.

Bunker, E. & Luna, E. (2003). Rethinking kindergarten to maximize all children's learning. Paper presented at the International Reading Association Annual Conference, Orlando, FL.

Burns, S., Griffin, P. & Snow, C. (Eds.). (1998). *Starting out right*. Washington, DC: National Academy Press.

Calkins, L. (1986). *The art of teaching writing*. Portsmouth, NH: Heinemann.

Calkins, L. (2001). *The art of teaching reading*. New York: Longman.

Chall, J. & Jacobs, V. (Spring, 2003). The classic study on poor children's fourth grade slump. *American Educator*, 27 (1), 14-15, 44.

Chall, J., Jacobs, V., & Luke Baldwin (1991). *The reading crisis: Why poor children fall behind*. Cambridge, MA: Harvard.

Chapman, M. L. (1995). The sociocognitive construction of written genres in first grade. *Research in the Teaching of English*, 29, 164-192.

Chomsky, C. (1972). Stages in language development and reading exposure. *Harvard Education Review*, 42, 1-33.

Clay, M. (1991). *Becoming literate: The construction of inner control*. Portsmouth, NH: Heinemann.

Clay, M. (1993). *An observation survey of early literacy achievement*. Portsmouth, NH:Heinemann.

Clay, M. (1975). *What did I write? Beginning writing behaviour*. Portsmouth, NH: Heinemann.

Coleman, J. (1966). *Equality of educational opportunity*. Washington, DC: U. S. Government Printing Office.

Cooter, R. (2003). Teacher "capacity-building" helps urban children succeed in reading. *The Reading Teacher*, 57 (2), 198-205.

Cunningham, P. M.. (2000). *Phonics they use: Words for reading & writing*. 3rd Edition. NY:Longman.

Cunningham, P. M.. & Allington, R.L. (1999). *Classrooms that work: They can all read and write.* 2nd Edition. New York:Longman.

Cunningham,]. W. (1993). Whole-to-part reading diagnosis. *Reading and Writing Quarterly: Overcoming Learning Difficulties*, 9, 31-49.

Daniels, H. (2002). *Literature Circles.* NY: Stenhouse.

de Temple, J. & Snow, C. (2003). Learning words from books. . In A. van Kleeck, S. Stahl, & E. Bauer (Eds.), *On Reading Books to Children* (pp.16-36). Mahwah, NJ: Erlbaum.

Duke, N. & Bennett-Armistead, V.S. (2003). *Reading & Writing Informational Text in the Primary Grades.* New York: Scholastic.

Duke, N., Bennett-Armistead, V.S., & Roberts, E. M. (Spring, 2003). Filling the great void: Why we should bring non-fiction into the early-grade classroom. *American Educator*, 27 (1), 30-35.

Durkin, D. (1970). Language arts program for pre-first-grade children: Two year achievement report. *Reading Research Quarterly*, 5.(4), pp. 534-565.

Durkin, D. (1974-1975). A six-year study of children who learned to read in school at the age of four. *Reading Research Quarterly*, 1, 9-61.

Education Department of Western Australia. (1994). *First Steps Developmental Continua.* Western Australia: Author.

Ehri, L. (1991). Learning to read and spell words. In L. Rieben & C. Perfetti (Eds.), *Learning to Read: Basic Research and Its Implications* (pp.57-74). Hillsdale, NJ: Erlbaum.

Ehri, L.C. (1991). Development of the ability to read words, In R. Barr, M.L. Kamil, P.B., Mosenthal, & P.D. Pearson (Eds.), *Handbook of Reading Research* (Vol. 2, pp.383-417). New York: Longman.

Entwisle, D., Alexander, K., & Olson, L. (1997). *Children, schools, and inequality.* Boulder, CO: Westview.

Fountas, I. & Pinnell, G. S. (1997). *Guided Reading.* Portsmouth, NH: Heinemann.

Franzese, R. (2002). *Reading and Writing in Kindergarten: A Practical Guide.* New York: Scholastic, Inc.

Fu, D. & Lamme, L. (2002). Assessment through conversation. Language Arts, 79 (3), 55-64.

Fry, E. (2002). Readability versus leveling. *The Reading Teacher*, 56 (3), 286-291.

Gambrell, L., Mazzoni, S., & Almasi, J. (2000). Promoting collaboration, social interaction, and engagement with text. In L. Baker, M. J. Dreher, & J. T. Guthrie (Eds.), *Engaging young readers: Promoting achievement and motivation.* (pp.119-138). New York: Guilford.

Gorman, T. & Brooks, G. (1996). *Assessing young children's writing.* Available from the Basic Skills Agency, Commonwealth House, 1-19 New Oxford Street, London WC1A NU, UK

Graves D. (1994). *A fresh look at writing.* Portsmouth, NH: Heinemann.

Guthrie, J. & McCann, A. (1996). Idea circles: Peer collaborations for conceptual learning. In L. Gambrell & J. Almasi (Eds.), *Lively Discussions!* (pp. 87-105). Newark, DE: IRA

Hall, S. & Moats, l. (1999). *Straight talk about reading.* Lincolnwood, IL: Contemporary Books.

Hanson, R.A., & Farrell, D. (1995). The long-term effects on high school seniors of learning to read in kindergarten. *Reading Research Quarterly*, 30, 908-933.

Hart, B. & Risley, T. (Spring, 2003). The early catastrophe: The 30 million word gap by age 3. *American Educator*, 27 (1), 4-9.

Heibert, E. H. & Taylor, B. M. (2000). Beginning Reading Instruction: Research on Early Interventions. In Kamil, P.B., Mosenthal, P.B., Pearson, P.D., & Barr, R. (Eds.), *Handbook of Reading Research* (Vol. III., pp. 455-482). New York: Longman.

Heyns, B. (1978). *Summer learning and the effects of schooling.* NY: Academic Press.

Henderson, E. H. (1990). *Teaching spelling* (2nd Edition). Boston, MA: Houghton Mifflin.

Hildreth, G. (1936). Developmental sequences in name writing. *Child Development*, 7, 291-303.

Hoover, W. & Gough, P. (1990). The simple view of reading. *Reading and Writing: An Interdisciplinary Journal*, 2, 127-160.

International Reading Association (IRA) & National Association for the Education of Young Children (NAEYC). (1998). Learning to read and write: Developmentally appropriate practices for young children [a joint position statement]. Newark, DE: IRA.

Invernizzi, M., Meier, J., Swank, L., & Juel, C. (2000). *Phonological Awareness Literacy Screening* (PALS-K). Charlottesville, VA: University of Virginia.

Johnston, F. (1999). The timing and teaching of word families. *The Reading Teacher*, 53 (1), 64-74.

Johnston, F., Invernizzi, M., & Juel, C. (1998). *Book Buddies*. NY: Guilford.

Johnston, P. (1987/1998). Teachers as evaluation experts. In R.L.Allington (Ed.), *Teaching Struggling Readers: Articles from the Reading Teacher* (pp.46-50). Newark, DE: IRA.

Johnston, P. (2004). *Choice words: How language affects children's learning*. York, ME: Stenhouse.

Lomax, R. & McGee, L. (1987). Young children's concepts about print and reading: Toward a model of word reading acquisition. *Reading Research Quarterly*, 22 (2), 237-256.

McCarrier, A., Pinell, G.S., & Fountas, I. (1999). *Interactive writing*. Portsmouth, NH: Heinemann.

McGill-Franzen, A. (1992). Early literacy: What does developmentally appropriate mean? *The Reading Teacher*, 46 (1), 56-58.

McGill-Franzen, A. (1993). "I could read the words!" Selecting good books for inexperienced readers. *The Reading Teacher*, 46 (5), 424-425.

McGill-Franzen, A., Allington, R., Yokoi, L., & Brooks, G. (1999). Putting books in the room is necessary but not sufficient. *Journal of Educational Research*, 93 (2), 67-74.

McGill-Franzen, A. & Allington, R.L. (2001). Kindergarten reading and writing: Good books, good teachers make the difference. Florida *Reading Quarterly*.

McGill-Franzen, A., Wishart, T. & Winstead, M. (2002). Evaluating homegrown change: Promise and peril of scale-up for literacy in kindergarten. Paper presented at the National Reading Conference, December, Miami, FL.

McGill-Franzen & Goatley, V. (2001). Title 1 and special education: Support for children who struggle to learn to read. In S. Neuman & D. Dickinson (Eds), *Handbook of Early Literacy Research* (pp.471-483). NY: Guilford.

McGee, L. (1996). Response-centered talk: Windows on children's thinking. In L. Gambrell & J. Almasi (Eds.), *Lively discussions: Fostering engaged reading* (pp. 194-207). Newark, DE: IRA.

McGee, L. & Purcell-Gates, V. (1997). So what's going on in research in early literacy? *Reading Research Quarterly*, 32 (3), 310-318.

Morris, D., Bloodgood, J., Lomax, R., & Perney, J. (2003). Developmental steps in learning to read: A longitudinal study in kindergarten and first grade. *Reading Research Quarterly*, 38(3), 302-328.

Morris, D. (1999). *The Howard Street tutoring manual*. York, ME: Guilford.

Morrow, L.M. (2002). *The literacy center: Contexts for reading and writing* (2nd ed.). York, ME: Stenhouse.

Morrow, L., O'Connor, E., Smith, J. (1990). The effects of a story reading program on the literacy development of at-risk kindergarten children. *Journal of Reading Behavior*, 22 (3), 255-275.

Neuman, S.B. & Roskos, K. (1993). Access to print for children of poverty: Differential effects of adult mediation and literacy enriched play settings on environmental and functional print tasks. *American Educational Research Journal*, 30 (1), 95-122.

Newkirk, T. (1987). The non-narrative writing of young children. *Research in the Teaching of English*, 21,121-144.

Nowak, R. (May, 2004). "Intentional talk:" Literacy coaching that empowers teachers. Paper presented at the International Reading Association Annual Conference, San Antonio, TX.

Olson, L. (October 26, 2005). "Value Added" models for gauging gains called promising. *Education Week*, p. 11.

Pappas, C. (1993). Is "narrative" primary? Some insights from kindergartners' pretend reading of stories and information books. *Journal of Reading Behavior*, 25, 97-129.

Phillips, L.M., Norris, S.P., & Mason, J.M. (1996). Longitudinal effects of early literacy concepts on reading achievement: A kindergarten intervention and five-year follow-up. *Journal of Literacy Research*, 28, 173-195.

Pinnell, G.S. & Fountas, I. (1999). *Matching books to readers*. Portsmouth, NH: Heinemann.

Purcell-Gates, V. (1995). *Other people's words*. Cambridge, MA: Harvard.

Richek, M. & McTague, B. (1988). The Curious George strategy for students with reading problems. *The Reading Teacher*, 42, 220-226.

Rosenhouse, J., Feitelson, D., Kita, B., & Goldstein, Z. (1997). Interactive reading aloud to Israeli first graders: Its contribution to literacy development. *Reading Research Quarterly*, 32 (2), 168-183.

Smith, M. L., & Shepard, L. A. 1988. Kindergarten readiness and retention: A qualitative study of teachers' beliefs and practices. *American Educational Research Journal*, 25, 307-333

Snow, C., Burns, M.S., & Griffin, P. (Eds.) (1998). Preventing reading difficulties in young children. Washington, DC: National Academy Press.

Spear-Swerling, L. (2004). A road map for understanding reading disability and other problems: Origins, prevention, and intervention. In R. Ruddell & N. Unrau (Eds.) *Theoretical Models and Processes of Reading*, 5th Ed. (pp. 517-574).

Stahl, S. (2003). What do we expect storybook reading to do? How storybook reading impacts word recognition. In A. van Kleeck, S. Stahl, & E. Bauer (Eds.), *On reading books to children* (pp. 363-383). Mahwah, NJ: Erlbaum.

Taylor, B., Pearson, P.D., Clark, K., & Walpole, S. (2000). Effective schools and accomplished teachers: Lessons about primary grade reading instruction in low-income schools. *Elementary School Journal*, 101, 121-165.

Temple, C., Nathan, R., Temple, F., & Burris, N. (1993). *The beginnings of writing*, 3rd Ed. Boston, MA: Allyn & Bacon.

Tierney, R. & Shanahan, T. (1991). Research on reading-writing relationships: Interactions, transactions and outcomes. In R. Barr, M. Kamil, P. Mosenthal, & P. D. Pearson (Eds.), *Handbook of Reading Research*, Vol. 2, 246-280.

Turner , J., & Paris, S. (1995). How literacy tasks influence children's motivation for literacy. *The Reading Teacher*, 48, 662-673.

Villegas, M. (April, 2005). *Full-day kindergarten: Expanding learning opportunities*. San Francisco, CA: WestEd.

Vygotsky, L. (1962). *Thought and language*. Cambridge, MA: MIT.

West, J., Denton, K. & Germino-Hausken, E. (2000). *America's kindergartners*. NCES 2000-070. Washington, DC: NCES.

Whitehurst, G. J. & Lonigan, C. J. (2001). Emergent literacy: Development from prereaders to readers. In S.B. Neuman & D. Dickinson (Eds.), *Handbook of early literacy development* (pp. 11-29). New York: Guilford.

Yopp, H. K. (1995). Read-aloud books for developing phonemic awareness: An annotated bibliography. *The Reading Teacher*, 48 (6), 538-542.

Rhyme Sort Record Sheet

Student _____ Teacher _____ Date _____

SORT 1

rug	bug

☐ _____

pail	mail

☐ _____

tube	cube

☐ _____

dig	pig

☐ _____

fan	can

☐ _____

SORT 2

feet	seat

☐ _____

tie	pie

☐ _____

cake	rake

☐ _____

sock	lock

☐ _____

moose	goose

☐ _____

Kindergarten Literacy © 2006 Anne McGill-Franzen

Beginning Sound Sort Record Sheet

Student _____ Teacher _____ Date _____

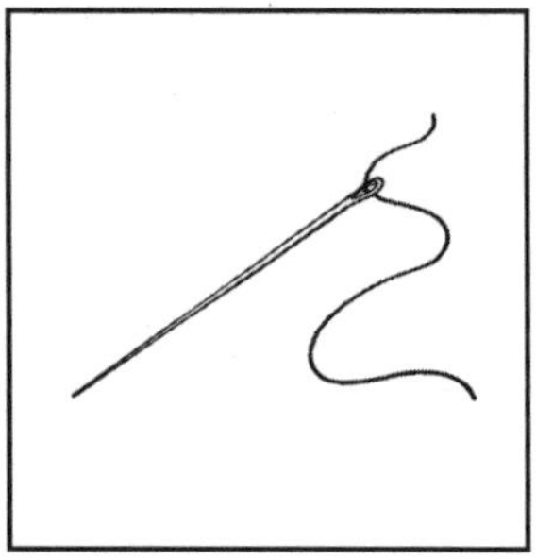

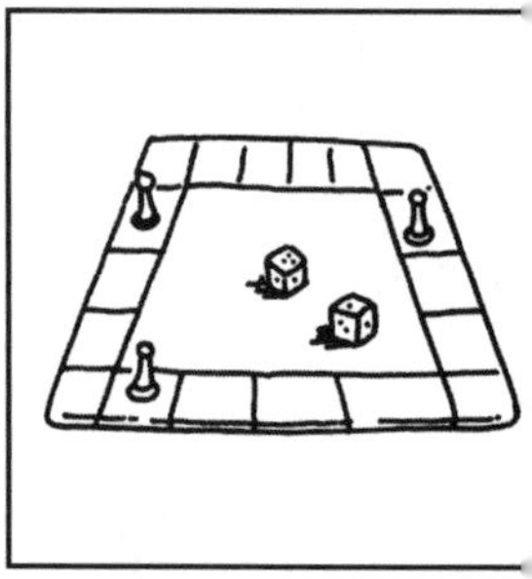

neck ☐

pencil ☐

feather ☐

gate ☐

note ☐

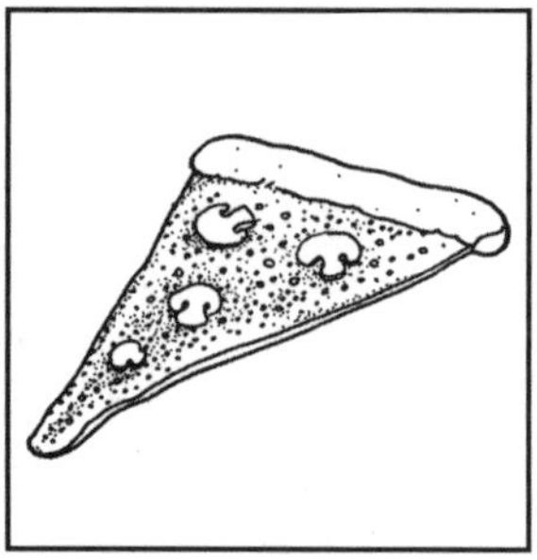

pizza ☐

fish ☐

guitar ☐

nest ☐

pan ☐

frog ☐

goose ☐

Kindergarten Literacy © 2006 Anne McGill-Franzen

Kindergarten Literacy © 2006 Anne McGill-Franzen

Kindergarten Literacy © 2006 Anne McGill-Franzen

Kindergarten Literacy Assessment
Spelling

Student _____ Teacher _____ Date _____

a b c d e f g h i j k l m n o p q r s t u v w x y z

A B C D E F G H I J K L M N O P Q R S T U V W X Y Z

1. _____

2. _____

3. _____

4. _____

5. _____

Total Phonemes _____

Kindergarten Literacy © 2006 Anne McGill-Franzen

Kindergarten Literacy Assessment
1. Letter-Sound Identification

A F K P W Z B H O J

U C Y L Q M D N S X

I E G R V T

a f k p w z b h o j

u a c y l q m d n s

x i e g r v t g

A F K P W Z B H O J

U C Y L Q M D N S X

I E G R V T

a f k p w z b h o j

u a c y l q m d n s

x i e g r v t g

Index